Write Home for Me

Jean Debelle Lamensdorf

Write Home for Me

A Red Cross Woman in Vietnam

Jean Debelle Lamensdorf

RANDOM HOUSE AUSTRALIA

Random House Australia Pty Ltd
20 Alfred Street, Milsons Point, NSW 2061
http://www.randomhouse.com.au

Sydney   New York   Toronto
London   Auckland   Johannesburg

First published by Random House Australia 2006

National Library of Australia
Cataloguing-in-Publication Entry

Lamensdorf, Jean Debelle, 1940– .
Write home for me.

ISBN 978 174051 393 7.

ISBN 1 74051 393 2.

1. Lamensdorf, Jean Debelle. 2. Vietnamese Conflict, 1961–1975 – Personal narratives, Australian. 3. Vietnamese Conflict, 1961–1975 – War work – Red Cross. 4. Vietnamese Conflict, 1961–1975 – Women – Personal narratives, Australian. I. Title.

959.7043394

Cover design by saso design & content
Internal design by Midland Typesetters, Australia
Typeset in Sabon 12/17 pt by Midland Typesetters, Australia
Printed and bound by Griffin Press, Netley, South Australia

10 9 8 7 6 5 4 3 2

For Barry Harford
And for all the men and women who served in Vietnam

Contents

South Vietnam, as it was known during the Vietnam War, and some places I mention.

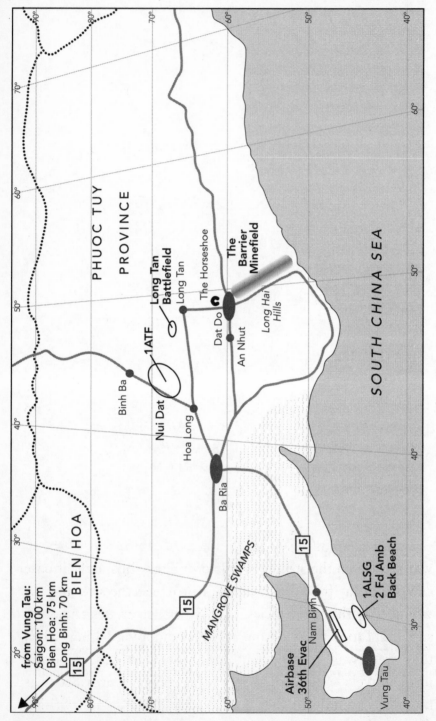

Phuoc Tuy province

Introduction

FOR ONE YEAR I WAS IN LOVE with 5,000 men. Dirty men, their shirts wet with sweat, their bodies caked with the red soil of the rubber plantation or with the gritty sand of the base camp, where they lived out of tents for that long defining year. Men who were rank with jungle mildew, who might curse through each day as soldiers do, but men who were strong and fit and in the prime of their lives. They were the men of the Australian and New Zealand forces – ANZACs – fighting what became known as the Vietnam War.

My part in the Vietnam War, from June 1966 to June 1967, was easy – comparatively. Brave front-line warriors no doubt will find my war story comic. In that one year though, in what was then South Vietnam, I experienced life more intensely than most people do who live to be a hundred. Working as a Red Cross officer with the Australian Military Forces to care for the non-medical welfare of wounded and sick Australian and New Zealand troops, mine was a view of war seen from the stifling wards of military hospitals at base camps not far from the fighting. I provided the sick and the wounded with toilet articles, newspapers, cigarettes and other supplies. I took those on the mend on shopping outings when they were well enough. But for those who were seriously ill or gravely wounded, the greatest service I provided was listening carefully to their sick or dying words and writing to their loved ones. They'd ask: 'Would you write home for me?'

I must make it clear that I was not a nursing sister – not the figure remembered in the World War I song: 'Mid the war's grave curse, stands the Red Cross nurse.' That distinct honour belongs to the Australian army nurses – all of them women – who arrived just one month before my term was up. (American nurses of both sexes were in Vietnam before I arrived.)

Like most people who were there, when I returned home to Australia from that extraordinary year, I told almost no one about the lives we led or the work we did. The fact is, almost no one asked. As a result, those of us who served kept our memories to ourselves. We built an impenetrable firewall so as to avoid the scorn of those who protested the war and said nothing. Even had there been words – which can be such positive agents of healing – no one would have understood, unless he or she had been there. As we grow older though, telling people about that time and place has become important – not to celebrate war, but to inform. The history of the Vietnam War must not be written only by politicians, journalists and historians who were not there. Nor must we forget those for whom the war lingers by way of wounded minds or bodies.

When anyone did ask, 'What was it like in Vietnam?' I'd answer briefly. I casually told of hair-raising flights in helicopters with no doors, of a dizzying social life and of the education gained by living and working with the ubiquitous American forces. I never once spoke of what war relentlessly does to the bodies and souls of men. Or that war is accompanied by indescribable sorrow. To do so would have contradicted what my generation learned from our British history: to die for one's country is glorious. Nor did I tell that, despite the daily atrocities associated with it, war builds friendships among those who were there that bind them forever. I didn't even mention the time spent trying to win the hearts and minds of the Vietnamese, so culturally rich but so different from us. Least of all did I mention the swirling gossip that enveloped me as one of the only young Australian women among so many men.

Sadly, and the greatest omission of all, I never spoke of the courage of the dedicated soldiers – ordinary people doing extraordinary things. Nor did I speak of the hope and the humour that can help a body and soul stay anchored in reality and thus endure overwhelming adversity. Living so close to the battlefield and working the wards of wounded soldiers, I thought I had understood what those men were going through, but for the most part, I hadn't. Only those who walked in their sturdy black boots understood.

When I returned home from Vietnam, I had almost no knowledge of what had happened to most of the Diggers, those brave Australian soldiers I knew there. Many who faced combat suffered the long-term curse of Post Traumatic Stress Disorder (PTSD), a term for what in earlier wars had been called combat fatigue or shell shock. PTSD is not difficulty in remembering – it is being unable to forget. That remains the Vietnam War's legacy for many men and women. Today, help is available, but that hasn't always been the case. After returning home, some men and women medicated themselves with alcohol and drugs, both pharmaceutical and otherwise, to alleviate their misery. The rest of us pushed the war deep down inside.

As for the National Servicemen, conscripts who were not

part of the Regular Army, they – like me – found a job and got on with the normality of life. They woke each morning to the sound of birds instead of cannon fire, but they didn't all sleep in peace. Some of them wandered with tortured hearts from job to job, marriage to marriage, for years. Others, the luckier ones, managed to move on from the horrors of war to hold down jobs and have a loving, stable and fulfilling family life. A number of them became the leaders of large and successful companies. Almost none of the people I write about could be described as famous, but I would like to think readers will hold them in higher regard than many of the so-called celebrities of today. These men have earned all the honour a nation can give.

It was nearly forty years before I met the man to whom this book is especially dedicated. On my first day in Saigon, I saw photographs of soldiers on operation scattered on a captain's desk in the army public relations office. A picture of one Digger caught my eye. He was dog-tired; rivulets of sweat carved paths down his dirt-smeared face; exhausted eyes focused on nothing. His dog tags were taped over to prevent a glint of sunlight from making him a target. His rugged masculinity, combined with the image of sheer exhaustion, sweat and dirt, represented every Digger to me.

'What are you going to do with this one?' I asked.

The captain shrugged. 'Nothing particular.'

'If you don't want it, may I have it? To me, he is every soldier here.'

With an understanding smile, the captain put the photograph of the unidentified man in my hand. 'He's yours, Jean.'

Three weeks later, when I had a permanent room in Vung Tau, I pinned the photograph on the wall over my bed, where it stayed for the full year I was in Vietnam. Each night before falling asleep, I prayed that God would keep my unknown Digger safe, along with *all* the Diggers, for I have great faith in prayer.

One evening a man whom I was dating came to pick me up. He glanced around my room and asked (a little jealously): 'Who's that on the wall?' I told him I wished I knew. I continued to watch out for the Digger, but we never crossed paths.

I had been in Vietnam about nine months when an engineer with whom I was having dinner stopped by my room. 'What's Barry Harford doing on your wall?' he asked.

'You know him?' I gasped, astonished.

'Yeah, Sapper Barry Harford. Comes from Broken Hill.'

As I packed to leave Vietnam, I took down the photograph carefully. Back in Australia I placed it on the front page of the first of my albums of Vietnam photographs. Sapper Barry Harford was written beneath the familiar image, punctuated with a question mark.

Through the years I remained unsure who the man in the photograph was; unsure if he was alive. More recently, as I prepared to write this book, I sought a positive identification of the picture through the veterans' Web networks. My unknown Digger was known to many.

It was Barry Harford! He had been a Tunnel Rat with the First Field Squadron's renowned 3 Field Troop at Bien Hoa and later at Nui Dat. Although I had kept my eyes open for him, he had gone home in September 1966. We had been in the same country just three months.

Compact and strong as only a former shearer can be, Barry had one of the most frightening jobs imaginable. Tunnel Rat is the proud title given to those men who dropped, often head first, with a torch in one hand and a bayonet in the other, into the eerie darkness of artfully camouflaged Viet Cong (VC) tunnels, where the only sound was the loud beating of a man's own heart. Barry Harford and his mates knew with dreadful certainty that lethal booby traps, poisoned bamboo spikes that would rip out a man's innards, deadly reptiles strategically placed, or a barrage of gunfire from hidden VC could await them. As Barry's long-time friend and fellow Tunnel Rat Les Colmer put it: 'We were pigs to the slaughter.' In those tunnels, which could stretch for miles, the Viet Cong lived and planned strategies against their enemies above ground. Before a VC tunnel could be destroyed, it had to be searched for enemy documents, men and supplies. So horrendous was their task that each Tunnel Rat had to psych himself before entering a tunnel. So valorous was their action that many other soldiers have claimed that famous name – so many that true Tunnel Rats scoff: 'It would need a heap of tunnels to accommodate all the men who say they were there – the surface of Vietnam would have collapsed!'

Barry Harford, today still haunted by his experience, is not well and spends a lot of time at the Adelaide Repatriation General Hospital (RGH), 'battling on,' as he says, endeavouring to rid himself of deeply rooted demons. When his social worker, Louise Checkley, showed him the photograph I had mailed him, he went off alone – silent for almost a day. Then he returned to Louise, again wanting to know who I was and how I had obtained his picture. He wrote to me, expressing amazement to hear the story and asking if he could keep the photograph.

'I'm glad you were able to track me down,' he wrote.

'It was great to hear how the photo helped you through a difficult time in Vietnam.'

Tears stung my eyes so that I could scarcely read. *My difficult time in Vietnam?* Barry's words reminded me of the standout characteristic of my unforgettable year: the brave and selfless spirit of those Australian men, fighting in an increasingly controversial war. No matter the conditions, no matter how gruelling the task, no matter how serious his wounds, he never worried for himself. He was only concerned and anxious for his mates, his family, his sweetheart . . . even me.

The process of researching and recalling those days of forty years ago has been an emotional experience. Once veterans start to think about Vietnam, it is impossible to stop. By email, letters, faxes and phone calls across the Pacific, I received information and warm sentiments. Many of the letters and notes were written in the block capitals the army required for filling out forms. I was transported back in time to the days when we were young and lean, into the months of caring, partying and heartbreak. We stood tall with the hubris of youth. We thought we were invincible. In our minds, none of us has grown older or heavier. Each of us sees the others as we were then, perpetually frozen in time – slim, suntanned and in the prime of our lives.

This story is not about why the soldiers were there, or the history of Vietnam – a country as beautiful and, at that time, as troubled as any on earth. You will find no discussion on whether this controversial war was justified. Wiser people than I have debated the question of war since antiquity. This is simply the story of a young woman who went to support men who did not ask to be sent to Vietnam. Men who went unflinchingly, many to be wounded, many to be killed. I went there naïve and returned home physically unscathed, but with increased wisdom and a fuller appreciation of the human spirit in the face of brutal destruction.

It is all true, as I recall it. If there are any factual mistakes, I take responsibility. Anecdotes were written as I believe, or was told, they happened. Even with events burned into our memories forever, the mind is not always an accurate recorder of information; our memories are amalgams of what we experienced, read and heard afterwards, or perhaps of what we might wish to be true. One thing I am sure of, though, is that in writing this account, I have come to respect and revere, even more than I did when I was there, the resilience and sheer guts of those courageous men and women who left a part of themselves in the land that was South Vietnam.

1

Off to War

IN 1966 I WAS A REPORTER FOR a morning newspaper in
Adelaide, South Australia. I was tall, fair and twenty-six.
I had toured three continents and had a satisfying career.
On the radio Frank Sinatra crooned 'It Was a Very Good
Year', but May of 1966 was not a very good month. In
Vietnam, more men than ever were being killed, including
the first Australian conscript, Private (Pte) Errol Noack. His
death seemed even more troubling to a concerned people
than the loss of men who had chosen to enlist in the army.
Australians were starting to protest their country's participa-
tion (and that of the United States) in a war thousands of
kilometres away.

And one May morning my beloved father died suddenly of
a heart attack, leaving our family feeling desolate and vulner-
able. More than that, there were unexpected and pressing
questions. Would my brother Geoffrey be able to continue his

1

university course? Would my youngest brother Robert be able to stay at private school? How would Mum cope? So with my family in turmoil, each of us struggling with the emotional and financial blow of Dad's death, what was I doing getting jabbed like a pincushion by army medicos – for every disease known to man except kennel cough – in preparation to go to Vietnam?

I was embracing my heritage.

People are attracted to war for many reasons: belief in an idea, the chance to prove oneself in battle or the camaraderie among those fighting a common foe. For me it was a mixed bag of emotions. I was disturbed that a lottery system decided which men were being sent to fight a war few of us knew anything about. People were protesting conscription but weren't doing anything to support those who had been sent to fight – and maybe die – for their country. I had grown up in a privileged country leading a life free of trauma and never had helped anyone in my life. I felt it was time to earn my place in the world.

That wasn't all though. Undeniably, I had a giant-size thirst for adventure. Like so many women who volunteered to go to Vietnam, I'd never had daydreams about marrying one of the boys I'd known from school days and raising children in a suburban home. My dreams were of mysterious lands and exotic experiences.

And I had been born to go to war. My father, his four brothers and my mother's three brothers, like so many Australian men of those days, had volunteered to fight in World War II. Dad was near the upper edge of the recruiting age on 3 September, 1939, when Britain and France declared war on Germany. When he heard Australian Prime Minister Robert

Menzies' immediate radio announcement that 'as a result, Australia is also at war', Dad was ready to put on his hat and head to the nearest recruiting station.

My family was living then in Port Pirie, South Australia, where Dad and Mum, as newlyweds, had moved from Sydney for my father to become town engineer. Mum was pregnant with me, her second child, in a town where she had friends, but no family. As Dad prepared to enlist, Mum begged him to wait until after the baby was born.

I arrived on 29 January, the Monday holiday on which Australia's founding (26 January, 1788) was being celebrated in 1940. Very soon after, Dad enlisted in the Royal Australian Air Force (RAAF) and was dispatched north to Darwin to defend our country against an imminent Japanese invasion. In Darwin, despite enemy bombs raining down, his skills as an engineer and surveyor were put to work building airstrips and charting the extensive north coast of Australia (few maps of much of that coastline had been drawn since Matthew Flinders charted it in 1803). I wasn't to know my father until the end of the war, when I was almost six.

Shortly after Dad's departure, Mum boarded the train with my brother Bruce, not yet two, and me, a babe in arms, for a three-day, 1,600-kilometre trip to live with her parents on their wheat and sheep property, Silverweir, near Tamworth, New South Wales. There we had an idyllic childhood, roaming the vast paddocks, one day merging peacefully into another. There was the occasional memorable day, like the time we saw Mum trapped by a snake near the back door with no big stick handy to break its back. With the ingenuity of every woman bred in the Outback, she picked up a large pumpkin and tossed it at the deadly reptile, killing it instantly.

Bruce and I, terror-struck and cowering at a safe distance, watched the accuracy of the bombing with awe.

One time we took the North-West Mail train to Sydney to visit my father's parents. Tamworth was a busy station, with troops and equipment moving through to North Queensland for jungle training. My mother wrestled us on board a train crowded with men in khaki. Just as the Red Sea had parted for Moses, the sea of khaki miraculously divided, and Mum was ushered into a seat. A strange man with an even stranger accent asked: 'Would the little girl like some candy?' He was the first American I'd met. I didn't know that nearly forty years later I would marry one.

At day's end at Silverweir, Grandfather sat on the back porch rolling his own cigarettes in the glow of hurricane lamps. As he smoked, he taught me army songs from World War I. 'It's a Long Way to Tipperary' and 'Pack up Your Troubles in Your Old Kit Bag' were only the start of it. I knew nothing about war. It was simply the backdrop to our lives.

The day the news came that the Japanese had surrendered was so different from the norm that I remember its tiniest details. First we collected Grandfather from the far paddock where he was working. Then, grabbing the curried egg sandwiches that had been packed for his lunch, we hurried into Tamworth to join the celebration of the war's end. The kerosene-fuelled car (petrol was scarce in wartime) belched fumes all the way as though it, too, were celebrating. My father, with whom Mum had lived for only three of the nine years they had been married, was coming home soon – and he was safe.

In 1946 we returned to Port Pirie and a year later moved to Adelaide. Dad took a job as city engineer for Woodville, then the largest designated 'city' area in Adelaide. With a government war service loan, Mum and Dad built our home. We were raised to believe in God, ANZAC Day and cricket great Don Bradman – and also to be independent and free spirited. Each ANZAC Day was marked by Dad's departure into the chilly early morning darkness for the Dawn Service to remember those of the Australian and New Zealand Army Corps killed in all wars. Only once did I brave the cold to get up and go with him. Later in the morning we stood as a family along the sidelines, watching proudly as Dad, in his business suit and hat, marched through the streets of Adelaide at the end of the parade with the RAAF.

When my two younger brothers, Geoffrey and later Robert, were born, I became tough and self-reliant. Then, in the worldwide poliomyelitis epidemic, the disease interrupted my hop, skip and a jump life. Stricken in 1950 with a mild case of polio, I had to lie flat on my back for six months, unable to go to school, unable to raise my arms to hold a book. With luck and good nursing I recovered to live the busy life of a teenager, wondering what career path I would adopt.

I had toyed with the idea of joining the armed services but knew I could not take the discipline of conforming. Instead I went into journalism. At a time when newspaper Help Wanted advertisements still were classified under 'Men' and 'Women', I was stirred by the exploits of Marguerite Higgins of the *New York Herald Tribune*, a heroic female pioneer in front-line reporting during the Korean War.

On staff at Adelaide's morning daily newspaper, *The Advertiser*, I toiled of course on the women's pages. Each afternoon, though, I found myself escaping to the rough-and-tumble of the main newsroom two floors below, where the air was thick with cigarette smoke. There, hard-talking, hard-drinking veteran male journalists could pour out a river of alliterative words all with the same meaning and not draw breath. Sometimes they'd refer to their World War II adventures. I was dazzled by the exploits of an older journalist, Lawson Glassop, whose book *We Were the Rats*, a revealing portrait of the Australian Digger at Tobruk, had just been re-released. The book had been banned for many years because the language of soldiers describing the brutality of war was considered obscene.

I had struggled to save for an eighteen-month working holiday in Europe and the United States, not unusual in pre-jet days for those wanting to know the world outside our South Pacific island. And in the benevolent way of the newspaper business then, my job was waiting for me on my return. It was all too comfortable. The turmoil of the sixties rocked the United States but made little impact on sleepy Adelaide. We worried about nuclear weapons and the Berlin Wall, but we also worried about how quickly we could get the latest Beatles record and whether Australia would win the Davis Cup. The little war that was starting to heat up in South-East Asia was, at first, too far away to contemplate.

For a reporter, though, Vietnam was the story of the decade. My curiosity about that mysterious country was whetted by a journalist who had worked there. My intense romance with him didn't last, but the gripping stories he told me sent my thoughts spiralling northward. I could imagine the reaction if I, a relatively inexperienced female journalist and a mediocre reporter at best, were to ask to be sent to Vietnam. The Managing Editor (male of course) would say: 'Are you crazy, Jean? We send only our top men to Vietnam.

And where would you go to the loo?' I would be the joke of
the office.

Beginning in 1965, Australian men were conscripted into the
army to boost its strength. Selected birth dates were pulled
from a lottery, and those who turned twenty in that period –
unless they did not meet the army's fitness standards or temporarily were deferred – were committed to enlist. The
National Servicemen, as they were known, were chosen right
across the board, from all sections of the community. Except
for theological students or the clergy, there were no occupa-
tional exemptions. Nor was any attempt made to classify a
conscript according to his value to the community, as happened
in the United States. Officially very few National Servicemen
did not 'volunteer' for Vietnam, perhaps for fear of letting
down 'the team'. The shotgun marriage between the National
Servicemen and the men of the Regular Army to boost the
army's manpower proved to be more of a success than anyone
could have hoped. The Nashos teamed seamlessly with the
Regs to become, as Regular Army Sergeant (Sgt) and Vietnam
War hero Bob Buick MM said, 'Bloody great warriors.'

In those early days of the war, nearly every Australian
believed the government's claim that our military was helping
the Vietnamese achieve freedom to pursue their daily lives in
peace. However, anti-war protests were starting, particularly
from the labour unions that were withholding military
supplies needed by the fighting men, and people were
marching, albeit in a small way then, in the streets of our
capital cities. Don't only vent your anger at politicians, I
thought. Do something to help the soldiers in danger! I didn't
want to remain uninvolved.

As with everything of importance in my life, I stumbled

into my Red Cross work with no definitive plan. My boss sent me to interview a local woman, Thea Cawthorne (now McCabe), who was just back from Saigon where she had worked with what is now the Australian Department of Foreign Affairs and Trade. Thea told stories that thrilled me of *coups d'état* and of cocktail parties with machine-gun-toting guards hiding behind the potted plants. She spoke of being trapped in the Australian Embassy on the seventh floor of the Caravelle Hotel when a bomb went off on the fifth floor, damaging the staircase and lifts. Flying windowpanes, dust and rubble were everywhere.

'How many Australian women are there in Vietnam?' I asked.

'Most married staff is unaccompanied because of the danger,' she replied, 'so it's only the secretaries at the Embassy, some civilian nurses and church workers, a whole crowd of dancers entertaining the GIs, and one Red Cross girl.'

'What does the Red Cross girl do?'

'She hands out newspapers to the soldiers in hospital, plays cards with them, that sort of thing,' Thea said casually.

Anyone could hand out newspapers, I thought. And as for cards, my game had been sharpened by a mother who learned card skills from the shearers at Silverweir. An idea was fermenting in my brain. I would apply to Red Cross to work for them in Vietnam, and at every spare moment from my Red Cross duties, Brenda Starr, Star Reporter, of comic book fame, would send home feature stories to *The Advertiser*.

In no time flat, my letter of application arrived at Red Cross headquarters in Melbourne, and I was summoned to the Adelaide office for an interview with a senior executive. He peppered me with questions: 'What work have you done for Red Cross? Have you taken a first aid course? Can you drive? Have you experience in hospital work? Can you teach handcrafts?' Not only was it jarringly apparent that nearly all my answers were in the negative, but I had never even given blood or sold a badge on the streets. Clearly I was not the person they were seeking. Red Cross wanted an experienced worker. I put the idea out of my mind and told no one.

However, Adelaide being the small city it then was, I soon began to hear rumours that my interview had not been the disaster I imagined. Unknown to me, I already had been security cleared and accredited to the military. One afternoon in late April 1966, my boss was standing by my desk talking to me when the phone rang. In a newspaper office, you never ignore a ringing phone – there might be a big story at the end of the line. The call was Red Cross, asking if I could go to Vietnam in six weeks.

Dazed, I hung up the receiver and confessed: 'Red Cross wants me to go to Vietnam.'

'Then your photograph and story must go on the front page of *The Advertiser* tomorrow,' my boss shot back.

The next day, when the plop of *The Advertiser* landing on Adelaide driveways called people from their beds, they saw my picture on the front page. The accompanying story announced that I was joining the Red Cross Field Force to work with the troops in South Vietnam. Television and radio interviews followed – and phone calls. An American woman living in Adelaide phoned to tell me to look out for her good friend Vi Auer, who was working for American Red Cross 'somewhere' in Vietnam. And I had just been a bridesmaid for a friend whose brother, Lieutenant (Lt) Roger Wain-wright, was already in Vietnam with soldiers from the Fifth

Royal Australian Regiment (RAR), preparing for the arrival of the rest of the Battalion. Would I take a cake to him?

There was also a sobering phone call from a lawyer I knew through work, Roma Mitchell, who the previous September had become the first female judge in the British Commonwealth when appointed to the Supreme Court of South Australia. (Dame Roma Mitchell later became Governor of South Australia.) At a legal conference in South-East Asia, Miss Mitchell had become friendly with a highly-regarded female lawyer from Saigon. As recent letters to her friend had gone unanswered, Miss Mitchell feared that the lawyer might now be in gaol, or killed – another victim of the war – perhaps for criticising the government. 'Will you make some enquiries?' she asked. Although I promised I would try, the circumstances of war made the task impossible.

My parents appeared to take my 'going to war' news placidly. They *were* worried, of course, but just as they never had done anything to stop their children from following a rainbow, they said nothing to discourage me. Forget about my dreams of being Brenda Starr. From the moment of the announcement, my brother Rob – still at school and heavily into rock music and surfing – dubbed me Florence Nightingale, and then simply Flo.

Because of his age, Rob was a prime candidate for conscription. He clearly remembers the day when the postman delivered the letter informing him that he was not, for the time being, required by the army. He was greatly relieved. My mother cried with joy. Everyone kept quiet though, in case someone they knew was not as lucky. My middle brother Geoff, then a twenty-year-old second-year medical student at the University of Adelaide, was less likely to have been called up, but could have been. Both he and Rob were confused about the war and later opposed it. Nevertheless, they always thought it despicable that some people would take out their opposition to the war on those who had fought. Neither brother, however, was confused about my sense of duty and adventure.

My eldest brother Bruce, then a young lawyer, and his wife, Barbara, were full of admiration and pride. 'There goes Jean again, always doing something different from everyone else.' Then almost twenty-eight, Bruce was too old to be conscripted himself. Although he felt Vietnam was America's battle, he believed we were supporting an ally. Not unlike so many others, he later began to have some doubts that the war was right. Regardless of their feelings about Vietnam, all three of my brothers felt I was brave in volunteering and never questioned my motives. I don't know about brave, but certainly I was naïve. But that was okay. Without naïvety, I would have been afraid.

The Advertiser allowed me to continue to work there until departure day and willingly gave me time off to be measured for the grey Red Cross uniforms. Army medicos inoculated me against cholera, plague, yellow fever, tetanus, typhus and more – about thirteen different injections, some of which required three doses. I was officially DP1, Draft Priority One, a non-combatant, though I was to work with the military. I was to wear the uniform of the Australian Red Cross Field Force, which differed from the more neutral International Red Cross.

I was abysmally ignorant of military life. I had a notion that men saluted women and thought that would be fun. I swotted up on military rankings, practised the Alpha, Bravo,

Charlie, Delta alphabet, and learned how important it was to take a Paludrine anti-malaria pill each day. I studied the Geneva Conventions of behaviour relating to members attached to the armed forces, learned first aid and about Red Cross activities in general. Since World War I, the Australian Red Cross has supplied comforts to our sick and wounded soldiers: non-essential articles such as a comb, toilet articles, playing cards and games that mean so much. Soldiers get the necessities, their food and equipment, from the military but those essentials often can be Spartan. I was to be part of the Red Cross effort that intended every soldier to feel well cared for. As one soldier put it: 'As long as we get the luxuries, we will manage without the necessities of life.'

With the Red Cross, I visited Daw Park Repatriation General Hospital, and I initiated a visit to the casualty section of the Royal Adelaide Hospital. Never having seen injured people, I didn't want to embarrass anyone in a war zone by looking shocked or maybe even, heaven forbid, fainting at the sight of a wounded man.

As I was dressing for work one morning, just four weeks before I was to leave, my mother told me Dad wasn't feeling well. After his shower, he had returned to bed, his face an alarming grey colour. Mum had called the doctor, who was on his way. When the doorbell rang, I said to Dad, 'The doctor's here.' As the doctor hurried down the hallway, he could hear Dad's laboured breathing, yet when he got to the bedside, Dad was dead. That hard-working, courageous man, who valued truth and honesty above everything, had suffered a massive heart attack.

As well as feeling the grief of an only daughter, and anger that Dad was no longer around to answer so many of my questions, I was feeling guilty. There had been two cars in the driveway and a major hospital within a quarter of a mile, yet none of us had known enough to rush Dad to hospital ourselves. Normally strong and resilient, my mother took Dad's death hard. Almost a teetotaller, she stunned us after the funeral by downing a large glass of brandy in one gulp.

After a week of upheaval, tears and uncertainty, I debated whether I still should go to Vietnam. How could I abandon Mum at such a time of upset and change? But my parents had raised me in the spirit that 'life goes on', and Dad, in particular, lived by the maxim 'life is not a dress rehearsal'. More simply: go for it! That's what he would have wanted. I showed up on schedule for my final uniform fittings and was embarrassed to hear I had given Red Cross officials some anxious moments. They had been too polite to ask if they still were part of my plans. Next I packed as though I was going to the other side of the moon. My luggage contained enough hair spray, tampons, toothpaste and cosmetics to last a year, or so I hoped.

Then the farewell parties started. My boss had a weekend cottage in the Adelaide Hills that she generously offered to my work colleagues for a party the night before I was to depart. After a riotous evening I hardly remember, and leaving my friends to clean the claret stains from the boss's carpet, I set off next morning at first light by commercial aircraft on the greatest adventure of my life. I had no sense that I might be putting my life at risk. I felt only exuberance. As I excitedly said goodbye to my family, Mum struggled to hold back her tears. I felt only a tinge of remorse that I was leaving her within weeks of Dad's death. It just didn't occur to me that for the second time in her married life Mum was saying farewell to a loved one she might never see again.

After an hour in the air I was in Melbourne. At Red Cross National Headquarters (NHQ), I was introduced to the top officials, including the kindly, considerate Secretary General, Mr Leon Stubbings. Various department heads explained the workings of Red Cross's many areas, such as the Enquiry and Tracing Bureau, about which I knew so little. I was too nervous to remember all the names and the departments, but everyone wished me well.

I was intrigued to find my new boss, Commander John Crabb, was an ex-Royal Navy man. His ability to combine naval efficiency with a joyful sense of the *bon mot* and a wicked wit made him a formidable yet delightful commanding officer. He graciously invited me home to dinner that night. Tall and pretty Pam Spence (now Werner), Red Cross's first Saigon Field Force representative, was there also. We sat together at the kitchen counter chatting and drinking numerous gin and tonics with the Commander's wife, Hilary, while she calmly prepared a gourmet meal after working hard all day herself.

A year earlier Pam Spence had astonished even Brigadier O. D. Jackson, the senior officer of the Australian troops in Vietnam, when she arrived in Saigon, for the First Battalion had been in country only a few weeks. 'He warned me to observe all safety precautions and to keep in touch so that he would know I was okay,' Pam said. It was reassuring to hear that the military cared about the Red Cross women. 'Cared', I was to discover, was an understatement. 'Revered' was more like it.

Pam's stories held me spellbound. 'In Saigon I lived with the American nurses in a French villa next door to 3 Field Hospital,' she said, 'and I shared an office with the American Red Cross.

Just down the street from us was an American helicopter unit of Dust-Off (casualty evacuation) pilots, so there were constant alerts and bells ringing as they scrambled into their jeeps and raced to their choppers.' That was the first I had heard of these pilots, famed as heroes of the Vietnam War for their extractions of the wounded, often in the face of heavy fire. Pam, as the only Red Cross woman to care for any sick or wounded Aussies, had been on duty all day, every day. She never had the luxury of a day off. Six months later she was replaced by Hilda Zinner, and I was going to work with Hilda. We were to be the only Australian women with those 5,000 men.

Next day at Albert Park Barracks, I was introduced to the Director-General of Army Medical Services, Major General A. J. Clyne, who ushered me into his office with flattering eloquence. I was issued a pay book in which my salary of $36 a week (about $180 in today's money) was credited, enabling me to make withdrawals in South Vietnam. My meals, lodging, health care and transport were to be taken care of by the army. I was handed travel documents and a free passport before I flew on to Sydney for a third day of Red Cross orientation.

That was the extent of my basic training for life in a war zone. As I was to find out when I reached Vietnam, I was *so* unprepared for what lay ahead.

2

Sydney to Saigon

O N THE 15TH OF JUNE, THREE DAYS after I had left
Adelaide, Red Cross officials drove me to the RAAF
base at Richmond, 55 kilometres from Sydney at the
edge of the Blue Mountains. From then on I was in the hands
of the army and one of the many cogs in a splendidly oiled
machine.

As I was officially part of the military, I was given the
temporary ranking of Second Lieutenant (2 Lt). The rank,
marked by stripes on my uniform epaulettes, carried with it
military status and many privileges, the most valuable being
the freedom to mingle with all ranks, yet I had received no
military training. Nor did I ever feel like I had any more
importance than anyone else. I unknowingly accepted all
privileges as standard for a woman. But I was still just Jean;
if anyone ever had called 'Lieutenant,' I never would have
turned around.

We waited on the tarmac in the cool darkness of a winter evening to board the Qantas Boeing 707, taking off from Richmond to avoid any anti-war protesters. There were a hundred men around me in jungle green uniforms and shiny black boots, fully armed. They seemed the tallest, handsomest, fittest men I ever had seen. I was to travel with men of the Third Special Air Service Squadron (3 SAS), the elite Phantoms of the Jungle, whose exploits are legendary. There were no families seeing them off.

The SAS is based in Swanbourne, Western Australia, and the men had made their farewells in Perth. As I climbed the stairs to the aircraft and took my seat, the reality of what I was heading for was beginning to sink in. There were no pretty Qantas air hostesses. All the crew was male. And I was the only woman aboard. Although I was setting off into the unknown, strangely I was calm – probably because I didn't have a clue as to what lay ahead. Nor in my ignorance did I give a thought to the fact that any one of us on Qantas that night might not return home alive.

With the cake I had been entrusted to deliver placed safely in the overhead locker, I took my given seat in the centre of the plane where the emergency exit doors offered extra leg room. We sat in rows, three abreast, on each side of the aisle. In keeping with my new officer status, I was positioned between the 3 SAS second-in-command (2 I/C), Captain Geoff Chipman – the only captain in the small unit – in the aisle seat, and a Royal Australian Engineers captain, assigned to work as a staff officer in Saigon, by the window. Across the aisle from Geoff Chipman was the Commanding Officer of 3 SAS, Major John Murphy. Sophisticated, confident and smoking a cigarette, Major Murphy could only be described as drop-dead gorgeous. If Hollywood had ever wanted a new swashbuckling hero, he was it.

The 707 revved its engines and we were on our way. Qantas, in a manner befitting troops going to war, treated us to first class service. There was no in-flight movie in those days, but who needed it when the most delicious delicacies kept arriving on our food trays. Free drinks flowed. One time, when I went to the toilets at the back of the plane, Juvy Matten took my arm and pulled me into the aisle to dance. I was happy to sway to the music with a handsome young soldier, especially on a jet plane. His mates did not call Pte John Matten 'Juvy' (for 'juvenile delinquent') for nothing. Juvy loved music and anything with a beat got him going, especially if he had some jumpabout juice inside him. And in the looks department, Juvy could give Major Murphy a run for his money. Were all SAS men chosen for their devilishly handsome looks? The thought intrigued me.

At Townsville, shaking off the crumbs and debris of the trip, everyone left the plane while it was refuelled. The sticky tropical air settled on us like a welcome blanket after the chill of the Blue Mountains that we had left behind. As we flew on another five or six hours to the Philippines to refuel at Manila, all the free drinks meant the aircraft was becoming noisy. But some of us were trying to sleep. Captain Chipman went back to the revellers; there was a quick word and then absolute silence. Army discipline was impressive! The aircraft's engines kept up a soothing rumble, and I drifted in and out of sleep, anxious that my head might droop onto the shoulders of the men on either side. Both were absorbed in their own thoughts, as they had left young families behind. Geoff particularly was concerned for his wife and for the daughter born to them that day. How many of the soldiers would sleep, I wondered, setting off as they were for the biggest poker game of their lives?

President Ferdinand Marcos recently had imposed martial law in the Philippines. At Manila International Airport in the early morning light, I felt jolts of fear as menacing-looking men with machine guns swarmed around, altogether too close for comfort. I looked longingly at the towers of the capital in the distance, knowing there was time for a quick taxi ride into town, but I wasn't there to see the sights.

The officers and I were the last to board the aircraft for the final three hours or so to Saigon. As I entered the cabin, I gasped. One hundred rifles, each with a bayonet sheathed in a scabbard, projected from all Qantas seats except mine. The carousers of the earlier hours were quiet, and everyone was alert. The soldiers had been trained to know what to expect: war is serious business. Was each one thinking about what lay ahead and how he would conduct himself in combat?

From the safety of an aircraft seat it is always exhilarating to make landfall after hours over water. Crossing the coastline into South Vietnam, though, meant we were looking down on enemy territory, yet what we saw were scenes of great beauty. Beneath our aircraft were golden beaches and blue sea, vibrant green paddy fields brimming with silvery water, red-tiled roofs of towns and brown-thatched roofs of villages. The rubber plantations, the mountains, the jungles and the rivers of the country flashing below would be our home for the next twelve months. The landscape looked lush and inviting, but I sensed that the practised eyes of the SAS men were already checking out what awaited them in the green canopy of foliage and distant hills. Soon the sloping roofs of

Saigon appeared. Quickly the 707 banked and landed at the city's airport, Tan Son Nhut, the pilot not wanting to spend any longer than necessary within reach of enemy fire.

As I first stood on Vietnamese soil there was no time to be apprehensive, for Tan Son Nhut was a whirl of sensations. Sandbags, to protect buildings from gunfire and mortar, and uniformed troops were everywhere. The variety of aircraft on the runways included the huge Pan Am passenger jets that flew into Saigon all through the war, World Airways, Air Vietnam (the nation's own airline), and our Qantas 707. All shared the tarmac with fighter bombers, huge military transports, tiny Cessnas, and helicopters of all shapes and sizes, including the enormous twin-rotor Chinooks. The slim white planes of Air America, I was told, were used for CIA operations.

Inside a terminal choked with people, there were no Customs to clear – an unnecessary formality for troops arriving to help save a country from communist domination. Western men in bulky military uniforms towered over the slight figures of the Vietnamese. American Military Police (MP) and the civilian police of Vietnam, known as White Mice because of their white uniforms and white gloves, moved among the teeming crowd. The White Mice were feared by visiting troops as much as by the Vietnamese: they had a reputation for ruthless brutality.

I soon noticed a small posse of Australian soldiers impatiently waiting to fly home on the Qantas jet. One of them, Lt Jim Irvine, was the last member of the First Battalion RAR to leave Vietnam, and he explained why. 'Someone in a vehicle I was commanding on Route One on the way back from Saigon killed a nog who tried to drop "something" into our vehicle from his bicycle,' he said ruefully. 'We should have buried the guy on the side of the road. Instead we visited every medical facility in the area trying to get rid of the body properly. So I ended up in a combined US MP and White Mice investigation as the area was not a free (open) fire zone. I had to stay on as the chief witness instead of going home with the main party.'

I knew without asking what the Lieutenant meant by 'nog'. The Australian soldiers called the Vietnamese nogs or noggys, and the Americans used equally demeaning names such as gooks, dinks, or slant-eyes. We Westerners were, of course, the round-eyes. It is one of the oldest human instincts to make oneself feel superior by disparaging others, especially if they are the enemy.

I had spoken to Jim for only a moment, but during that time my fellow travellers from 3 SAS – in keeping with their secretive reputation – seemed to have vanished into the hot steamy air. They were to fly 100 kilometres to Vung Tau's American-operated airbase, and from there they were to travel in a convoy of trucks to make their homes in the tents of the Australian Task Force base at Nui Dat, about 35 kilometres north-east of Vung Tau. There was no airstrip at Nui Dat then, and the road was unsafe, necessitating the convoy. Months went by before I saw any of them again.

Hilda Zinner, my supervisor in Vietnam, met me at Tan Son Nhut airport in Saigon. She wore the same grey Red Cross uniform as I wore, but she had three stripes, equivalent to a captain's rank, across her shoulders. Hilda, who was German-born but had settled in Double Bay in Sydney, was big, boisterous and brusque. She had worked with the Red Cross in Malaysia and Borneo, and I guessed she was about twenty years older than I. We loaded my luggage into a grey

Volkswagen station wagon with *Uc Dai Loi* (Australia) and *Tan Tay Lan* (New Zealand) Red Cross painted on the sides. Hilda drove expertly through the eye-popping Saigon traffic, chattering non-stop. I hardly heard a word. There was too much else to absorb, and it was overwhelming.

Traffic flowed along the busy streets like water, in and around itself in an unordered, chaotic way. Speeding buses and trucks that should have been put out to grass long ago, and with no sense of what side of the road was which, jostled for space with sinuous waves of cyclo pedicabs. Arthritic blue and white Renault taxis spewing toxic substances honked aggressively at clopping buffalo or pony carts. Military vehicles shared the tamarind-lined roads with Vietnamese on bicycles who came straight at us with an unconcerned air. Crossing the road on foot would be impossible – or so I thought. I discovered that those wanting to cross didn't dash but proceeded slowly. Amazingly, the traffic flowed safely around them like a river around rocks. Sandbags and barbed wire protected most buildings, except those of the shanty towns of refugees just outside the airport. White Mice, in former French gendarme stands, attempted to control the traffic with frantic arm waves and whistles. If that failed, the trigger-happy White Mice fired the guns at their waists to achieve their purpose.

'You can have a shower and lunch at the General's house,' Hilda said. I was grateful on two counts as she spoke: that she didn't take her eyes off the frenetic traffic as she weaved the Volkswagen in and out, and that I was to get a welcome shower. Already the sticky air had turned me into a sweat-soaked rag.

Major General Kenneth MacKay, Commander of the Australian Force in Vietnam, lived in a suitably spacious villa in the centre of Saigon. I was too overwhelmed with tiredness and the humidity to take in its comforts. If his family was still in Saigon at that time, I can't remember. Senior Allied military personnel originally had been allowed to have their families with them in Vietnam, but all American wives had been sent home for safety reasons the previous February. An Asian servant beamed at me with a mouth of crooked teeth and ushered me wordlessly to a bathroom and bedroom. I emerged clean in a fresh but creased uniform for lunch. Hilda chatted with the General while I sat silently, trying to digest my impressions so far. At the time I didn't appreciate that the simple but elegant lunch would be the last hint of sophistication I was to enjoy for many months.

Vietnamese shopkeepers pull down their shutters between midday and three, and all citizens retire for a siesta, but not personnel fighting a war. Again Hilda slid behind the steering wheel of the Volkswagen, and we set off for Military Assistance Command, Vietnam (MACV). Headquarters for all US military activity in Vietnam, MACV provided assistance to the armed forces of South Vietnam. The building was known to the military as 'Free World Headquarters', the Free World forces being those of the United States, Australia, New Zealand, Thailand, Korea and the Philippines. What the rest of the world said about that title, I don't want to know! At MACV I was introduced to more top brass, the 'Saigon Warriors', as the Diggers sardonically called them. And in the public relations office, I discovered that riveting photograph of Barry Harford. I was glad to let the Australian army postal system take delivery of the cake I had successfully transported, knowing it would be in Roger Wainwright's hands the next day, unless he was out in the bush on operation.

Next we visited 3 Field Hospital, the big American hospital in Saigon that had, on occasion, cared for the wounded from the First Battalion when they were based at Bien Hoa, 30 kilometres north. There were no Australians there that day, but we toured the wards to give me a feel for what my work would be like. I saw female American nurses for the first time. How can they allow themselves to be so messy just because there are more men around than anyone can handle, I thought, looking at their shiny faces and untidy hair. What a prig I was! Soon I would look equally messy within half an hour of setting off each morning.

Hilda kept the worst until last. Our final visit was to the psychiatric ward for shell-shocked men. They sat on the sides of the beds in the customary American blue pyjamas. Just sitting, blank eyes staring at nothing. They offered no response when I spoke to them. 'A lot of them are faking so they won't be sent back to the battle,' a nurse whispered. Even if that was true, I didn't care. The room was a picture of such indescribable sadness that it is burned forever into my memory.

Saigon lies well inside the Tropic of Cancer, about as far north of the equator as Darwin is south, and the sun sets abruptly about six each evening. Enveloping darkness signalled the end to our work day. We had whirled around like dervishes, me in a zombie-like trance induced by jet lag and the torpid air of the wet season. Hilda took me for a quiet dinner, then to my room for the night at the beautiful old Hotel Majestic overlooking the Saigon River. Built in the French style, with five-metre ceilings, the hotel stood at the far end of Tu Do, one of Saigon's most famous streets. I could see the river's meanderings as it flowed east, eventually to

meet the South China Sea near Vung Tau. The Majestic's
rooftop bar and restaurant was a popular place for people to
sip a gin and tonic and watch the war: tracer bullets lighting
up the sky, ammunition dumps exploding, helicopter gunships firing at enemy targets. I was too tired, dirty and sweaty
to linger.

My room of faded elegance on the sixth floor was spacious
and appealing. After a hot soaking bath, I expected to fall
asleep instantly but as my exhausted head hit the pillow my
mind shifted into overdrive. The myriad sights and sounds of
the day chased each other around in my brain. Unfamiliar
noises – gunshots and the distant thunder of artillery – drifted
in from the windows. Worst of all, I was in a hotel room in
wartime Saigon, where no one knew exactly who was enemy
and who wasn't. I had no idea where Hilda was staying,
except that she was with friends. I was alone, and I was scared
sleepless. Would a sex-starved soldier get into my room and
rape me? Would I die from getting some non-drinkable water
in my mouth when I washed my face? Even worse, would the
Viet Cong attack in the night? Would I live to see another
tomorrow? It seemed my eyes didn't close all night. I was later
to find that most women, and maybe the men too, had similar
fears their first night in South Vietnam.

When Hilda arrived next morning to pick me up, I had been
dressed and ready for hours. Breakfast was lovely: coffee and
a crusty fresh baguette loaf, a legacy from French colonial
days. So far I had spent no money; there had been no need.
Our first stop was to change my Australian money into
Military Payment Certificates (MPC). The scrip, worth 118
piastres (P) to the Yankee dollar, was given in equal exchange
for my money. MPC, the coin of the realm for US and

Australian forces in Vietnam, was issued to contain rampant inflation and to halt black market foreign exchange dealings that were destroying the Vietnamese economy – already in danger of collapsing under the huge military presence. I took the crumpled MPC handed to me, and noticed that it smelled of mildew. Then we headed to the American military supply area to collect five pairs of olive-green American army issue fatigues (shirt and trousers) and heavy black army boots for me to wear when I visited the more dangerous forward areas. No women's Aussie jungle greens were yet available as there were no Australian servicewomen then in Vietnam.

'I look like an elephant in these baggy fatigues,' I groused to the crewcut Private First Class (PFC) who served me. 'Ma'am, any of the local Vietnamese tailors will fit them for you,' he answered in a tone that suggested I wasn't the first person to complain. So *that* was the secret! I'd noticed that the basically shapeless fatigues when worn by the American gals clung to their bottoms and showed off their waistlines. I'd get mine tailored to fit too. PFC Crewcut handed me an army helmet and a Yank cap for a head cover, and I was outfitted. I wanted to pass on the Yankee cap, but I needed *something* to wear until I met up with the Aussies and could get my hands on a true floppy bush hat. I still had to have my name monogrammed in black on the right front of the fatigues, in the white space left empty for that purpose, and to have Australian Red Cross stitched on the left. The PFC had Crewcut block-lettered on his right front and US Army on his left. Even General William C. Westmoreland, commander of the US military advisory group, wore his name for all to see. But that job would have to wait until I got to the Long Binh/Bien Hoa military complex. I was to work there for three weeks until there was suitable accommodation for a woman in Vung Tau – a tent was *not* considered suitable by the powers that be.

I knew of Bien Hoa, for that was where the First Battalion had been based, and Long Binh was adjacent to it. I also had seen Bob Hope's Christmas special from Vietnam when he had joked: 'Here I am in Bien Hoa. That's Vietnamese for duck!'

Australian Army advisers had been working with the Army of the Republic of [South] Vietnam (known to us as ARVN) since 1962, and the RAAF had flown in transport planes to support the advisers. In 1965, Australia's Prime Minister announced that a battalion of troops was to go to Vietnam. The First Battalion settled in at Bien Hoa, just north of Saigon in May 1965, working with the American 173rd Airborne Brigade in defending the base and reacting to any enemy activity in the area, including Saigon. Their year up, the First Battalion was relieved by the Fifth and Sixth Battalions, whose mission was to clear and secure a different area, Phuoc Tuy province south-east to the coast, including the vital port of Vung Tau. By June 1966 the Australian forces had established a rudimentary Task Force operational base in the middle of an abandoned rubber plantation which they named Nui Dat. The base was logistically supported from Vung Tau, on the coast 100 or so kilometres from Saigon and Bien Hoa. As the change in location took place, mention of Bien Hoa faded from Australian newspaper headlines, to be replaced by Vung Tau and Nui Dat.

'We will live in Vung Tau with the Americans when they finish building a place for their doctors and nurses,' Hilda announced as I stowed my new fatigues and boots in the Volkswagen. 'Meanwhile, the 93rd Evacuation Hospital at

Long Binh looked after the Australians when they were at Bien Hoa, and the staff needs extra help. I'm sending you there.' She saw my look of disappointment, so to soften the blow she continued: 'The Australians have a great reputation there.' Long Binh, she explained, was the biggest military compound in the world. It was to be an ideal place to orient myself to the war before joining the Aussies at Vung Tau.

3

Long Binh, Bien Hoa and Battle Casualties

Highway One, known so poignantly as the 'Street Without Joy', ran the length of South Vietnam. By mid-afternoon of my second day in Vietnam, our Land Rover, with an army private at the wheel, hurtled at breakneck speed along the wide Saigon–Bien Hoa stretch of Highway One toward the 93rd Evacuation Hospital at Long Binh. All military traffic was speeding, as the area was not considered safe – Jim Irvine's 'incident' had happened there. How dangerous was 'not safe'? I didn't know but was relieved that the army driver kept his foot hard on the accelerator as he dodged in and out of the pony carts and cyclists, and on through the shabby ribbon of villages lining the road.

The 93rd Evac hospital supported a huge area, ranging from Pleiku in the Central Highlands, south to Bear Cat, and west to the Parrot's Beak, a notoriously dangerous area of neighbouring Cambodia near Tay Ninh that jutted into

Vietnam. The Viet Cong were known to transport equipment from North Vietnam to the South by way of neutral Cambodia, Cu Chi and Bien Hoa. Those place names quickly became familiar to me, although none of the patients could explain exactly where they were. As roads were too dangerous to travel, soldiers moved around by air unless they were slogging on foot through the jungle or rice paddies.

The hospital was a huge sandbagged area of quonset huts with wards, sleeping quarters, mess halls and chapels sheltered under the semicircular corrugated metal roofs. What was not in a quonset hut was in a tent, rows of which appeared to stretch for miles. Once again the 93rd Evac was prepared to continue its proud history of nursing under extreme hardship. A generation earlier its nurses had followed troops into the World War II invasion of Sicily and a few months later had been in the thick of the Anzio tragedies that followed the Allied invasion of Italy.

No sooner had the Land Rover sped away than I was greeted by a short, trim woman of about fifty in the candy blue uniform of the American Red Cross. She held out her hand and said: 'Hello, I'm Vi Auer!' My chin hit the floor. Of all the gin joints in all the towns in all the world, I had walked into hers! Come to think of it, Saigon in war time was not so different from the throbbing intrigue and corruption in French wartime Casablanca. Of the hundreds of American Red Cross (ARC) women, affectionately known as Donut Dollies, working in South Vietnam, Vi Auer – the only one I had been asked to look up – was the first one I met.

'It's time for Happy Hour. We've got Mai Tais,' she said. Was she speaking a different language? Happy Hour was a new expression to me then, made popular by the Americans.

And what was a Mai Tai? Vi introduced me to the three or so other ARC women at the 93rd, all of whom had known each other from working in Korea, Japan and the Philippines. No doubt that's where they developed their taste for the rum-based Mai Tais. Worn out from the heat and the previous two sleepless nights, I was happy to sip a Mai Tai or two or three, and listen, with eyes shining, to their talk – tough but caring women's talk of war experiences, patients and exotic postings. I was entranced.

The women told me I must shower between 6.30 and 7 pm each day, the only time women were allowed to shower. They showed me the toilet block, a line of three or four boxes of cheap timber, with a roof to keep out the rain but no doors. Anyone walking along the line of latrines had a clear view of what the occupants were doing – only a fence in front shielded us from the rest of the world. Looking at the muddy path that led to the latrines, I vowed to make sure I never would need to go there between lights-out and dawn. My 'room' in the women-only quonset was a stretcher cot alongside many others, all covered with white mosquito netting. A wooden box was my bedside cabinet, and on top of that sat a tin basin for washing. My only other furniture was a narrow, grey metal locker in which I could hang a few clothes and lock any valuables. But who had valuables? We shared everything and wanted nothing in return.

We lined up in the mess hall cafeteria-style – plastic plates and tin cutlery in hand – for the lima beans, mashed potatoes and Salisbury steak dinner, an unappetising staple of US army cuisine. That night, on my thin mattress, I listened to the non-stop chop-chop of helicopters overhead and drifted into my first good sleep in two nights. I was unbothered by the knowledge that the hospital was under high alert for a mortar attack, for I was surrounded by capable women who would know what to do should that happen.

When day broke at six, the clang of alarm clocks all around woke me. Everyone quickly was astir because work started at seven. I made haste to get ready. I poured a splash of water into the tin bowl on top of the box to wash my face, spread double the usual amount of deodorant under my arms as I was already beginning to perspire in the humid air, and pulled a uniform over my head. Teeth were cleaned by using potable (fit for drinking) water poured into a cup from a jerry can by my bed. Makeup was applied by peering into a mirror hanging from the metal cabinet, but hanging far too low for my tall frame. I smeared on lipstick and pulled a comb through my already sweaty short hair. I still had to visit that dreadful toilet block, but for all intents, I was ready for work. We were to go straight to the hospital wards after breakfast. Working hours officially started at 7 am, but we were often at work from 6.30 am onward. I was excited at what lay ahead – and, oh, so innocent.

The 93rd served one of the busiest war zones in Vietnam. Venereal disease and malaria added to the patient load as well. It would be a hectic day, especially as one of the ARC women was ill with 'fever unknown', a common complaint in Vietnam. Vi handed me boxes of yellow pencils with erasers on the ends. 'Most of the men don't have anything to write with,' she explained. 'They come to us straight from the jungle, with nothing except what they've been wearing for days. They'll all want a pencil.' I beamed with pleasure at having a job to do.

Vi led me to the door of a ward full of American wounded, lying on narrow beds in their hospital-issue blue cotton pyjamas, and left me. I walked in and nervously introduced myself: 'Hello, everyone. I'm Jean Debelle from Australian Red Cross, and I have pencils with rubbers for you!' The sound of silence that followed would have stunned Simon and Garfunkel. As soon as the words were out of my mouth I would have given anything to take them back. I wanted to flee at supersonic speed but blundered on, handing out pencils as though my life depended on it. Finally I escaped into the next ward. Great start, you *idiot*, I chided myself. You just told them that you had pencils with condoms! Or did the Americans know what we call erasers in Australia? Maybe no one had heard me. Maybe I'd be forgiven because I talked with a funny accent. Maybe the Pope is a Protestant.

Part of the work of a Red Cross girl was to write, at the dictation of a wounded patient, a letter to his family or friends when he was unable to write it himself. That day I wrote and mailed several letters to American families. Then Vi directed me to a soldier whose head was swathed in bandages; tubes were attached to all parts of his body. My heart ached to give him comfort and support. Together we struggled through a letter to his family on an Ohio farm. Because he could hardly speak, it took a long time. The ward had grown quiet; only male nurses or medics bustled up and down. I looked at my watch: it was 6.30 pm. I had to get to the shower. I was sweaty from the tropical heat and dirty from the muddy ground, but how could I leave him? I can shower later, I reasoned. Patiently I continued with the letter until it was done; I wasn't allowed a shower until 6.30 pm the next day.

John Wayne, of your movie screen and mine, was to visit next morning. The hospital's chief, Lieutenant Colonel (Lt Col) Walter Gordon, honouring the Australians he had known before, invited me to be among the few personnel to meet him. At ten o'clock, unshowered and quite sure that I smelled, I left the wards and joined the half circle under the blazing sun to welcome the giant of Western movies. John Wayne in green army fatigues, his rangy body looking larger than life, moved along the line, saying a few words to each person. I was introduced as being from Australia. 'I didn't know Australians were here,' he said in that often-imitated, deep, slow voice, while giving me a steady look from his compelling eyes. 'We are helping you win the war, Mr Wayne,' I replied politely, but he already had moved on to shake the next hand. Although suitably star-struck, inwardly I wanted to slog him. How dare he not know the Aussies were there!

That evening at six-thirty I was first in line for the showers. As in the latrines, there was no privacy. Everyone was clearly visible. But how good it felt to have smooth skin at last, instead of the gritty, sticky feel I had endured for the previous two days. I pulled my gown around me, slipped a pair of rubber thongs onto my feet, and padded back to my hut to dress for dinner. Each step in the thongs kicked mud up the back of my showered legs. Was it impossible to stay clean in Vietnam? 'Here's mud in your eye' was taking on a whole new meaning.

We got used to always being dirty. Vietnam, surely one of the world's most beautiful countries at any time, was also a dusty, dirty place, made worse so by the war. In the monsoon season from May to October, rains turned the dust into mud that could bog a tank-like Armoured Personnel Carrier (APC). Always it was hot and overwhelmingly humid.

One day during my first week, a man wearing the familiar bush hat of the Australian troops came across the compound.

'G'day. I heard you were here.' After only five days surrounded by Americans, I was so homesick to hear that
familiar flat accent I nearly hugged him, but didn't of course.
He was from a small unit of the Sixth Battalion, moving First
Battalion stores and vehicles to Nui Dat. I begged him for a
floppy bush hat, and he followed up on his promise that
I'd have one next day. Then I was happy to toss away my
American cap. As far as uniform went, at last I was properly
outfitted.

Each day there was barely time to have lunch. Some
evenings, refreshed by a shower and dinner, we returned to the
wards to play bingo or for other arranged entertainment with
the patients. Other nights we would sit outside to catch any
passing breeze, but inevitably that meant swatting at the mosquitoes and other creepy-crawlies that also came out at night,
for even the bugs knew better than to come out in the heat of
day. I hadn't yet seen any mail from home, but I would sit and
write to those who had given me such a wonderful farewell.
Inevitably the letters were dirty, bug-stained and sweat-
streaked. The first few I wrote over and over, trying to keep
the page clean, embarrassed that anyone might think I was
exaggerating the dirt, 'bunging on' the hardship. Most of all,
I wanted letters to my mother to be pristine. It was impossible.

One constant, somewhat bitter statement was made when the
GIs heard I was from Australia: 'Your President has been here
to see your guys. It would be nice if ours came here to see *us*.'
Our 'President', Prime Minister Harold Holt, had visited our
troops at Bien Hoa on ANZAC Day, two months earlier,
before going to Washington to promise the President of the

United States Australia would go 'all the way with LBJ'. 'I'm sure President Johnson will come soon,' I hastened to assure them – as if I could do anything about it.

There were a number of things I could do something about, however. In addition to writing letters for the wounded and giving out supplies, I learned to navigate my way through the American field phone system, going from exchange to exchange; at the 93rd we had to call the units to sort out a patient's mail, pay and personal belongings. I learned to scrounge whatever I needed from anywhere I could. And I became totally unfazed by the constant mortar alerts. After hearing of the dangers combat soldiers faced daily, why should an incoming mortar round or two throw me?

Each day I did my best to assist Vi and her team. After a week of non-stop work, she decided I had earned some time off. With nothing else to do, I did what any young winter-white Australian girl would do when surrounded by a sea of suntanned bodies. I put on my two-piece swimsuit – commonplace for a young Aussie woman in the sixties – grabbed a book, lay down on my tummy on one of the benches where soldiers watched outdoor movies at night and set about getting a tan. Totally absorbed in Graham Greene's *The Quiet American* – a melancholy story of the French war against the Viet Minh and obligatory reading for any visitor to Vietnam – I was unaware that in windows and doorways people were gathering to look at me. If I had been lying there naked, I could not have caused a greater reaction. A hastily summoned Vi arrived. Gently she suggested that in an almost totally male environment, where many men had not seen a woman – let alone a woman in a swimsuit – for many months, it might be wise to go inside and change. I was mortified. Another giant clanger. I had travelled the globe, I had worked hard to become a cosmopolitan woman of the world, but no matter how one sliced it, I was utterly green. I hadn't grasped yet that doing what came naturally in Australia was not done in a camp full of bored and sex-starved soldiers. Later in Vung Tau the American nurses told me with amazement that they never had seen bikinis and Speedos like the ones Aussies of both sexes wore at nearby Back Beach. Lt Annie Philiben of the 36th Evac said: 'Your nurses wore those long nun-like uniforms and Victorian veils, and then we would see them frolicking in next to nothing at the beach!'

That night at Long Binh it poured. Vi, no doubt as a way of reinforcing her point, took my arm and drew me to the door. Outside, in the torrential rain, a movie was screening, and about twenty GIs (or 'grunts', as the American infantry-men called themselves) sat on the backless benches, huddled in their ponchos. Their eyes never left the movie screen, and they seemed oblivious to the rain beating down on them. The movie must have seemed like heaven compared to the horrors they had come from, and would return to, in the jungles and rice paddies.

One such place was Cu Chi. It was from there that casualties constantly filled the beds at the 93rd. About 36 kilometres to the west of Saigon, Cu Chi was headquarters of the 25th Infantry. Its emblem, a yellow slash on red, signalled both its origin in Hawaii, where it had returned fire against the Japanese at Pearl Harbor, and its name 'Tropic Lightning'. Running beneath the 25th Infantry base, and largely unknown to its men, was a network of carefully concealed Viet Cong tunnels. They extended 200 or so kilometres around and into the base. There the VC lived, slept and ate, surviving for years in an elaborate 'township' of hospitals, dining rooms and kitchens, right below the 25th Infantry camp. The massive Tet offensive of 1968 against the Allied forces was said to have been planned and launched from those tunnels. Australian engineers, the venerable Tunnel Rats, working near Cu Chi, were the first to discover and explore the tunnels and the first to blow up underground VC headquarters, no matter what anyone else asserts. It is likely that there was very little the VC didn't know about the 25th Infantry, and daily I witnessed evidence of their intelligence in the wards.

The days rushed by, punctuated far too regularly by the chop-chop-chop of Dust-Off helicopters landing with their wounded in a swirl of debris right alongside the 93rd, just as they did next to every major military hospital in Vietnam. The sound of the helicopter is one of the most memorable sounds of Vietnam. The Dust-Off pilots, angels of hope to the wounded, flew Iroquois helicopters (universally known as Hueys), each with a big red cross painted on the olive-grey fuselage. Often, under hostile fire, the pilots had to chop their way down into a jungle clearing, rotor blades whirling, to pick up the wounded. In twenty minutes or less, the casualties were being cared for in a modern hospital, increasing their chances of survival from the kinds of injuries that would have killed them in past wars. Immediately after handing their precious cargo to a hospital's stretcher-bearers, the crew took off again for more wounded. It was said they made an average of about eight trips before they got 'zapped', a very final proclamation for 'killed'. Was it any wonder grey hair crowned most of the pilots' young faces? They had everyone's heartfelt admiration.

To partially offset the sadness that we faced each day, there was always plenty of male attention. On ward rounds I'd share a joke with a 93rd Evac doctor who, like most of the American doctors, had been drafted. He invited me to dinner one evening 'on the economy'. That meant eating off-base at one of the local restaurants believed to have food clean enough for Westerners to eat and thought to be safe from VC attack. I hadn't been off-base in the ten days since I had arrived from Saigon and accepted with delight. Over dinner I learned he was a married man. When he rushed the meal along, I was grateful. I didn't feel totally safe off the base. I presumed he was anxious to get back in case of an influx of casualties. We returned early to the 93rd.

'Have you seen the operating theatre?' he asked. I hadn't seen an operating theatre anywhere so jumped at the chance. To my horror, when we entered the room, he shut the door firmly and pinned me to the wall. He began to grope my body, but I fought back, fiercely pounding him with my fists to get free of his grasp. In his frustration he got angry. I fled, leaving him to his anger. I was angry, too. I hadn't as much as touched his hand! Again, I chided myself for being so naïve. Would I never understand that life was different in a war zone? I avoided speaking to him again. I did see him, though, many months later, spending a weekend with a woman in Vung Tau. I was glad he'd found some company.

Sometimes the bloody aftermath of battles that filled the hospitals was bizarrely juxtaposed with a reminder of our ordinary lives at home. One day I watched astonished as an American nurse took a snowy tennis dress from her metal locker. She was playing tennis that day on the court of

American Ambassador, Mr Henry Cabot Lodge. And I was told that people were water-skiing on the VC-threatened Saigon River!

One Sunday the female nurses and I were invited to a party at the 173rd Airborne Mess in Bien Hoa. The GIs were to go out on a big operation next day and wanted to celebrate while they could. We arrived about four o'clock in the afternoon, and immediately the girl from Down Under who talked funny was the centre of an interested group. Many of the Airborne had known Australian First Battalion soldiers whom they esteemed highly. We chatted over drinks for several hours and then returned to the 93rd.

'That was a great party,' I said to the nurses as we jolted our way home on the back of a deuce-and-a-half (a two-and-a-half-ton truck with the white star of the US Army on the front doors). There was silence for a moment, and then one nurse said quietly: 'I'm glad you thought so. You won't see half of them again. Only half will come back from the operation alive.' Stunned, I sat silent for the rest of the trip.

My days were a swirl of new patients, dreadful food, and almost nothing for me to do for recreation except drink, so after two weeks, I was happy to be asked to teach English to Vietnamese teenagers who had lost their parents and homes near the Cambodian border. They were living at an orphanage and school run by nuns of the Roman Catholic church in a village about eight kilometres from the 93rd. I struggled through an English lesson, sweating with each look at their earnest faces hanging on my every word. The last half hour was left free for play. I panicked. How could I amuse Vietnamese teenagers? All I could think was to teach them the Hokey Pokey; they could use their English and have fun at the same time. To my relief they loved it, especially when we turned around and bumped bottoms. Squealing with laughter, they pushed and shoved to bump their thin buttocks against my ample Western rump. I wondered what the nuns thought of it all. The next day a speck of dirt scratched the cornea of my left eye, and I was forced to take some days off work on bed rest. Then a huge influx of casualties arrived, and I was too busy to visit the school again. I was disappointed and felt that I had abandoned my new friends.

Wearing an eye patch in the sticky climate was not pleasant, but it made me aware of how much more uncomfortable a wounded man must feel. As soon as the patch came off, I hitched a ride on a chopper to see Hilda in Vung Tau. 'I'm so busy and happy, but I want to be with the Aussies,' I told her. I'd had dinner the previous evening with the men and women of the Australian civilian surgical team from the Alfred Hospital in Melbourne who worked at Bien Hoa's Vietnamese hospital. The evening had made me even more homesick for my own countrymen.

Within days Hilda sent word from Vung Tau that there was, at last, accommodation for us there. During my three weeks at the 93rd I had been welcomed warmly. Before leaving, I was introduced to another American custom, the PG (a parting gift), and it was not to be the last time I was made aware that Americans are some of the most generous gift-givers in the world. The gift is long forgotten but the gesture is not.

On 11 July I hitched a ride with an American in the next jeep going to Saigon, and together we faced the speedsters along the Bien Hoa highway. He left me at Tan Son Nhut, where I waited in the heat of the afternoon for the four o'clock RAAF Caribou, an olive-green short takeoff and landing transport of 35 Squadron, to take me to Vung Tau, at the southernmost tip of Phuoc Tuy province.

The loadmaster helped me scramble into the open back of the Caribou (not easy in a skirt – there were no ramps then) and I belted myself into a space on the webbed seating that lined each side. Efficiently and quietly, the load crew went about their preparations for takeoff. As we raced along the runway and lifted into the air, I realised, horror-struck, they had forgotten one vital job – the back of the aircraft was wide open! I could see the ground rushing away beneath me. Only my seatbelt prevented me from tumbling out that gigantic hole onto Saigon's red rooftops, which were rapidly receding and being replaced by menacing jungle and paddy fields. I looked around in a panic but no one else seemed concerned, and it was impossible to talk because of the noise of the engines. I sat with sweaty palms and racing heart for twenty minutes until I felt the aircraft descend for landing into Vung Tau airbase.

I never once flew in a Caribou in Vietnam that did not have the back wide open.

4

So This Was Vung Tau

THREE WEEKS AFTER SETTING FOOT IN VIETNAM I arrived
in Vung Tau. Unlike the huge US military base at Long
Binh–Bien Hoa, Vung Tau was a seaside town, pretty
but somewhat down-at-heel. Expecting my new home there
to be at best a quonset hut like that at the 93rd, I was astonished when Hilda drove me to a three-storey stone building.
The Villa DuBois, as it was known, had been constructed to
house the medical officers and senior enlisted staff of the
American 36th Evacuation Hospital. There were a few spare
rooms for visiting medical personnel and for the American
and Australian Red Cross (during my year, New Zealand Red
Cross was not yet in Vietnam). Majors and above had rooms
to themselves; everyone else roomed with one other. The 36th
Evac enlisted men, as Americans call Other Ranks (ORs),
were housed in tents near the hospital.

Named after the popular second commander of the 36th

Evac, Lt Col James DuBois, the Villa sat behind a low white fence on one of the main streets that ran parallel to the Vung Tau beachfront. Surrounding the other three sides of the Villa was a two-metre-high stone wall painted the soft yellow so loved by the French and topped by a spiral of barbed wire. At the front gate stood a sentry box with a tin roof and four sandbagged sides, but open from the waist up. The guard, his only armament an M14 rifle (the more advanced and compact M16 rifles were not available to US hospital personnel), was protected from the rain but from little else – least of all from an enemy attack. Another sentry watched over the front door. From five o'clock each night, an additional 36th Evac enlisted man patrolled up and down along the back wall, which was about three metres from our bedroom window. There was almost nothing to stop the VC from attacking us in the middle of the night; not a situation that made me feel secure. Our accommodation was a palace, though, compared to that of most other officers.

Room 116 that I was to share with Hilda was like many an unadorned motel room, but to me it seemed the ultimate in splendour. We entered through a tiny hall. The bathroom to the right had water that ran hot or cold into a porcelain wash basin (no more tin bowls on a wooden crate). There was also an overhead shower, a jerry can of drinkable water, and an inside flushing toilet! Luxury! Another step on the red and white tiled floor and we were in a room with two single beds parallel to each other. A cheap wardrobe stood against the near wall, and on the far a large window looked out over the barbed-wire-topped wall to the green foliage and red-roofed villas beyond.

A rustle at the door signalled the arrival of two American

Red Cross women from the room next door. Eleanor Koops, known as Koopsie, and Vivienne Ollila, both hugged me. 'Honey,' Eleanor drawled in her Alabama twang, 'this is for real here. You'll need someone to look after you, and we're going to do it.' Hilda, one of the few people with transport, offered to drive us all the short distance along the road to the Pacific Hotel – a large seafront establishment surviving from colonial days – for dinner. The hotel had been converted into Bachelor Officers' Quarters (BOQ), where personnel of both sexes and marital status who lived in central Vung Tau ate their meals. I took my plastic tray and lined up for the taste-less food slopped onto my plastic plate. Every army grumbles about the chow, but in Vietnam our food was limited to what could be brought in from other countries. We didn't dare eat local food, contaminated as it was with faeces and flies. To do so was a quick road to hepatitis or dysentery.

At dinner I met Harry Janssen, the first male Field Force officer Australian Red Cross had sent overseas to work with our troops since World War II. He was to become a good friend. A Dutch immigrant and a boyish father of two from Melbourne, Harry was a former pilot in the Royal Nether-lands Air Force and an accomplished musician. He had boundless energy and enthusiasm, and spoke animatedly, leap-frogging from subject to subject in his strong Dutch accent. Harry lived in a tent with the men of 2 Field Ambu-lance hospital at the First Australian Logistic Support Group (1 ALSG) encampment. The role of ALSG was to supply the front line troops at the 'sharp end' at Nui Dat. The ALSG camp was built on sandhills along what became known as Back Beach, on the eastern edge of the Vung Tau peninsula, about six kilometres from Vung Tau. Harry warned me about life in the camp: 'When the wind blows off the sea, the sand bites into your skin like needles!'

Many Villa residents were also at the Pacific for dinner, as it was the closest place to get a meal. I was introduced to Dr Jim Fenton, an American radiologist who, with Sam Byland, an ophthalmologist, and later David Kitchin, another medico, had a room next door to mine. I was glad to know I had a secure male presence so close. Jim's first words grabbed my attention: 'My wife wrote me about the anti-war protests in Australia after your first draftee was killed.' When Private Noack's death was reported in the American papers, Jim's wife in Detroit had mailed Jim the clippings. I was amazed to hear that the political impact in Australia of Errol Noack's death had reached all the way to Detroit.

Nancy and Bill Lee were a married couple who owned the two bicycles I'd seen parked in the hallway along from our room. Faced with the perennial transportation shortage, they had sensibly 'gone Vietnamese' and bought bikes. Nancy explained that it was not common in Vietnam for a married couple in the military to share a room. 'When we were first in country we were posted to Long Binh. I lived in the nursing quarters and Bill lived in the men's barracks.' Then she started to laugh: 'When one of the Special Forces men found out we were married, he "acquired" an ambulance and arranged for a four-point guard to be posted around it so that Bill and I could have an evening together.' It was a case of, if this van is a'rockin', don't come a'knockin'!

Next morning when we returned to the Pacific for breakfast, I had the first of hundreds of servings of greasy fried eggs with bacon dried into scrappy pieces, the way the Americans preferred it. 'Why do the eggs taste like petrol?' I asked

Koopsie. 'Honey, they're preserved in ether,' she drawled. Sometimes the eggs were powdered. In fact, most of the food was powdered, dehydrated or tinned.

After breakfast Hilda drove me the six kilometres from the Villa to the Vung Tau airbase, where the 300-bed (400 by year end) 36th Evacuation Hospital was located. The hospital was a series of quonset huts, linked by roofed concrete walkways. Nine or so rows of sandbags reached half way up the walls of the wards to help protect the hospital from mortar fire. Victor Charlie's welcome message for newcomers was often an incoming round, and the hospital had been shelled severely three months earlier. There were two showers and two toilets for the entire hospital and no other running water except in the operating theatre and the laboratory. To 'scrub' between patients, doctors, nurses and medics washed their hands in a bucket of germicide, then rinsed in another bucket of water. Only the operating theatre and the post-operative ward were airconditioned. This meant that if it was 43 degrees Celsius outside, it was probably no cooler than 38 degrees in the post-op ward.

Dust-Off choppers stood ready on the hospital helipad, located alongside the shed that housed the Agent Orange supplies. We didn't know then that every time the choppers took off and landed they sent clouds of Agent Orange into the air we breathed. The chemical sprays used to defoliate the jungle, which gave cover to the Viet Cong, had more deadly effects than anyone thought. They upset Vietnam's whole ecosystem and caused severe medical problems.

A stately and charming blonde, Hazel Honeycutt (known unofficially as Honey) was in charge of the American nurses at the 36th. She had a silver oak leaf on her lapel, signifying she was a Lt Col. 'We are so thrilled to have you here,' Honey welcomed me in a Southern drawl as smooth as silk. Portraying every positive cliché written about Southern women, Honey was gracious and elegant (even in her army fatigues) and her staff said she was a magnificent nurse. Honey's administrative assistant, Sergeant First Class Jerome Faux, noticed my surprise that the Vietnamese secretary was dressed in Western clothes. He told me that the young woman arrived at work each day in the traditional Vietnamese *ao dai* and then, to everyone's amusement, disappeared beneath her desk to change into a dress! 'We are so tickled that anyone is tiny enough to change clothes under a desk,' Jerome said.

As often happens with a good leader, Honey's kindness and caring spread down through her staff. I met Lt Jackie Kennedy and Lt Geraldine (Polly) Parrott – unforgettable names for obvious reasons – among a host of others I remember fondly after forty years. Male nurses worked along with the women, for men had entered the American Army Nurse Corps ten years earlier. The female American nurses were attired in the same green army fatigues as the soldiers, and the American and Australian Red Cross women stood out prominently in our blue or grey dresses. There were some Australians already being treated at the 36th for gunshot wounds, malaria and the occasional accident.

The American 36th Evac and the Australian 2 Field Ambulance (hospitals with similar responsibilities despite the name variation) had first worked together at Milne Bay, Papua New Guinea, during World War II. In Vietnam their relationship was extraordinarily close again. Although both hospitals cared for the sick, 2 Field Ambulance was still under construction. Before 2 Field became fully operational several months later, the most severely wounded Australian soldiers were operated on at the 36th Evac by our surgeon and anaesthetist, who had the run of all its facilities. Then the soldiers were cared for devotedly by the splendid American nursing staff – a privilege paid for by the Australian government.

There was a small office that I was to share with American Red Cross. Hilda's plan was that I should have responsibility for our wounded at the 36th Evac at the Vung Tau airbase; Harry Janssen with 2 Field Ambulance at the ALSG camp atop the sandhills at Back Beach, as well as with the Task Force dug in at a rubber plantation at Nui Dat; and she would supervise and report our activities to NHQ and help out when needed.

As we returned to the Volkswagen for our trip to the ALSG camp, I saw a group of untidy, mud-covered soldiers in an even muddier Land Rover with a gold kangaroo patch on its front doors. Unmistakably they were Diggers, our fighting men from the Task Force base, about 35 kilometres to the north-east. I yearned to know more about them and where they lived, but there was no time for more than a shy smile and a wave.

Hilda drove us the six kilometres along a dirt road, past a few scattered ramshackle houses and clumps of bananas trees, to the camp in the sandhills. ALSG's Commanding Officer, Lt Col David Rouse, was a friend of Hilda's from Sydney, so she had a direct line to the top. I thought that would make our life easier but what it meant, in fact, was that if I strayed from Hilda's somewhat rigid ideas of correct behaviour, Colonel Rouse heard about it before I did! He shook hands with me warmly, as did all the officers I met.

The captain in charge of Administration, Kevin Hawthorne,

immediately flattered my tall, broad-shouldered frame by
calling me Little One. A tough and soldierly man on the outside, Kevin was all melted butter underneath. During the
coming months he was to take me under his protective care
with fatherly gentleness, although he was probably only a few
years older than I. He advised me of army procedures and
generally set me straight with shrewd advice and insights
which, as a novice, I welcomed. I began to think of him as my
Guardian Angel in olive green.

ALSG and 2 Field Ambulance were built on the only land
available in the seaport of Vung Tau – the land that no one
else wanted. The steep sandhills, some 30 metres high, were
dotted with clumps of foliage on the highest dunes. Behind
the dunes a wide and beautiful beach, Back Beach, went on
forever until it disappeared into the haze of the Long Hai
hills. And joy of joys for the Australians, even the surf was at
times challenging. There were no permanent buildings yet in
the camp – only tents along the ridges and the endless hills of
sand. The Officers' Mess tent was placed on the highest sand
hill to catch any breeze from the South China Sea that might
ruffle the sticky air, but the ubiquitous sand penetrated every
crack, crevice and orifice available and made life miserable
for all. After a windy night, men – like huskies in snow –
would wake up and shake off the sand. 'Cleaning your teeth
with sandy toothpaste is not bloody funny,' I was told.

Pte Jim Townson said the ALSG camp reminded him of the
French Foreign Legion when he arrived to work at 2 Field
Ambulance. A ruined French fort, with thick walls scored by
slits through which the French had once fired their rifles,
stood like a decrepit old guard house on the left of the main
gate. The advance party, who had arrived three weeks before

Jim, had erected canvas tents on the sandhills. Jim's first task was to fill the sandbags used to protect against incoming mortar fire. The back-breaking job continued for months. The hospital's tented wards were the last to be built, and once they were in place, the patients started coming. Jim told me how business was done there. 'We wanted a truck from the Yanks, a ten-wheeler, because our trucks couldn't get through the sand. Bill Rodgers went to see them, a slouch hat changed hands, and we had our truck!'

Lt Col Bill Rodgers, CO of 2 Field Ambulance, who carried a swagger stick in old British army style, was adept at getting the better end of the bargain when swapping with the Americans. The Yanks had so much, but what they in turn wanted, only we had. As well as the famous slouch hats, Owen machine guns were a desirable item for barter. Colonel Rodgers was once offered a Huey helicopter plus flying lessons in exchange for his Owen. 'I had to decline on the grounds I couldn't take the helicopter home, but the Americans offered to pack it into crates and ship it to Australia. Full marks for persistence,' he told me.

Unlike the comparatively well-equipped American hospitals, 2 Field Ambulance consisted of two concrete slabs each supporting a large canvas marquee to form two 25-bed wards that later were expanded to hold a total of 60 patients. Occasionally snakes, scorpions or other venomous creatures crawled their way across the concrete floors. Another smaller tent held an operating theatre, where for only six weeks minor surgical work had been going on; the more serious work was done at the 36th Evac. The amenities the Americans had in Vietnam often seemed the height of luxury to us from Down Under in our rag tag shambles of a camp.

Engineering the ALSG camp at Back Beach from a series of sand-dunes wasn't a simple task. ALSG had to be readied quickly before the Fifth and Sixth Battalions arrived there to get acclimatised before moving to the underdeveloped and not yet secure camp at Nui Dat. Building speedily and effectively sometimes led to lines being drawn aggressively in the sand. Lt David 'Digger' Brandie, a 17 Construction Squadron engineer with an exuberant spirit and a smile to match, told us how, in the stress of those early days, he had come to blows with Colonel Rodgers.

David was in charge of the bulldozer operators, who were to cut some of the sandhills down to a plateau and sometimes fill in the valleys. David said his first priority at ALSG was 'to build roads and provide access for the immediate crisis of troops and equipment on the ground, and to plan for the expansion of units which were to operate from Vung Tau. We also had to work with what we had,' he said, 'which wasn't much. About half of my troop, 100 in all, were National Servicemen. Many didn't know how to push sand with a bulldozer. So not only were we working three shifts around the clock, but we had to train the guys as well.'

Like all unit commanders, Colonel Rodgers believed his hospital should have first priority. But the problem was the location of the hospital. 'Everyone knows,' as David explained, 'that hospitals are supposed to be quiet areas, and bulldozers are known for making a din. We had two or three bulldozers working alongside each other, running at full throttle. At night we had generators running construction lights, and the lights from the bulldozers themselves would bounce up and down as they worked. It must have seemed like thunder and lightning to someone lying in a sick bed nearby.

'Well, not long after we started and in the middle of the night, Colonel Rodgers had had enough. He sent one of his sergeants onto the site and ordered my lance corporal to shut the machines down or go somewhere else to play. This lance corporal was not one of my most experienced leaders, so he closed down the machines and everyone scattered to find me.

'Bear in mind that the responsibility for commanding three shifts, twenty-four hours a day, had gone on for months,' Dave mused. 'I was always on call, but occasionally I managed to find a good watering hole. By the time they found me, I may have been a little more vocal than was normal. The corporal left knowing he was to get back on the job or I'd have his guts for garters. I was the only one who gave him orders to start or stop, so the job went on. But an hour later the corporal was back. This time he'd been ordered off by the colonel himself – and lance corporals are inclined to do what a colonel tells them, particularly when *their* boss is only a second lieutenant.

'At this point I decided I should take care of the situation personally, so in my impetuous youth, pride stamped all over me and flamed by a can or two of Budweiser, I set out to put the medico in his place. The machines were going when I got there. Suddenly the colonel appeared in the dark, running up the sand-dune breathing flames of fire. He was about to tear the strips and stripes off the lance corporal when he ran into me. That's when the war of words began. Bill was going to court martial me, and I was going to turn one of my 'dozers on him. Somehow in the midst of this mayhem the job went on. In the morning I had to apologise to Bill, the ALSG Commander told Bill to move the hospital or accept the noise, and the troops had another story to justify the madness of the military officer!' David walked off leaving me laughing, as he was to do so many times.

The humidity of that July day when I first saw the camp was oppressive. As it was the wet season, water lay everywhere, further hampering the development of the camp. Bulldozers continued to roar day and night, attempting to smooth out the sandhills, yet there were deep valleys between them still. There was little hardstanding; the hard rock mixture and the Marsden metal plates, which formed a strong surface across the sand on which to walk or drive with relative freedom, were still far in the future.

By mid afternoon the sun was blazing. Together Hilda and I ploughed our way through the deep sand, stopping frequently to shake the grains from our flat, black leather, Red Cross shoes. It was tough going. Sand stuck to our sweaty bodies, making our skin like gritty sandpaper. The only plus in the dismal scene was that the sand meant the South China Sea and its lovely beach were only a short distance away. I was yet to learn about the mosquitoes, the pit vipers and the scorpions that were at home in the sand and plagued the men living in tents.

Hilda drove me back the six kilometres to the centre of Vung Tau, my home for the next year, and left me to explore. Vung Tau, or Cap St Jacques as it was known by the French, once had been a lovely seaside resort. As the closest beach resort to Saigon, it was still a popular weekend destination for Saigon's rich. It also served, however, as the in country 'relax away from battle' area for both the Free World forces and – to keep the balance in that incomprehensibly complex battleground – the Viet Cong! No area was secure.

Vung Tau's tree-lined, horseshoe-shaped Front Beach –

dotted with its Ba Moui Ba (the Vietnamese 33 brand beer) bars and with a long stretch of golden sand around the headland to the north-east – looked more than a little like Victor Harbor, Adelaide's traditional beach resort. Front Beach was also a popular swimming area for the locals, but there any similarity ended. Front Beach was off limits to us and to the Americans. It was there that the Vietnamese washed themselves, urinated and defecated, oblivious to anyone who might look. They had no choice, for there were no sewers in Vung Tau, and most houses had no toilets. Their only alternatives were the streets or the fields, where their most private functions could be seen by all. After some months there, I realised I never again could hear *Moon River* without thinking of Vietnam!

Still lovely in parts, Vung Tau was also a dirty, rat-infested, disease-ridden town of about 20,000 Vietnamese. At what was obviously the town centre, a large white board known as The Flags stood in the middle of the crossroads. It turned out that The Flags, which listed the Allied countries offering humanitarian aid to Vietnam, was where everyone chose to meet. Across from the sign, I saw the ramshackle sprawl of a smelly market and an assortment of shops with motorbikes parked inside and rubbish strewn outside. I was stunned. It was not the town I had been expecting. Where would I get my hair cut? Even more vexing: where would I get my legs waxed?

Life in Vung Tau was lived on the streets. They were everyone's backyard and thoroughfare, with the pavements used for everything except walking. There the Vietnamese squatted, knees wide apart, cooking noodles and soup, which they ate from hand-held bowls as they sat on low wooden stools. They drank coffee or beer while they read a book, smoked, chatted or watched the world go by. Or they might wash their hair, repair a motorbike, breastfeed bare-bottomed children (some as old as four), urinate and more. No one took any notice except me. Barbers worked outside as the customer sat in a chair surrounded by shorn dark hair, measuring progress in a mirror nailed to a post. Sidewalk 'dentists' and 'doctors' took care of their 'patients' with rusting surgical instruments. People were even having their ears cleaned with those same dirty tools. Everywhere were curious children who surrounded me and playfully pulled the blonde hairs on my arms, giggling because my arms were different from their hairless limbs.

Modishly elegant Vietnamese women with elaborate hair-styles strolled leisurely under parasols, some in long cotton gloves to protect their hands from the sun. Others, with backs rigidly upright, rode bicycles, securing their flowing skirts on the seat behind. Sturdy, poorer women carried colourful vegetables or even pails of water in two circular baskets on the ends of a bamboo pole bent over their shoulders. They hurried along in rubber sandals at a fast clip despite their heavy burdens.

Travelling salesmen, predecessors of Meals on Wheels, pedalled bicycles with carts on the front that contained appealing fried delicacies wrapped in banana leaves – snacks that no Westerner dared sample without dire consequences. Other salesmen on bikes peddled pots and pans, cane furniture, stacks of sugar cane, house plants in fancy ceramic or clay pots, even huge baskets of firewood or bricks.

The tree-lined streets were littered with trash, and military vehicles competed for room with cyclos (from the French cyclo-pousse) and Lambrettas (the local version of a minibus), both of which were the only public transport. Cyclos – the reverse of Chinese rickshaws, for the passenger seat is over the two wheels in front of the driver – roamed the streets like taxis seeking passengers. To ride a cyclo-pousse is, for my money, the most magical way of travelling there is. As you glide along, a muscular man, cigarette hanging from his lips, pedals languidly from his seat behind. It is the gentle sound-less movement that makes it so special. The hustle and bustle of the streets is there in front of you to see, to hear, to smell, even to touch.

It was common for the Vietnamese to squeeze a whole family – mother, father and perhaps four or five children – into the passenger seat, a sight that never failed to astonish us. Similarly, families of that size could be seen around town on a two-person motorbike – one child across the petrol tank at front and both parents sharing the seat while the mother held one child, and another child or more sat on the back over the wheel. For Western bodies though, sweating in the heat and humidity, two in a cyclo was more togetherness than any of us wanted.

Despite its drawbacks, Vung Tau giddily filled my senses. The spicy food smells and the attractive stacks of fruit in the market that gave off a heady aroma in the late afternoon sun enthralled me. Steam rose from the verdant foliage that hung heavy and gleamed brilliantly after rain. Everywhere there was the pungent fish smell of *nuoc mam*, the yellow fish sauce made from fermenting anchovies that enhances almost all Vietnamese food, no matter whether the food is served in a fancy restaurant or at a takeaway food cart. To uninitiated Western noses it smelled dreadful.

In the market I stopped to buy two bananas, tiny ones just the size of my fingers. As I quickly discovered, bananas were sold by the bunch. When I broke off two, there was so much shouting of 'troi oi' and agitated arm waving that I was terrified I'd be shot by the gun-happy White Mice who lurked everywhere. Then explanations flew. Eventually everyone smiled, and I was handed the whole bunch for the price of the two bananas.

It was starting to get dark, and I turned towards home. I was stopped short by what was the first of many offers I was to get in the Vung Tau market. A boy in shorts and rubber sandals, hardly more than eight years old yet smoking a cigarette sophisticatedly, said with a cheeky grin: 'Miss, 'ello, 'ello! *Uc dai loi* Number One. I take you through market. I be your fren'. You gimme five P?' His words rushed at me in a manic torrent. Then he got my attention. 'You want man? I have very nice big brother.' Taking my laughing 'no thanks' for uncertainty, he persisted. 'He ver-r-r-y good. He know many tricks. Or maybe you wan' GI?' I kept walking. After flashing me another wicked grin, he disappeared. Was he joking? The Vietnamese loved a bit of fun, but I never knew if the joke was on me.

Suddenly, as happens in the tropics, it became totally dark, and there were few lights around Vung Tau. I was starting to get scared again. I folded my weary body into a cyclo and let the tireless legs of the driver pedal me back to the Villa.

5

Sense of Humour Needed

Boooom! A huge explosion right inside the Villa jarred us awake at 5.30 on my third morning in Vung Tau. Each night I had fallen asleep exhausted – the constant struggle through the deep sand at camp, the long days trying to help the soldiers, and the enervating climate all took their toll. And at night I wrestled with the nagging thought that VC might attack the Villa.

Boooom! Hilda and I shot upright in our beds.

'VC!' Paralysed with fear, my voice could only manage a squeak. Oh God, don't let me die. I have only just got here. Then reality overcame my terror, and I threw on a dressing gown. I was damned if I was going to be shot in my nightie. Hilda and I were unarmed, untrained at what to do in an attack. Hearts racing, we stood immobile, straining to hear more sounds. The Villa was eerily quiet. Then footsteps came running along the tiled hallway.

'Is anybody hurt? Is anybody hurt?' The sweet sound was the southern voice of Colonel Honeycutt, checking that all her precious chickens were okay. I opened our bedroom door and saw other anxious faces appear at doorways along the corridor. Colonel Honeycutt was still tying the sash of a white robe over her nightgown as she ran, long blonde hair flying loose down her back. Off she dashed again, nightwear flapping, and relief made me giggle. Until then I had seen Colonel Honeycutt only in crisply starched fatigues, hair pulled into a chignon, looking as well groomed as a *Vogue* cover girl.

The Villa's hot water system had exploded, shooting water all over and blowing away an entire wall of the room where two male nurses were sleeping. Amazingly, they escaped unhurt. All water to the Villa was cut off, so Hilda and I used the jerry can of potable water for a sponge bath. That day all 36th Evac women wore perfume, and happily, the boiler was fixed by evening. I never was frightened about the VC attacking us again.

Hilda and I began to settle in at the Villa DuBois, each taking over one side of our room. On the wall above my bed I taped the photograph of the Unknown Digger that I had been given in Saigon. Except for the beds, there was almost no furniture, and we needed to do a lot to make our quarters comfortable. The rooms of the American nurses, who had been in Vung Tau several months, already had bookcases, straw mats on the tiled floor, and curtains at the windows for privacy from the patrolling guard. Hilda and I took turns dressing in the tiny bathroom so as not to give the guard an eyeful. Longing for the niceties that make life easier, I bought a straw floor mat and some fabric agreeably cheap in the market, and an American nurse, Kay Triplett (now Battles), transformed the material into nifty curtains on her sewing machine that had been shipped from Tokyo. The machine had arrived marked '999', which meant Urgent Medical Supplies. From ALSG we scrounged a wooden rod and proudly hung our curtains. Other soldiers painted three planks of timber for us that, together with some bricks I found lying around the Villa, became a three-tiered modernistic bookcase for family photographs, cameras, writing materials and the few books we had.

The Vung Tau market had wonderful decorating items. I bought baskets in different sizes for waste paper bins and to hold dirty laundry. Small blue and white rice bowls tied together with string into sets of twelve, a cent a bowl, were perfect for peanuts, pins, and myriad other things. I found a small hotplate on which to boil water for tea or coffee and eventually used it for heating combat rations (C-rations) or tinned food. Our room was shaping up to be home.

Baby-san, a Vietnamese girl of about fifteen who spoke little English, cleaned our room, made our beds and did our laundry for a small fee, which we paid to the GI who managed the Villa. Many of the long-serving Americans had spent time in Japan and had brought the Japanese form of address with them. Baby-san worked hard willingly and, it seemed, happily. Before work each morning, we threw our laundry into a basket, and when we came home at night, she had washed and crisply ironed everything.

The maids had a novel way of laundering uniforms. They'd drape them wet over the disease-infected back area where stray chickens, pigs and sometimes cows roamed and then stamp on them with bare feet to get out the dirt! David

Kincaid, my neighbour next door who was in charge of procuring items for the 36th, eventually arranged for washing machines to be purchased from the US base on Okinawa, a nearby Japanese island. The washing machines also arrived marked Urgent Medical Supplies. We were spoiled, but the reality was that we would not have had time to do our own laundry because we began work no later than seven each morning. I confess that today I long for the luxury of returning home each day to find my clothes hanging newly washed and ironed in the wardrobe.

Baby-san always made our clothes look fresh and appealing, but as soon as we dressed, the clothes wilted and gave off the stench of rank humidity. That odour clung to everyone. Along with *nuoc mam*, it was the smell of Vietnam. When I pull out my floppy bush hat forty years later, the same musty smell is still there. Of necessity we almost always wore perfume, bought at the PX (post exchange), our best supply store.

But there was a bigger problem. Our clothing, particularly our underwear, was disappearing with increasing frequency. I had clothes and jewellery stolen twice in the first three weeks. Carol Settimo (now Law) ran the United Service Organisations (USO) club in Vung Tau. The USO supplied hot meals, snacks, phone calls home, and other amenities for the US troops. Carol was a feisty Manhattan gal, and she'd had enough. 'I didn't come to Vietnam to supply the locals with lingerie,' she steamed. 'I'm going to complain to the boss Mama-san.' When Carol got home that night, all of her lacy underwear had her room number, 231, written in huge black marker across the crotch. She came downstairs to show us, tears of laughter streaming down her olive-skinned face. That wasn't the end of it either. At the time, Carol was engaged to a doctor serving elsewhere in Vietnam. One night, in a moment of intimacy, he saw her underwear and said, 'What's this for? In case you get lost going home?'

I had arrived in Vung Tau no longer a Red Cross novice, but there was a lot I still had to learn. I plunged into my work with gusto, seven days a week, doing all the non-medical work a nurse was too busy to do. I wrote letters for those too seriously sick or wounded to do it themselves. I welcomed new patients with the prestige toilet kits that Red Cross provided in the early days. I sent telegrams and I mailed letters, always through the military system. Often the letters were marked on the outside 'SWALK' (sealed with a loving kiss), 'Ho Chi Minh is a Rat Fink' or 'Please Mr Postman, Don't be Slow, Be Like Elvis and Go Man Go'. I gave soldiers cigarettes and matches if they smoked, sorted out any queries they had about mail or about property misplaced when they arrived in hospital, arranged for flowers to be sent for a wife's birthday, and shopped for those about to return home for further treatment. All the time I tried to calm the patients' worries and fears, often by doing no more than simply listening. It wasn't easy to find the right thing to say, particularly when a man had lost one or more of his limbs or eyes. Occasionally I tried to lift flagging spirits by handing out advice: 'Try to see the good side of life. You have so much to be thankful for.' But as I spoke, I felt embarrassed at the banality of my words.

I adored my job. But under my smiling shell, I was shy and insecure and never felt completely at home in my role. I had gone to an all-girls school, and I was still not at ease having men as friends rather than as boyfriends. I approached each patient as apprehensively as a swimming novice approaches the deep end. I was neither a nurse, nor girlfriend, nor a soldier's wife or mother. I knew, though, that it was important for me to be there.

To forget my own self-centred anxieties, I put on my biggest smile and hoped I was saying something helpful when I chatted with the patients or sent army signals on their behalf. When a soldier was wounded, his unit notified army headquarters. The official message, in formal military terms, was relayed to the man's loved ones. Devastating news often was coldly brief:

> Pte Loved One suffered gun shot wound yesterday and left leg amputated. Condition satisfactory.

The Red Cross went further. Through army channels we sent signals that were warmer, more personal and explanatory and, we hoped, more comforting to those at home so far away:

> Pte Loved One is recovering well after having his left leg amputated below the knee yesterday by an Australian surgeon in an airconditioned American hospital. Today he sat up in bed and enjoyed his first cigarette. His friends have visited him, and he hopes to be home soon. He sends love to all, especially his girlfriend, Jenny, and wants to know if you bought the new car.

Letters we received from mothers and wives testified to how much those Red Cross messages were appreciated.

The comfort kits we handed out were far superior to anything the Yanks had for their soldiers, and the Americans envied our men. When the wounded were admitted to hospital, they had been days or weeks on operation. They had nothing with them but the dirty uniforms they wore. Our kits held shaving materials, toothpaste and a brush, soap, a comb, a tin of talc, deodorant, rubber thongs, notepaper and pen, tissues, summer pyjamas and, in the early days, a singlet, which some of our men liked to wear.

At first we purchased Australian cigarettes for the patients, because that's what they wanted. We soon found it wasn't a wise use of Red Cross money – too many patients smoked – so we saved the coveted cigarettes for only the neediest. Eventually, as the load of wounded soldiers increased, we had to compromise with less generous toilet kits, reduced to a small cotton dillybag holding basic toilet articles. But no matter what we gave or did for the soldiers, they were always grateful.

To offer a patient a newspaper from home was like offering a banquet to a beggar and could be topped only by giving him Australian cigarettes. Eventually the Red Cross established a regular supply of newspapers. New Zealanders raced to the lead in getting the *New Zealand Herald* to us in a mere three days. Australian papers were generally no more than eight days old, and that was fine for patients who had been on operation, sometimes for weeks; in many cases they had not seen a paper for months. Our library of books came much later.

I welcomed the days after patients had been discharged or sent home, when there were a few empty beds. It meant there was more time to chat with the rest of the men to ease their boredom. Every day a patient begged me: 'Have you got anything I can do?' It was unsettling for a soldier who had been kept constantly busy for months to have nothing to do but rest. Sometimes, but only sometimes, we had jigsaw puzzles and playing cards available. Before I left Australia, the Red Cross had taught me some simple handcraft ideas using materials they believed would be readily available at the hospitals in Vietnam but without such basics as newspapers and flour to make paste, and with the 36th Evac's rulings about patients having only their toilet requisites with them, I was frustrated in my attempts to get handcrafts organised.

The days dragged for our patients, as they had so few visitors. Their mates could visit only when they had time off and transport; both were rare. The Diggers at the sharp end were either on operation or busy securing their home in the plantation, known simply as 'the rubber'. Daily truck convoys of supplies were the only form of road transport available, and each day's convoy brought reports of scattered enemy activity or dead Vietnamese found on the road.

Koopsie and Vivienne included our wounded in all the recreational activities they planned for the Americans, and many times the Australians shared in the goodies that arrived non-stop from the States. The two women were unstinting in their help to me. It was just as well – the conditions of our shared office were crowded and difficult and they, both trained social workers, had a better understanding of what was needed than I did. Sometimes when they were desperately busy, I'd return the favour by helping them.

Both the Fifth and the Sixth Battalions at Nui Dat had started operations, and new wounded constantly arrived at the 36th Evac. Some of the men had walked over what they thought was a pile of leaves, only to fall into a cunningly camouflaged pit of sharp bamboo spikes that had been dipped in faeces. The spikes slashed the skin like the sharpest knives.

The VC were expert at using everyday jungle materials to fight a modern-day war.

As well as the wounded, there were men who were ill. Beds were filled with patients who had contracted malaria, hepatitis, dysentery and fevers unknown, as well as those suffering from venereal disease. I hesitated to ask who was being treated for what.

Although the army issued every soldier a condom before he was given a pass to leave the camp, some patients had caught venereal disease from bar girls in town. Apparently bars with names like Yellow Bird, Melody or Venus looked respectable from the outside, but were houses of prostitution. With resignation a doctor told me: 'Most soldiers are hopelessly drunk at the time they contract the disease and either forget to use, or are totally incapable of using, a condom.' Around town I saw Australians dating Vietnamese women, but few to my knowledge married them. One soldier described a liaison as 'like f--king an ironing board'. As unpalatable as their line of work may be to some, I think many of the local women who prostituted themselves hated what they were forced to do to put food on the table for their families.

The hot, moist climate and many swampy areas scattered throughout the region provided ideal conditions for malaria. Soldiers contracted the debilitating illness despite a daily or, for some, a heavier weekly dose of the anti-malaria pill. Unlike most of us who took a daily pill, the RAAF men took the malaria pill weekly. Outside the airmen's villa was a sign showing a shapely Vietnamese girl and the words:

You'd go crook if she forgot HERS, so don't forget YOURS.
Thursday is Pill Day.

As a malaria precaution, Australian officers decreed that after sundown, the soldiers must wear long-sleeved shirts and long pants. After dark our men were clearly identifiable – arms covered, sleeves buttoned – on the streets and in the bars of Vung Tau. No one, though, ever said anything to Hilda and me about our sleeveless dresses! The edict also extended to the men's nightwear. The summer pyjamas that were part of our Red Cross kits could no longer be given out, although the doctors suggested we keep them for patients suffering from skin complaints and for those with damaged lower limbs. Troops out in the scrub on ambush, however, could not sleep under a mosquito net, and there were strains of malaria in Vietnam resistant to the pills we took. Malaria continued to be a haunting problem no matter what precautions were taken.

During the day, though, dress code was a different story for the Diggers. In the timeless way of the bush, Aussie soldiers saved on laundry by going shirtless when they were not on operation. This state of undress was allowed as a preventative against skin diseases, a common occurrence for men who worked in sweaty conditions, often wearing wet clothing for long hours, uniforms and equipment chafing their bodies. And the Diggers' lean, suntanned backs got them many an admiring look from the American nurses!

The American nurses were a great group. Many of them were hardly older than their patients and had been tossed into a situation where they knew they had to sink or swim. They swam as though they were chasing an Olympic medal. They loved the Aussies because they were so friendly, appreciative, and uncomplaining. As Ben Harmon, an orthopaedic surgeon serving with Uncle Sam, told me: 'Caring for the Australians was one of the best experiences I had in my life.'

Often I was called to serve as an interpreter for the Americans, for there were many times the language didn't jibe. 'Sister', for instance, was the correct form of address for a female Australian nurse; the GIs called their female nurses 'Ma'am.' A Digger could earn a black look from an American nurse called 'Sister' for the first time. Each morning the American nurses greeted me with new communication howlers. Kay Triplett gleefully told me about a conversation with Australian Pte Lyall Black, who was seriously wounded on operation with the Sixth Battalion.

'Sister, can I have a rug?'

'We don't have any rugs here,' Kay said. 'We have bare cement floors.'

'Sister, you don't understand. What I want is thick and woolly. You put it over your bed when you're cold, and I'm cold.'

Kay said, 'Uh huh!' and hastened off to get him a blanket.

One afternoon Lt Anne Philiben said, 'Jean, I've just had a couple of your lot come in and ask "Where's me mate?" I know what "mate" is, but when I asked what was wrong with him so I could send them to the right ward, they said, "He's crook."

"Well, don't bother me if he's a crook." I said. "Go to the MPs!"'

On another occasion Ben Harmon told me about one of the nurses who came to him, shaken, after an Aussie said to her sympathetically, 'Sister, you look all knocked up.' After Ben had stopped laughing, he explained to her that the Digger meant 'fatigued', not 'pregnant'.

There was a splendid Aussie who took care of military matters for the sick and wounded at the 36th Evac – Warrant

Officer Colin Avery. As medical liaison officer, Col solved a patient's worries about his pay or equipment. His primary job, though, was to organise the RAAF evacuation of the sick and wounded and to see that the dead were transported properly to their home soil. A true gentleman who had the respect of all his men, Col had been in the Regular Army most of his life and had fought the Japanese in New Guinea in World War II. At age forty-eight, Col Avery was jokingly called 'the oldest Nasho in the Australian army'. Ian Merrilees, of 2 Field Ambulance, told me how Col had acquired his moniker.

'Bert "Fergie" Ferguson, our quartermaster, was entertaining some Yanks in the Sergeants' Mess and was spinning a yarn about how it was impossible in Australia to escape National Service. He pointed to Col sitting across the Mess and told the Yanks that the bloke sitting there had dodged National Service during World War II, and the government had caught up with him and conscripted him for Vietnam. The Yanks listened wide-eyed. The following day Col had to go to Saigon and, upon entering the Commander's office, was greeted with: "Here comes the oldest Nasho in the Australian Army." The bush telegraph was even faster than at home!'

The joy of working in a camp along the seashore, with its tantalisingly clean and salty air, soon changed to exhausted resignation as we struggled daily up and down the steep sandhills. I got so fed up with stopping every few steps to shake sand out of my shoes that I wrote to NHQ seeking permission, which was promptly given, to wear black sandals instead of the uniform flats. All facilities were basic and minimal. Our Red Cross hut was a tent in the sand, and sand got into our typewriter, our radio, everything.

In the steamy climate, I was always hot and thirsty. With no drinkable water readily available, I was never without a can of Coca-Cola in my hand. There were no toilets yet for women at ALSG, but that was no problem – no matter how much Coke I drank, I sweated it away. It did take careful planning, though, not to be caught short with a monthly period or a case of diarrhoea, as the Villa was a long six kilometres from where we worked. And there was nowhere to wash my hands unless I was at the Villa.

Constant visits from generals and parliamentarians provided a welcome break in the daily routine, and I met them all. Dr Jim Cairns, Australia's fiercely anti-war politician visited on the last day of July. I wasn't impressed. I was gratified, though, when he said, 'I'm glad to see Red Cross here.' Gough Whitlam, then Leader of the Opposition in Federal Parliament and later Prime Minister, was in Vung Tau two weeks later.

Task Force soldiers were working long hours to establish and make safe the Nui Dat camp; some units spent as much as eighty-six of their first ninety days in Vietnam out on patrol, and the strain was beginning to show. We were starting medical evacuation (medevac) of soldiers with injuries from accidents along with the battle casualties. In 1966 it took a full three days for a patient to be flown to Australia for medical treatment, as the RAAF had only the smaller Hercules planes. A patient would overnight in 4 RAAF Hospital at Butterworth in Malaysia, then overnight again at RAAF Pearce, Western Australia, before making the 4,000 kilometre trip across the continent to Richmond, outside Sydney. There was still a drive from Richmond to nearby 2 Military Hospital at Ingleburn. To complicate matters further, and to lengthen the journey, planes couldn't fly over Indonesia at that time. When

Indonesia eventually opened its air space to Australian military planes, direct flights from Butterworth to Richmond alleviated some of the patient's travel discomfort.

The day before medevac was always my busiest. Soldiers had very few chances to go shopping for presents for their loved ones, and they all wanted to take home something special. Nui Dat soldiers, particularly, had no opportunity to buy the Seiko watches, transistor radios, cameras and tape recorders available in the American PX, where the Aussies were privileged to shop. The PX was a department store of sorts, with one on every base it seemed, and with prices one-third of those in Australia. But in those early days, supplies at Vung Tau's American PX were unpredictable. If goods *were* there, the line of customers would reach way out the door, so clever Harry Janssen arranged for us to get early notice of goods available from the PX and a chance to shop in the store before normal opening hours. And the American colonel in charge of the Vung Tau area gave me permission to buy the patients PX cigarettes without a ration card, as the wounded had no ration cards with them.

Shopping for the wounded wasn't easy. I drove those who were ambulatory to the American PX and later, when it opened, to the Australian PX. I took money and orders for purchases for the rest. If the American PX had but few goods, we were left to haggle for the best price in the inadequate local market; nothing ever went smoothly. Bargaining in the market was the most time consuming of all. I wouldn't dare return to a patient having paid too much for something. Besides, I had to uphold the proud and well-deserved *Uc Dai Loi* reputation of Number One Cheap Charlie versus that of the more free-spending Americans. Eventually learning what the cheapest price was, I saved time by adopting a take it or leave it attitude with the stall holders. They soon learned to take it. At the market we bought silks, Vietnamese dolls – the poor-quality souvenirs in which the market abounded – and the ever-popular sexy, transparent, two-piece sleep attire for the wives and girlfriends at home. At first I couldn't figure out which piece went where. The top and bottom looked to be alike, with the bottom piece open for . . . um . . . business!

On the way back to camp we'd stop for a much needed cool drink at a roadside shack, built like so many others from packing cases and flattened-out beer or Coke cans. There we'd buy models of the Huey choppers, complete with whirring propellers, crafted from the same flattened cans. Most important of all was a bag for the patient to carry home his purchases. It became a familiar sight to see each patient being loaded onto a RAAF Hercules flight with a market-purchased Air Vietnam travel bag stuffed with homecoming gifts beside him on the stretcher.

Eventually, when supplies became more regular, a visit to the PX was an eye-popping treat. With many items not then seen in Australian stores, the PX was a treasure-trove of goods, both basic and luxurious. Most anything you wanted to buy – including the latest trend from America in clothes, music or cosmetics – the PX had it, provided you didn't want anything as necessary as soap, toothpaste or deodorant. Those basics you'd probably find in the Vung Tau market, but for black market prices. Top brand basics were diverted mysteriously from their PX destination into the hands of those wanting to benefit financially from war. The first Aussie beer, Swan Lager, that was shipped to Vung Tau disappeared briefly, then turned up on the black market the next day.

But more often than not, what the PX had in abundance was what we could do without. Like T-shirts emblazoned with 'When I die I'll go to heaven, as I've spent my time in hell, Vietnam!' or joke greeting cards proclaiming: 'Hi, here I am in VIETNAM defending you, your loved ones, and our country . . . Frightening isn't it?'

6

Living in a Goldfish Bowl

SWISH, SWISH, SWISH. SNAP, SNAP, SNAP. EMERY boards swished back and forth across my nails, and scissors snapped at my hair to shorten it. I sat spread-eagled in the market beauty shop, four manicurists working on my hands and feet simultaneously while a male hairdresser trimmed away. When he finished snipping, he pulled my hair onto rollers while two more women rolled my hair on each side. I was the eye of a cyclone of focused activity, seven beauticians working on me at once. Enjoying the soothing background of their singsong chatter, I luxuriated in the novelty of it all. In less than an hour I was done – a new woman for a couple of dollars' outlay.

A strange form of shampoo had started the treatment. My hair, still dry, was tantalisingly massaged for about twenty minutes with at least half a bottle of shampoo. Water was used only for rinsing. There had been a moment of consternation when I jerked up my soapy head as a motorbike roared across the shop floor, inches from my chair, to park in the back of the shop. Dogs and chickens roamed freely through the salon, yet the beauticians – no evidence of a licence or certificate of training to be seen – brought talent and skill to their work. They could twist my short hair into a passable French roll (a style then fashionable) with the aid of many bobby pins. 'Buyer beware' was the watchword though. One time my hair was about to be sprayed with lacquer from an aerosol can covered in brown paper. Suspicious, I ripped at the paper. What the Vietnamese unwittingly had bought on the black market as hair spray was spray starch!

To be a Western woman in war-torn Vietnam was to stand out like a ski lift in a wheat field. No woman was short of a date, although I knew that was simply a matter of numbers. I had determined not to single out any Australian by dating him solely, for I was there for the welfare of *all* men. And I had too much respect for the wife left behind to cause a war at home by dating her husband. I had no idea who was married and who wasn't anyway. No sensible soldier would wear a wedding ring as it might cause him to lose a finger if it caught on something; most Diggers tied their rings onto their dog tags.

Stories of American nurses contracting venereal disease or being sent home pregnant were enough to reinforce my high-minded principles. Understandably, for women seeing death each day, sex was a celebration of life – and an opiate. There were a lot of 'transactions' going on at the Villa, or so I heard, but while I was in Vietnam under the proud banner of Red Cross, there was to be no new meaning of Room Service in room 116!

Doing what comes naturally when girl meets boy had to be put on hold. Of course, that didn't mean I wasn't interested. But none of the Australians asked me out! Instead of swarming like bees to a honey pot around the only Aussie woman for miles who was remotely near their age, in the beginning not one as much as asked me to share a drink. So much for my carefully thought out plans. I was perplexed. I knew that in the baking heat and oppressive humidity I looked about as sexy as a dead snake, and the rain or the sweat left my hair like a wet rag. Even worse, my face was starting to explode in acne from the heat and the dirt. Nevertheless, the Yanks thought I was okay. So why were the Australians so reluctant to speak to me? Surely living in an all-male environment meant that they'd want to talk to a woman. And they couldn't all be married. Were they all too busy setting up a secure base in the Great Sandy Desert of Back Beach or the VC-infested rubber plantation area to think of anything but existing? That was part of it I knew. But still I didn't understand: there were so many of them and just one of me.

It turned out that the reasons were complex, as different as each and every man. Some men said they didn't want to be reminded of home and all it represented, so they avoided all contact with women. Others didn't want to stand out from the rest by dating, even innocently. Some men spent so much time on operation they felt they had forgotten how to be 'civilised'. They rarely saw a woman, and if they did, they felt awkward at the strangeness of it all. Others lusted from a distance. One Digger told me recently: 'I just had horny thoughts as I looked at you from afar.' Another man settled for going to Mass every Sunday in Vung Tau and sitting where he had a good view of any round-eyed women present; that was the only place he'd see them.

Dr Tony White, the engaging and unassuming young doctor with the Fifth Battalion, further enlightened me when he showed me a letter he had written to his mother on 2 November, 1966:

Things are going along well here now. The concrete floor of the new Regimental Aid Post is being poured at present. It should be up soon. Yesterday we had the first woman visitor to the RAP, the Red Cross lass called Jean Debelle, from Adelaide – very pleasant. Most strange having women around here. The Brigadier has only just permitted women to come up from Vung Tau on day visits. No overnighters as yet! Seriously, though, I do find it a tremendous novelty talking to a woman for a change. God knows what I'll be like when I get home again!

A more fanciful reminiscence came from Lt Dave Sabben, a National Serviceman who, at twenty-one, had married his long-time girlfriend before leaving for Vietnam. Dave was awarded a Mention-in-Despatches (MID) for his bravery at Long Tan, the worst battle in which the Australians were involved in the Vietnam War. Years later he wrote me the following:

It's stinking hot. The Caribou stands on the tarmac apron, its idling engines buffeting the group of a dozen or so soldiers waiting to board. Thoughts dance in my head. Saigon. A first for me – a platoon commander plucked yesterday from an operation, dressed in clean polyesters and

off to Saigon for five days to command the small detachment of soldiers who protect the living quarters of some
Saigon-based pogos.

I see two women separate from the nearest building and
approach. I haven't seen a round-eyed woman since getting
to Vietnam eight months ago. Oh, yes, there were those
nurses, so cool and professional, when I visited my
wounded guys after Long Tan. And, yeah, there were those
two whom Harry, my company commander, had invited to
the Mess a month or two ago, but, hell, you couldn't see
them for all the majors and captains flocking around.

All the soldiers turn to watch the two women approach
the Caribou. They're in uniforms which, I think, are only
an impediment to the imagination. I flick a glance around
the group, self-conscious, but see that unspoken idea has a
resounding quorum.

The younger one's looking at me. Me! And she's smiling.
She's coming directly towards me. Her face is only a foot
from mine now. And she's saying something I can't hear for
the noise of the Caribou engines. Our cheeks touch as she
shouts in my ear: 'Congratulations on the MID'.

Christ! It's Jean Debelle – one of the two ladies Harry
had invited to the Mess. How the hell did she recognise me?
I'm flattered but mystified. She has hundreds of male faces
to recognise. The loadmaster shouts for us to board. We file
in and she ends up sitting opposite me. The low canvas seats
that line each side of the Caribou are not designed for ladies
in knee-length skirts. Even with her legs demurely together,
there's a clear view of the way to the Promised Land.
I suddenly need to study the rivets of the Caribou airframe
in great detail.

Conversation is impossible in a Caribou in flight. Our eyes meet from time to time and we exchange smiles. I am sure she's reading my mind. What do women make of male fascinations? Are they aware and just ignore them? Or are they really unaware? Nah! I decide they must know. They're just more mature than we are, year-for-year, and tolerate our relative immaturity. Bless 'em!

Jean gives me a smile and a little wave as she leaves, as if to say good luck. For my time in Saigon? For the rest of my tour? For life? For the pursuit of the Promised Land? I don't know. I never see her again to ask.

So here's to Jean, I think, and the hundreds, maybe thousands, like her. Women with the courage to participate in a man's domain like war and endure. They live their life in a goldfish bowl, yet maintain their dignity and good humour. And they leave a legacy behind them, the extent of which they cannot possibly be aware. Memories trapped within a young man's development, in which they're innocent, unknowing participants.

I admit I was aware, after the accidental bumping of cheeks, of some electricity in the air, for even to brush hands with a soldier could generate a spark. I was blissfully ignorant though, of how much I may have revealed to Dave Sabben in the Caribou. I always took great care to ensure that never happened.

With no Aussies asking me out, I began to date some of the more than half a million Americans in Vietnam. Going out at night, I'd put on my prettiest cotton dress, with pearls and French perfume. It was important to feel feminine. First, I shared no more than a couple of dinners with Ted, a flat-topped, ginger-haired captain in the Green Berets who made my mind race with stories of secret excursions into neutral Cambodia. That was at a time when President Johnson repeatedly denied that any American troops were there. I met Ted through his American army friend, Bill, who was one of the more unusual patients at the 36th Evac. A short, wiry man, Bill had worked with the Vietnamese in an undercover rural cadre aimed at rooting out the Viet Cong. His usual work attire was the black cotton pyjamas worn by both the Vietnamese peasants and the Viet Cong, who were often one and the same. Bill had lived off the land with the Vietnamese, scavenging edible plants and fruits, until he discovered his painfully malnourished body could no longer absorb Western foods. He remained in hospital until he could eat normally again.

Then there was a US Navy lieutenant, Dave Welch, who was a popular date with some of the American nurses. Dave had dark hair, dimples that looked oddly out of place with his strong jaw, and the manners and bearing of an Eastern Seaboard Ivy League man, which he probably was. Dave and his team worked with the Junk Force, patrolling in absolute darkness the tiny, well-hidden channels – only large enough for a junk – that criss-crossed the Mekong Delta and were used extensively by the VC as supply routes. His craft was similar to a conventional local fishing junk of the type used years later by the fleeing Vietnamese boat people, with eyes painted on each side of the bow for the boat to see its way. The only difference was that his had large machine guns mounted on the bow and around the decks.

On Sunday afternoon Dave – or Nguyen Van Welch, as his buddies called him – made a Navy 'junk' available to the

36th Evac staff for a Medcap, as medical civil action programs carried out by the armed forces were known. A Medcap usually ventured into unsafe areas, but the Viet Cong had the sense to leave us alone while we were providing their kinfolk with medical care. Dr Ian Favilla, leader of the RAAF medical team in Vung Tau, and an assortment of RAAF men went with us. As we motored across the water, the South China Sea shone splendidly in the midday sun, and there was a cooling offshore breeze. I turned to RAAF cook Tony Huntley and said: 'If I shut my eyes, I could be on Sydney Harbour.' Tony agreed: 'It doesn't get any better than this.' The peace of the moment was broken by a sleek flying fish that leapt from the sea and back again with streamlined grace. 'You wouldn't see that in Sydney,' Tony said in awe.

Our destination was a sleepy town of palm trees and villas that the VC hoped to win from the influence of a young bespectacled and highly motivated Roman Catholic priest and some nuns. Medcaps, a rare and precious luxury for the Vietnamese, were a curiosity for the children and they mobbed us, giggling excitedly and caressing my arms as we made our way to the town square. Barefoot children in shabby clothes – hair matted, bodies covered by sores, little bellies bloated – pushed and shoved for attention. We stood them in an organised queue to await treatment, with the priest and nuns trying to keep order. The medical staff formed into well-practised groups and got to work, checking for tuberculosis, malaria and general malnutrition among a host of other ailments.

Before the medical staff saw the patients, the children had to be clean, and that's where I came in. Having no medical skills, I was handed a bar of soap and a basin of water. I stripped any Vietnamese up to the age of about ten, stood the child naked in the basin and scrubbed each one clean all over. The children wriggled and screamed with glee or fright, the soapy water made them slippery to hold, and we all had a picnic. At the same time, I had to break the scabs on festering sores and boils, a common ailment. The task pained me almost as much as it did the children.

There was no shortage of soap. A 36th Evac nurse, knowing of the scarcity of soap in Vietnam, had written to the personal-care products giant, Procter & Gamble, who sent her nearly enough soap for us to bomb Hanoi. There was a constant line of glossy-haired patients to be treated – all women and children. The priest was the only man we saw that afternoon, except for a few toothless old men with wispy beards and heads wrapped in dirty cloths. All the fit men were away from home – in a foreign university, in prison for protesting the government, or off fighting, who knew on which side. We never knew if those Medcaps were beneficial as the Vietnamese had no choice but to endure the poor sanitation in the smaller villages and surrounding countryside.

We treated the villagers for hours and then, hot and sweaty from our labours, we started for home in the late afternoon. Halfway across the water the navy boys dropped anchor for an onboard barbecue. 'Anyone wanna swim?' Dave asked. As one, the Aussies roared 'Yes'. The RAAF boys and I went over the side so quickly that I forgot to remove my contact lenses. The gods shone on me and the lenses stayed put. Just as well – it would have been weeks before I could have obtained replacements from Australia.

Only the Aussies swam. The Yanks looked on as though we were crazy. They knew the deep water was filled with sharks and other ominous creatures and didn't understand our passionate need for a dip. However, I was first to clamber out. Far from the water's edge, I had begun to worry that a hungry shark might circle. Two men hauled me over the steep sides of the boat, and I flopped inside with total lack of dignity.

Dave moved on to dating a nurse, and I took up with Bud, a Dust-Off pilot of about thirty. A friend told me that Bud had gone totally grey in just three months, such were his dangerous duties. He was stationed near Tay Ninh and came to Vung Tau about every week for a break. I knew when to expect him, but he'd phone me a day or so before to confirm.

A phone call over the army field phone system was complicated. The Villa sentry would knock on my door to say there was a call for me on the communal phone in the entrance hall. By then the call had gone through four or more military telephone exchanges. Both of us had to shout to be heard. 'I'll see you about five on Friday,' Bud said. 'Okay,' I replied. Then he said something else. 'I can't hear you,' I said, and he yelled louder. 'What was that?' I said, and again he tried, and I repeated, 'I can't hear you.' Then somewhere along one of the exchanges a male American voice chipped in: 'He says he loves you!' Surprised – we had only dated twice – and too embarrassed to talk further, I finished in a rush, 'Oh, oh, okay, bye.' Had everyone along the line been listening to our conversation? Had even the Aussie on the Emu telephone exchange heard? I had grown used to lack of any privacy with bathing and toilet facilities, but were even my emotions open to public scrutiny?

It was no time before word about my dating habits got back to me from the Australian camp. 'You're getting a reputation, Jean, for your Yank boyfriends,' an officer told me. 'You should date Aussies, you know.'

'None of you ever ask me out,' I retorted.

Slowly the Aussies began to pay me more attention. I had already discovered that if I as much as had my hair styled differently, they'd have heard about it at Nui Dat by sundown. There was so little else to talk about. I also knew that for most men who went to war there were wives or sweethearts waiting at home. Women for whom the daily routine of life went on; who shopped for Cornflakes, coped with the bills that never stopped coming, dealt with the toilets that blocked, and put a brave smile on their faces to give their children birthday parties. For a soldier in the rubber or at the beach, those loved ones were never far from his thoughts and his yearnings.

I understood all of this – but that didn't stop my social life from being a giddy whirl. I was hankering for a date with my fellow countrymen as much as the next person, so I dated single men – and certainly I dated married men. I never knew one from the other, though, unless I got to know them as close friends. Either way, I was always careful not to get deeply involved, because I was still determined to lead a life of which a Mother Superior would approve. Many men were lonely for their wives and families, whom they missed dreadfully, and just wanted to be with someone from home to talk about anything other than army chit chat. I was happy to listen. After talking about their families and showing me their photographs, the soldiers seemed more relaxed for an hour or so.

Despite my circumspect behaviour, the gossip grew daily, and generally I was an innocent victim. The rumour mill, with little else to feed it, found its grist in me. If I did anything, people talked. If I did nothing, people speculated. I was helpless to avoid the attention, so I forgot about it. I understood all too well the aphorism attributed to Winston Churchill: 'A lie gets halfway around the world before the truth has a chance to get its pants on.' The soldiers might have gossiped then, but today they have nothing but compliments for the women in Vietnam. I have letters and email messages praising the work of Red Cross women, and the gist of them is: 'Jean, you were up on a pedestal for the work you did. All of you girls were.'

On all levels, we lived in a man's world. Men urinated out in the open, although that was nothing new to me; I was raised in the country, and I had a father and three brothers. Any feminine trappings we had, Hilda and I had to provide for ourselves. Use of profanity was standard operating procedure for the men; swear words are as much a part of a soldier as his heavy black boots, but I scarcely noticed. Often the first indication that the air was blue was a soldier's contrite 'Sorry Jean, I didn't know you were there.' But in most cases I simply hadn't heard him.

There has been much written of the boozing, sexual carousing and drug use in Vietnam, most frequently among the American troops. Others have written that women in Vietnam were subject to sexual harassment from soldiers. All I can say is: I saw or experienced none, except for that operating theatre attack from the American doctor. Nor can I find anyone else in my time there who did. In fact, I found far more leering and suggestive comments in civilian life. In Vietnam, for the most part, I worked in an atmosphere of utter respect.

I asked American Red Cross veteran Sandra Fosselman, whom I had met at Long Binh, if she was aware of any sexual harassment. Her eighteen months' stay in Vietnam was in far 'hotter' places than mine, such as An Khe, where the ratio of women to men was 3 to 25,000 and Pleiku, with a 5 to 25,000 ratio. Sandra was astonished at my question. 'We were clearly

placed on pedestals,' she agreed. 'I knew of no incident of a
woman being approached or assaulted. The men really were
protective of us, perhaps because there were so few of us.'

Frankly, at first I did wonder if there was truth to the old
story that the army put bromide in the drinking water to keep
the soldiers under control. When I finally got up courage to ask
an officer, he hooted with laughter. No way. There *were* times,
however, when doing ward rounds among men at the peak of
fitness despite a wound or illness, that I was reminded of Mae
West's sly query: 'Is that a gun in your pocket or are you just
glad to see me?' It was easy to move on to the next patient.
Sometimes I'd hear the men talking about sex among themselves. I took it as a sign that they were getting better. They were
just being normal blokes, God love 'em. In Vietnam, sexual
tension was in the very air we breathed – the male/female ratio
saw to that – but it was never a problem for me.

What did bother me, though, were the Dear John letters,
or a wife's letter of apology that she had got drunk on New
Year's Eve and slept with her husband's best friend. Those
letters were devastating for a fighting soldier to receive. His
girl was his lifeline to home. Sometimes he'd have to go on
operation after receiving a letter that broke his heart. When
I heard about the Dear Johns (normal for faltering romances
at home, but nothing was normal in a war zone) my heart
broke also – but for the soldier. I wanted somehow to hurt the
woman in return.

Vietnamese women, I had been told before leaving Adelaide,
were the most beautiful in the world. I wasn't disappointed.
Women of all ages moved with grace, even with two heavy

baskets balanced across their shoulders. Most beautiful of all were the high school girls we passed as we drove along Vung Tau's streets to the 36th. Their silky, long black hair, cut straight as a die across the ends, glistened in the sun as they strolled to school. In their snowy white, ankle-length *ao dai* and billowing black, navy or white pantaloons, they seemed to represent all that was decent and good in that country where we witnessed so much hatred.

The *ao dai*, the Vietnamese national dress, is one of the world's most exotic and graceful fashions, one that manages to look extraordinarily innocent yet at the same time down-right sexy. The long-sleeved bodice with a straight skirt split down each side is all one garment. *Ao dai* fit snugly from neck to waist to emphasise the Vietnamese fine-boned bodies and small breasts. Vietnamese tailors know how to fashion bras and swimsuit tops to make the smallest bust look pin-up-girl-worthy. A trick they learned from the French? Some of those wondrously enhancing items were in my luggage when I returned home. My friends were puzzled at first by how my bust size had grown dramatically when the rest of me was thinner than at any time in my adult life! To my embarrassment though, when I had new uniforms copied from existing ones by a Vung Tau tailor, I discovered too late that he had put gathers along the shoulder line, presumably to emphasise what I had. The gathering caused a considerable amount of mirth among the soldiers, whose eyes missed nothing when it came to women.

As well as new uniforms, I needed to buy casual clothing as mine continued to disappear mysteriously in the wash. One Thursday in late July I heard there was a Caribou going that weekend to Bangkok, a shopper's dream, and anyone was welcome to ride on it. For six weeks I had worked until I dropped and I'd rarely had time off. I raced to the small Vung Tau post office and sent a telegram to Thea Cawthorne, who was then at the Australian Embassy in Bangkok, requesting a bed for Friday and Saturday nights. I hadn't seen Thea since I'd interviewed her in Adelaide, when she'd inspired me with stories of Vietnam and Red Cross work.

Excitedly I began to pack. 'You should tell the Brigadier you're going,' Hilda cautioned. I was too emotionally exhausted to think and shot back: 'I'm sure he is too busy planning a war to bother with my trip.' Until then I had worked unsupervised, unilaterally making giant-size emotional decisions, and the circumstances of war led to my feeling I was absolutely free. Hilda's warning was like the jerk of a leash on a dog, but she hadn't forbidden me to go. There was a saying amongst the troops: 'What can they do to punish you? Send you to Vietnam?' I was on my way to Bangkok the next day.

The two-hour flight seemed interminable. Conversation was impossible, and I had no book. Eventually we taxied along a runway at a military airbase outside Bangkok. I was soon hurtling towards the city in a jeep, sharing the road with Thai trucks, ornately carved and decorated with teak facades.

Bangkok is one of the world's most exotic cities, replete with artistic, culinary, cultural and other joys and treasures, and it is complemented by the remarkable gentle beauty of the Thai people. In 1966 it was also the raunch capital of Asia because of the troops spending their R&R (Rest and Recreation) there. When the Diggers referred to it as Thighland, I didn't know if it was a deliberate play on words or an innocent mispronunciation.

I arrived at the Australian Embassy at midday Friday, the worst time possible. The weekly diplomatic bag was being readied for its departure to Canberra within the hour. Thea was astonished to see me – my telegram had not arrived. 'Sit here and wait for about forty-five minutes,' she said. Exactly three-quarters of an hour later, the bag was on its way, and Thea took time from work to tell me the best places to shop. Thailand is famous for its gems, and almost next door to the Embassy was a jeweller who sensibly gave excellent value to his diplomatic neighbours. I never thought I could afford a sapphire on my budget, but how could I say no to a princess ring of deep blue sapphires and Australian opals for $12! It was on my finger before you could say *sawatdee* ('hello' in Thai). That was only the start. Brightly coloured Thai silks and cottons from American silk king Jim Thompson's wonderful teak-lined store followed, and those I could have sewn into garments for a song in Vung Tau.

Thea introduced me to the Thai culture. In turn I told her how different life had become in Saigon with the military presence; the Saigon each of us described was like two different cities. We saw the famous Bangkok floating market, where housewives bargain for fresh fruit and vegetables and catch up on the current gossip. We visited an assortment of glittering temples. We saw more whorehouses and GIs with girls on their arms than I ever saw before or since. By Sunday afternoon I was back in Vung Tau, and everyone was envious of my break from the war.

I always sought new ways to do my job better, and the abundance of fresh fruit in Bangkok gave me an idea. To see fresh fruit on a military menu was almost as rare as to see caviar. With the doctors' permission, I started to buy the patients pineapples and bananas in the market. It was the first fresh produce most soldiers had tasted since they'd arrived in country, and it was a hit. I also learned to put more than one razor blade in our welcome kits, for in the tropical climate a blade lasted only three days. Brushless shaving cream was preferred, because it was a struggle for a sick man to make shaving cream lather without a brush. Soap containers were essential; otherwise a patient had to wrap his soap in newspaper – if there was one. Loose writing paper blew around the breezy 2 Field Ambulance wards, so we changed to notepads. Envelopes stuck together unless they were self-seal. I learned that the men didn't want to read the *Women's Weekly* (although I liked it) but asked for *Australian Hot Rod*, *Sports Car World*, *King's Cross Whisper*, *Tom Thumb*, *Outdoors*, *Everybody* and, oh, so many *Man* magazines. NHQ acceded to my every request.

Delivery of Australian papers still took too long though. And mail service between Australia and Vietnam was not good, we were told, because of an airline dispute in the United States. For reasons unknown, our mail was reputed to go via Hawaii! Whatever the reason, it was a fact that almost all of the letters we wrote home between the end of July and the end of August were delivered to Australian households on the same day. The irregular mail service was particularly stressful for loved ones who knew their boys were going out on operation, while they tried to keep the home fires contentedly burning. None of us had access to a telephone, and sending a telegram from a local post office was futile, as I had found.

I wasn't always successful at keeping the patients from becoming bored. In the rubber the men had devised their own hobbies, when they had time. Some made pets of frogs or insects that they fed and cared for. Some tried to grow vegetables from seeds. There was always something to do to pass the time, but in hospital there was nothing. Once a week I served tea with Arnott's biscuits for a special treat. Shopping trips with ambulatory patients were a popular break from hospital routine. Those excursions expanded into beach visits and then, as I became more brazen, sight-seeing trips that were as much a break for me as for the boys. One afternoon I took three long-time patients to see an armed Chinook helicopter, a twin-bladed bus-like chopper. The colonel in charge of Vung Tau's Chinooks gave us a personal tour.

To give muscle to my market bargaining skills I decided to learn some Vietnamese. I joined Harry for language classes, held at the Vietnamese/American Cultural Centre in Vung Tau. Located in a school that was simply a row of shabby single-storey rooms, the Cultural Centre was extremely hot and poorly lit. Each Wednesday evening from six until seven-thirty, Harry and I sat with about twenty American men at tiny battered desks that, like school desks everywhere, bore the graffiti of past years. The large enrolment at our lessons may have been due to the beauty and vivacity of the Vietnamese teacher, Co Xanh, which means Miss Green.

The lovely Co Xanh never favoured a man over me in class; however, after we learned how to count (most useful for the market), our lessons developed a strong male bias. We learned how to say 'I love you' and 'My friend will buy the next round of drinks', neither expression being of the slightest use to me. I doubted any woman paid for a drink during

her year in Vietnam – I certainly didn't. Worn out from work
and the heat by the end of each day, with no ear for languages
and with Vietnamese desks built for small local derrières, I
lasted for six lessons only. Harry determinedly stayed the
course, his musical ear quickly becoming attuned to the tonal
sounds of Vietnamese. For an hour after class, the tireless
Harry then taught English to schoolchildren – if you can
imagine an Aussie immigrant with a broad Dutch accent
teaching English in Vietnam!

Harry stirred up excitement by getting a well-sited stage
erected at 2 Field Ambulance. On the second day of August,
Julia Bellares, an Australian dancer and juggler and the first
entertainer we had seen, was to do a show there. I filled our
VW with as many of the 36th patients as we could squeeze in.
As we drove along the rutted gravel road, the VW began to
shudder more than usual. We had a flat tyre, our first; an
amazing record considering the state of the roads. The sick
and wounded men, in their pyjamas, insisted on changing the
tyre for me. They, of course, could do the job a lot faster than
if I were to do it, although I could! I watched and fretted that
they might injure their healing bodies, worried that we would
be late for the show, and thanked the Lord no one had a
camera.

The show was good, but it was the gossip we picked up that
made the trip worthwhile. We heard about a patient in 2 Field
Ambulance who was not happy with his lot, all because of a
poorly conceived army procedure. Toilet facilities at the camp
were primitive. Urinals, known as piss-a-phones, were no
more than pipes stuck upright in the sand. For 'big jobs',
there were the Flaming Furies – deep lavatory holes with seats
across them that were burned for hygiene reasons at 0400

hours each day. The drill was that a soldier made the rounds putting range fuel in each hole, and then he went around again tossing in a match. The unhappy patient, a soldier who'd had diarrhoea, got caught short between the two rounds. He dropped a cigarette butt between his legs and was blown about two metres into the air. He was the one lying on his stomach in hospital with dressings all over his badly burned bum. Swift changes ensured that fuel and flame were dumped simultaneously into the Flaming Furies.

In the second week of August, Brigadier Jackson deemed the Task Force base at Nui Dat safe enough for women visitors, and we were invited as often as we wished. Hilda set off by chopper on August 17 for a morning call. I could hardly wait for my chance to see the 'sharp end', home base to most of our patients. My wait proved to be far longer than I anticipated.

7

Long Tan

VICTOR CHARLIE WAS NOT HAPPY WITH THE arrival of the Australians in Nui Dat and fired mortar shells and artillery into the tents in the rubber. There was no point in my asking how much damage had been done, for the reply was always jocular: 'They sure made a mess of the banana tree by my tent. I'd been caring for those bananas like a baby.' I didn't fall for the bravado, but if ever the soldiers' spirits were down, I hadn't noticed.

By mid August I had been in Vietnam for just two months. It was raining cats and dogs. There was no point in drowning on our way to dinner at the Pacific Hotel, so some American nurses and I waved a crowded Lambretta to a stop and somehow squashed in. There was always room for one more in a Lambretta. It magically expanded to accommodate demand, even if it meant some people clung to the outside. At the Pacific we got in line for chow and filled our trays with the by now familiar bland offerings. But something was different. There was a buzz in the air. I heard the word Aussies mentioned again and again.

'Why is everyone talking about the Aussies?' I innocently asked an American. 'Ma'am, they're in serious trouble. They're fighting for their lives.' Not the Aussies! That only happened to other troops. I remember shivering despite the hot, humid air. I *had* to find out more, but making a phone call was not easy. The Vietnamese system, for all practical purposes, was non-existent. Military phones were not plentiful. While sending jumbled prayers skywards, I bolted my dinner, then raced back to the Villa to use the field phone there. I was switched through the American signals system and then heard an answer at ALSG in the familiar Aussie accent: 'Emu'. I knew enough about the army by then to ask for the duty officer. That night he was Major Nat Salter.

'Are the Aussies in trouble?'

In the gentlest voice imaginable, Nat said: 'Yes, Jean, they are.'

'Are they being brought into the 36th Evac?'

'Yes,' he replied.

With quick thanks I hurried off the line. Fortunately I had been brief. That night ALSG and all Task Force units were going through what was to be the busiest night of the Vietnam War for the Australians: a night of welling sadness but also of lasting pride.

The Battle of Long Tan is now legendary in the annals of Australian war. Although other important battles were fought in Vietnam, never did so small an Australian force engage so large and formidable an enemy so fiercely and for so long. In the mid-afternoon of 18 August, 1966, on a routine search in familiar terrain, Delta Company of the Sixth Battalion – about

100 relatively inexperienced but highly trained men – encountered at least 1,500 Viet Cong troops in a rubber plantation during a blinding rain storm. The Australians had swept the area the day before without meeting opposition and were not expecting to be so vastly outnumbered. Suddenly, a determined foe attacked. The heavy rain and the low cloud prevented any close friendly air support. As it grew dark, the enemy massed for a final assault. The Aussies were down to their last rounds of ammunition. In the darkness and rain, the courageous RAAF crewmen – flying helicopters not yet bullet-proofed – were facing enormous difficulties in dropping more ammunition to the stranded troops. Through the chaotic noise of battle, the Diggers heard the thunder of the approaching Aussie cavalry: Armoured Personnel Carriers bringing troops and ammunition. The APCs crashed towards them through the dark jungle and torrential rain to rout the enemy, and the embattled men cheered. The Aussies had inflicted huge casualties on the enemy (at least 245 Viet Cong were buried by the Aussies) for the loss of eighteen Diggers.

At the Villa, Hilda was settling in for a night of reading. 'Are you coming with me to the 36th Evac?' I asked her. 'No,' she said forcefully. 'And you shouldn't go. Tomorrow is time enough.' I was dumbfounded. Wasn't this what we had been sent to Vietnam for? 'I'd like to go tonight,' I persisted, but Hilda was adamant that there was nothing that couldn't wait until morning and that I would be in the way.

I was bothered. The Villa was a whirl of doctors and nurses who, having just returned from their day shifts, were being called back to the hospital to await the heavy influx of injured Aussies. I felt I could be useful, if for nothing more than to hold a dying man's hand so he would not be alone in the chaos surrounding him. Perhaps I could pass on his last words to his loved ones. At least I could let the bewildered, battle-shocked men – surrounded by unfamiliar Americans – hear a voice from home. I pleaded, but to no avail. Inwardly pouting, but fearful of disobeying a direct order, I went to bed early, planning to be at the hospital at dawn. The decision not to go to the hospital that night still bothers me today.

Usually I slept like a drugged person, but not that night. Usually, for fear of my 'loose lips sinking ships', I didn't know – or want to know – when the Aussies were on operation and in danger.

But that night I did. Feeling utterly helpless, there was nothing I could do except pray that all would go well. I didn't know then that, in the Aussies' hasty regrouping to safety, two wounded men, Pte Jim Richmond and Pte Barry 'Custard' Meller, were unintentionally left behind, separated and alone but for the dead and dying VC all around. Their night was far worse than mine.

It was not the usual group of patients who greeted Hilda and me at the 36th Evac the next day. Those admitted late the previous night were silent. As I looked along the rows of casualties in the unnatural quiet, the stunned and wounded eyes, as much as the damaged bodies, identified those who had survived the battle in the rubber plantation. There were no friendly smiles, yet I heard no moans or crying. I was mentally prepared for tears from the men. I saw none. Some men avoided meeting my eyes, perhaps scared to reveal their emotions. A soldier might give way to grief in front of his mates, but not in front of an outsider. The only sound in the ward was the clump of army boots on concrete as the medical staff hurried about their work of healing.

Earlier, in the rubber plantation, there had been tears as the Diggers saw how many of their mates lay dead. They were not afraid to show their deepest emotions there – they loved each other like brothers and shared life's most intimate details. They knew the names of family members or pets, who got along with his in-laws and who didn't, whose girl dyed her hair; they knew each other's dreams and aspirations. But in the bustle of the hospital that morning, those Diggers held back their emotions until they could be alone.

I had no soothing assurances to offer. Words seemed so inadequate. Feeling helpless yet wanting to comfort, I gently touched the arm of each man as I moved around, handing each one toilet articles and cigarettes. 'Would you like me to send a message home?' I asked. 'What can I do to help you?' I tried to be a calm, steady presence at the side of those who were suffering. I was still ignorant of the enormity of the horror in the rubber plantation, but instinctively I knew those patients were different from any I'd yet seen. There were twenty-three men wounded badly enough to be admitted to hospital.

Other soldiers like Jack Peel of 32 Small Ships, who had been in hospital for minor surgery, could not get out of the place quickly enough when the real casualties started to arrive. Jack remembers: 'I felt I was an oxygen thief.'

Jim Richmond and Barry Meller, found sometime after daybreak and hastily choppered to hospital, were easy to identify. They were surrounded by the top brass who had flown in from Nui Dat and Saigon that morning to visit the wounded. How horrific the two Diggers' fears must have been, as they lay helpless and praying and wondering if the sun would rise.

In the face of such tragedy, I determinedly didn't cry, nor did I have the right words for the patients. As my training hadn't covered what to say to a man who has seen some of his best friends shot or blown away by a grenade, I resolved to ask a chaplain to help me find words to offer in the future. Hilda, who normally did not work at the 36th, assisted me in sending forty army signals to next of kin that morning. I was almost relieved when it was time for Hilda to drive me over the dusty back roads to the support camp to lunch there. All talk was of the events of the previous night, the worry of being able to resupply the trapped soldiers with ammunition, the number of casualties on both sides. A fragment of conversation drifted over to us. It was Nat Salter, the duty officer of the previous evening: 'The only sanity in the whole crazy night was hearing a lady's voice asking if the Aussies were in trouble,' he said. Undoubtedly mine had been the only female voice to crackle over the field phones on the night of 18 August.

The day the bodies of the Diggers who died at Long Tan were brought to the 36th, an Aussie soldier visiting there went crazy, threatening to shoot a Vietnamese who had been hired to sweep and clean the hospital. I had gone to the empty mess hall to get a Coke and found him there brandishing a gun and mouthing angry expletives at the Vietnamese. No one else was around. At first, I didn't realise how serious his threat was. Then I saw the venom in his eyes. With his finger on the trigger, he levelled the gun at the Mama-san, who stood motionless and blank-eyed beneath her conical hat, a straw broom her only defence. I believed he might shoot her – or even turn the gun on me. With knees shaking and with a voice as steady and soft as I could muster, I tried my best to calm him. 'Shooting her will get you in trouble. You don't want that. It's not going to bring your mates back,' I pleaded. 'Your family wouldn't want anything to happen to you. Here, let me put your gun safe. I know where we can get a cup of tea and cake.' I didn't, of course, but I couldn't think clearly. I only wanted to distract him until someone else could take over.

The soldier kept his weapon pointed at the Vietnamese. I stood in the mess hall, soaked with sweat, and feverishly repeated my mantra. My knees shook so hard I could hear my skirt flapping, yet I felt I was watching a television show in which I had no part. It seemed forever before a medic saw what was happening, spoke sharply to the soldier, and took his gun. As the medic and a doctor walked the man away, the soldier's shoulders slumped wearily, his eyes shiny with tears that did not spill. He was sent to the psychiatric hospital in Saigon.

Hilda told me later that she knew of the gunner and that, in talking to him about his family, I had seriously misread the tea leaves. In May, he had asked Red Cross to try to locate his parents. Perhaps there was no one who cared if he died in Vietnam. As with so many others, I never learned what happened to that troubled man; the nonstop intake of sick and wounded left no time for follow-up once he left the 36th.

The men of Delta Company, forever changed, went to the Rest and Convalescent (R&C) centre in Vung Tau for a few days to unwind. Few of us saw them. They kept very much to themselves. The events of 18 August were so horrible the men didn't want to talk about them to anyone but their mates. At the 36th, when they thought no one was looking, some patients cried into their pillows for days, some for as long as three weeks.

There is a well-known story of the Long Tan wounded – in pyjamas, on crutches or in wheelchairs, some with IV bottles attached to their arms – absconding from the 36th to a nearby

American club to get on the grog. The plan was temporarily
derailed when the patients were asked to leave the club, as
they were not properly dressed. With the scavenging resource-
fulness of the Aussie Digger, their mates soon returned
carrying enough pieces of uniform to secure everyone admis-
sion. The men proceeded to put away as many drinks as
possible until they were forcibly returned to the 36th under
MP escort. Meanwhile, the concerned 36th Evac medicos,
having no idea where to look for the missing men, patiently
awaited their return. As nurse Polly Parrott (now Bednash)
said: 'We tolerated shenanigans from the Aussies that none
of our men ever would be allowed to get away with. That
"escape" by rule breakers, living by their own code, was one
of the things that made the Aussies so attractive to us.' By the
time I heard about the booze-up next morning, the hubbub
had subsided, but the hospital staff was still laughing.

On 17 August, the day before the Long Tan battle, entertainers Col Joye and the Joy Boys, along with the diminutive
blonde singer Little Pattie, had given a show at the 36th Evac.
Those entertainers were huge on the Australian concert circuit
during the sixties. Col Joye had a string of top hit singles that
had taken the country by storm. In 1963 Little Pattie, only
fourteen at the time, had been at home doing her homework,
when she heard that her single, *He's My Blonde Headed
Stompie Wompie Real Gone Surfer Boy*, had reached the top
of the Australian charts. On the afternoon of 18 August, the
entertainers performed at Nui Dat while the battle raged
nearby. The concert party competed for some time with the
thunder of the artillery lending support in the Long Tan battle

before they were whisked back to safety in Vung Tau. Little Pattie was considerably shaken. Today she describes the Nui Dat gig as the worst she ever played.

The group was to give another three concerts on their return to Vung Tau – serendipitous timing as it took our minds away from the week's sadness. We were all looking forward to seeing them, but no visit to the patients had been planned. Why should our boys at the 36th miss out on the fun? After lunch I asked one of the ALSG officers where I could find Col Joye. He walked me through the sand to the tent that was home to Col while he was at Back Beach and called the singer's name. Not expecting to see a woman in the all-male camp, Col emerged from the tent in nothing but his cotton jockeys. Grinning wickedly, he ducked back under the tent flap to pull on his pants. In Vietnam I was accustomed to seeing men wrapped in nothing but olive-green army-issue towels making their way to the showers, or using the piss-a-phones that were dotted everywhere in the sand. A girl quickly learned when to look the other way. But Col Joye was a celebrity, one of the top Australian entertainers. Seeing him in his underpants in those days was to an Aussie sheila comparable to seeing Russell Crowe in his today! I wrote home about it.

Col promised he and Little Pattie would stop by the hospital. The patients were excited; a visit would help to make up for their having missed the Nui Dat concert when they were out on operation. Little Pattie took one look at the men, their clean faces beaming at her above their blue pyjamas, and started to cry. Smiles quickly turned to concern, and when I saw that dismayed reaction, I was concerned that the patients would be upset. It was my fault. I should have warned her that some men would have tubes or IV lines coming from unexpected places in their bodies. After all, she *was* only seventeen. I had forgotten that I had asked to see a casualty department before leaving Australia to prepare me for what I might see in Vietnam, and I was nine years older than Little Pattie. It was lucky I hadn't shown her the more frightening intensive care ward.

To get over the awkwardness, I suggested she sing for the patients. 'Oh no, I can't sing without a microphone,' she answered. 'But you're a singer! And the ward isn't very big,' I protested, anger rising inside me. Little Pattie shook her head. We toured the wards, with me struggling to introduce her brightly to the patients, but feeling the visit was a bust.

It wasn't at all. Col Joye had a long chat with every patient, and I am sure the men were thrilled to see Little Pattie. Her voice *is* small apparently, and maybe she didn't have the projection, resonance or, at seventeen, the confidence to perform live without benefit of a microphone. Rodger Eyles, a 2 Field Ambulance medic, who made a return visit to Vietnam in 1997 with a group that included Little Pattie, recalls that in a karaoke contest there: 'The talented Little Pattie scored less than I did, and modesty forbids me to suggest an Australian icon came second to this old Digger!' For the patients at the 36th Evac, however, the visit of Col Joye and the Joy Boys, and Little Pattie, could not have come at a better time. The happy diversion did much for everyone's morale.

The Red Cross broke a speed record sending us newspapers detailing the battle at Long Tan. When the papers arrived in a mere couple of days, patients eagerly grabbed them from my hands as I stepped into the wards. The front page of the August 20 issue of *The Australian* carried the headline:

EPIC COURAGE IN OUR BIGGEST VIETNAM BATTLE
17 DIGGERS DIE IN ACTION
But Australians kill 193 in three hours.
From OUR WORLD CABLE SERVICE: SAIGON, FRIDAY
In South Vietnam tonight the battle was being hailed as Australia's biggest since World War II. The Australian Task Force commander, Brigadier O. D. Jackson, said: 'The action was an epic of courage that will go down in Australian history.'

The Prime Minister, Mr Holt, said in Canberra last night: 'Australia is saddened by the loss of these splendid men. . . . With [my] sympathy will go pride in the fact that the Australians gave an outstanding demonstration of courage and military skill, and inflicted a sharp reversal on the Viet Cong.'

There was much newspaper and television coverage of the Long Tan patients in both the Australian and the American media. Often the TV cameras focused on Harry and me as we chatted with the wounded. None of us, of course, saw any of the coverage. Watching TV in Adelaide, Faye Meatheringham saw one of the broadcasts and recognised her friend Lt Bob Allen, a 36th Evac nurse, caring for some of the patients. A few weeks later Bob was surprised to get a letter from Faye – whom he had met two years earlier on board a ship to Tokyo – saying she'd seen him on TV and thanks for taking care of the Aussies.

Pte Ron Eglinton, the first National Serviceman to
be awarded the Military Medal (for his gallantry at
Long Tan), was among the wounded. In a letter to his
parents he described the battle: 'They came at us in great
human waves, just ambling along like a horde of zombies,
and we'd cut them down, and more would walk up and
over them in a seemingly endless supply.' When *The
Australian* asked Ron's parents for recent letters from
their son, understandably they handed over the account
Ron had written to them from his bed at the 36th. The
newspaper edited the long letter for its readers. Ron took
a lot of flack in the Nui Dat rubber when the letter was
published. The criticism of a letter written when Ron
was suffering, a letter never intended for public scrutiny,
was, in my opinion, unfair and hurtful. His colleagues
say his Military Medal never has been out of its box.
A good soldier and a team player, Ron remains unswerv-
ing in his belief that it should have been awarded
to others, unrecognised, but more heroic than he was at
Long Tan.

Ron's platoon sergeant, Bob Buick, also was awarded
the Military Medal for bravery at Long Tan. When the 11
Platoon commander was killed, Bob, a disciplined soldier
and down-to-earth leader, quickly took charge of the
savaged and trapped men. As he and fewer than ten of
the original twenty-eight men in 11 Platoon prepared for a
final assault, each man almost out of ammunition, some
took machetes and shovels in hand. Bob called on the NZ
supporting artillery to land high-explosive shells dangerously close to his men – positioned only 25 to 50 metres
from the enemy. The artillery's resulting spot-on accuracy

neutralised the attacking VC, enabling the platoon to withdraw and regroup with others.

Viet Cong propaganda regarding the Long Tan battle was astonishing. It portrayed their routing by the Aussies as a VC victory in which they had killed 700 Australians! I had become friendly with the Fifth Battalion intelligence officer, Capt Robert J. O'Neill, as I knew his wife's family in Adelaide. A graduate of the Royal Military College at Duntroon and a former Rhodes Scholar, Bob is now an internationally distinguished military scholar. In his book *Vietnam Task*, a detailed history of the Fifth Battalion's service in South Vietnam, Bob examined the VC claim that they had destroyed the Sixth Battalion, two infantry companies, and two squadrons of APCs. As Bob pointed out, the Task Force had only *one* squadron of APCs, and that squadron continued to make its presence known on the roads of Phuoc Tuy province. The enemy claims, he continued, also beg the question: if the VC really had killed so many Australians, why hadn't they moved in and taken the entire Nui Dat base?

On 21 August, there was a memorial service at ALSG. Feeling overwhelmingly sad, I joined Hilda and Harry in taking as many patients as we could squeeze into our vehicles. For days after the battle, the hospital was flooded with dignitaries of all stripes and nationalities. On 24 August, accompanied by school children, the Mayor of Vung Tau presented each man wounded at Long Tan with a Vietnamese doll. Later that day General Kenneth MacKay and Air Commodore Jack Dowling, the two men commanding the Australian forces in Vietnam, visited the men. Task Force commander Brigadier Jackson and company officers also stopped by.

In the weeks following the Battle of Long Tan, Hilda,

Harry and I received letters from grateful loved ones to whom we had sent Red Cross signals. It was satisfying to know that our messages gave comfort to those at home and fostered a clearer understanding of just how their boys were doing.

8

Expert at Not Facing Facts

WITH ALL THOSE GUYS AND SO FEW dolls around, and given the Digger's penchant for nicknames, it was inevitable that I, too, should be given one. Somewhere along the way I acquired 'Jean Jean the Sex Machine'. I don't know how it started, but it stuck. To my embarrassment (how could I explain it to my family?), the nickname made its way to Australia with returning soldiers. Ever since the surprise pounce by the American doctor in the operating theatre at the 93rd Evac, I had tried determinedly to live a circumspect life. Besides, I had the whole of the Australian forces who knew me, or of me, to put the brakes on my behaviour. Fat chance I'd get up to anything! I'm told, however, that at army reunions today, when my name comes up, it is always 'Jean Jean the Sex Machine'.

By early September we were taking enemy (or suspected enemy) soldiers the Diggers wounded in battle to 2 Field

Ambulance. It was disturbing to come face to face with our foe and find they were humans with the same hopes and fears that we had. I imagine they felt the same. There was one Viet Cong prisoner of war (POW) at 2 Field of whom many of us eventually became fond. He was given the nickname 'Stumpy', because his leg had been amputated after he was shot by Diggers during Operation Toledo, the follow-up to the Long Tan battle. The Americans had joined the Australians in the huge sweep aimed at driving any enemy remaining in a vast area of Phuoc Tuy province into the arms of several blocking forces. Toledo turned out to be an operation remembered mostly for the fact that no one had dry feet for two weeks. Corporal Bob 'Dogs' Kearney, a Fifth Battalion section commander at that time, believes it was his platoon that captured Stumpy.

Bob remembers: 'We were patrolling just north of Binh Ba, and the US Marines were the blocking force. We were in thick jungle and it was the wet season, very wet. Some of our blokes were suffering with monsoon blisters from continuous wearing of wet socks and boots. Out of the corner of his eye, the forward scout of our platoon saw a Vietnamese under a log. The man looked like a VC peering out of a bunker, so the scout hit the deck. The Vietnamese ran, and to the scout's surprise – and ours a minute or so later – he was completely naked. The scout yelled, '*Dung lai. Uc dai loi!*' (Halt. Australians!)

'Our Vietnamese was pretty bad, so the man kept running. A number of people opened up and hit the guy. When I got to the front, he was lying in the mud crying and saying '*Bac si, bac si*' (Doctor, doctor.). He'd been hit in the leg with a 7.62 round, and his lower leg was almost off. We called in a Dust-Off, but the chopper couldn't land since the only clearing in the area was waterlogged. It hovered about six feet above the water, and we bundled the Viet Cong in. We searched his little dugout and found an aluminium pot filled with cooked snails and nothing else – no weapon, clothing or eating utensils.

'The word came back to us later that he'd been a platoon commander at the Battle of Long Tan and had stuffed up seriously. Who knows? We were told that his punishment involved the loss of all kit and equipment and banishment into the jungle. Vietnamese are very modest, and he probably wouldn't have gone naked to the villagers for assistance. It wasn't long after we shot him that we heard he was all right and you all had nicknamed him Stumpy. I always thought how fortunate he was to have survived the contact, let alone the evacuation later. I hope he is still alive somewhere.'

Nguyen Van Ninh, a former ARVN officer now living in Sydney, told me that despite the Vietnamese being modest people, it was not unusual for a VC on a secret mission in Allied areas to go naked so that his clothes would not catch on anything. We will never know if Stumpy had 'stuffed up'.

When he was brought to us at 2 Field Ambulance, Stumpy was trembling all over with fear. Colonel Rodgers had an explanation: 'The enemy is told that Australians are cannibals, and so they're terrified of ending up in our cooking pots when they are captured.' Like all POWs, Stumpy was initially frightened and withdrawn, but it wasn't long before he softened towards us all, sensing he was among friends. He seemed glad for my warm greeting each morning.

Because of his engaging manner, the patients mellowed in their attitude towards him and included him in their activities.

Some taught him to play cards. Others tried to teach him English with an emphasis on the Australian vernacular, mostly profane. When I drove patients on sightseeing and shopping tours, Stumpy went too, squashed in the front seat between another patient and me. He showed no reaction when we passed the numerous American camps, but when we drove by the Republic of Korea (ROK) camp, we felt Stumpy go rigid with fear. The ROKs were reputed to be fearsome fighters.

One suffocating afternoon, when normally I would find the patients lying listlessly in their beds, I walked into a ward and sensed they all were waiting expectantly. They had coached Stumpy to say 'Jean Jean the Sex Machine' as I entered. Stumpy was all primed to deliver the line, with no clue as to what he was being put up to. He greeted me with a huge toothy grin and then, struggling in his accented English, he cried out: 'Jean Jean the Shit Machine!' The anguished bellows of the patients – 'No! No, Stumpy!' – drowned out my giggles. Some men were writhing and cursing. Others gasped their apologies to me. Some started to beat Stumpy over the head with newspapers and pillows. Stumpy's delighted grin at his accomplishment turned to bewilderment. He didn't know he had mixed up two of the most common words in a soldier's vocabulary.

Unknown to Stumpy, he had made a name for himself in top-level American army circles after a story about him appeared in the newspapers. When movies were shown at 2 Field Ambulance, Stumpy was allowed to watch them with the other patients. To our amusement, Stumpy, the underdog, would cheer loudly for the Indians in Westerns and would look doleful when they lost. Stumpy had a great sense of humour and no doubt put on his act deliberately to get at the

Aussies. The story of his antics at the movies was picked up by the press. When officials of the US motion picture industry, who had supplied the films, heard about it they shot off a stiff note: if movies freely provided to the troops continued to be shown to POWs, all Australians would have movie rights withdrawn. Rumour had it that the complaint was addressed at Embassy level. The curtain suddenly rang down for the luckless Stumpy: movie rights revoked. Show over.

Soon after Stumpy's arrival, we had our first North Vietnamese Army (NVA) prisoner of war in hospital. Unlike Stumpy, the NVA prisoner was sullen and seemed full of hate, prompting us, of course, to call him 'Smiley'. I gave the POWs the same toilet articles as the Australians and kept Stumpy and Smiley supplied with local fruit, as well as Vietnamese magazines and newspapers bought in the market. I always wondered if the reading material I gave them was appropriate. I encouraged Smiley to write to his parents in Hanoi – they had heard nothing of him for three months. I hadn't considered where I could mail the letter (after I had it censored, of course)! If I took it to the local South Vietnamese Post Office, all hell could break loose. Fortuitously, the International Committee of the Red Cross made an unannounced visit to 2 Field Ambulance. They reported great pleasure at seeing how well the Australians treated the POWs, and I was able to pass Smiley's letter on to them. I still wonder if his family received it.

Despite weeks of trying, I never could get Smiley to warm to me. He was an NVA captain, and perhaps his humiliation at being captured might explain his perpetual unwillingness to communicate. At first Stumpy was scared of Smiley, which intrigued us. Later, when we had an ARVN soldier in hospital for a few days, the South Vietnamese man was also terrified of Smiley. It took some months for Smiley to recover, and through it all he remained aloof and cold. As I heard it, after the Australians healed his wounds, he was handed over to the ARVN prison camp at Long Binh and was hanged as a war criminal. The only emotion he ever showed was when the ARVN came to take him away; he cried.

We all became expert at not facing facts, yet each day we saw what happens in war. People are wounded. People die. If there were recreational drugs around to alleviate that reality, I never saw any evidence, but I wasn't looking for it. One private of 2 Field Ambulance told me: 'US troops always seemed to have some marijuana in their pockets. I confess I smoked Mary Jane in the lines maybe two or three times, to experiment with the unknown. Just a whiff of drugs though, and the army sent you straight home and into *big* trouble. Drugs were absolutely forbidden.' The drugs that turned thousands of GIs into addicts had not yet become a problem.

Alcohol was another story. Top brand liquor from the PX was cheap. Most of our down time was spent drinking. Liquor offered a temporary refuge from the overwhelming tragedies we faced each day. Drinking and partying, we unwound on the good days and drowned our sorrows on the bad. Many a night we drank until the 11 pm curfew sent us home to our beds. We never needed an excuse for a party, and there was always a party somewhere. Women were booked up socially for weeks ahead, if they could keep up the pace. Often we celebrated a Grand Opening, as was the case with 176 Air Dispatch Company, who had constructed a canteen from pilfered American building materials. 'We have a three-piece band of American helicopter pilots that sounds like The Kingston Trio,' Frank Zuppar said enticingly as he invited me. I revelled in the unpredictability of our lives.

Most nights there were parties at the Villa, and they were wild. At that time there was nowhere else to go. Barefoot men and women in shorts and tops crowded into one room, sweaty skin against sweaty skin as we sat on the twin beds – the only seating except for the floor. Rock music played loudly, ashtrays were full and liquor bottles empty. The need to escape from our daily witness of the wounded and the dead inevitably led to people bonding and to liaisons forming. If I wasn't at a party, I was asleep – so tired that I could have slept with a brass band playing outside my door. Not once did Brenda Starr, Star Reporter feel the urge or have the energy to send a story home to *The Advertiser*.

The Americans loved the Aussies and thought that the Diggers all looked like Errol Flynn in a bush hat. They loved that we liked to party, that we were more informal and relaxed than they were. I briefly adopted the habit of wearing a bottle opener around my neck, where I should have been wearing my dog tags, and it was wanted at least ten times a day. Drinking contests between the Yanks and the Aussies were commonplace. The Yanks never won. They never seemed to learn that you can't outdrink an Australian. 'On one occasion,' American nurse Annie Philiben said, 'the Aussies counted the beers I had lined up in front of me, and I was nineteen rounds behind!'

Never knowing what the next day might bring, the hospital staff knew better than to drink to excess. Anxious moments were common, and they needed to be alert. The wounded were supposed to have weapons of all kinds removed from their bodies before they were loaded into Dust-Offs and lifted from the field. But accidents happen in war as they do everywhere. One time my Villa neighbour, Capt Jim Fenton, was standing by a nurse at the 36th when she removed a live grenade – pin out, ready to be tossed – from a wounded Yank's blood-soaked uniform. Jim quietly put one hand over that of the nurse and, with the other, grabbed the only tool nearby, a paper clip from a medical file, to disarm the grenade.

Some of the patients' injuries were less battle- than bottle-related. 'What happened to your ankle?' I asked L/Cpl Michael Croker, a radio operator with 161 Independent Reconnaissance Flight, when I found him at the 36th Evac.

'I fell into a weapon pit on Sunday. I ran into a friend from recruit training days, and we demolished a bottle of vodka,' he said, unrepentant. 'Our medics couldn't decide if the ankle was broken or just sprained. They put me into one of our Sioux helicopters, not a regular Dust-Off. Well, about five miles out, the pilot advised Vung Tau control tower that he was inbound to the hospital pad. When we landed, we were surrounded by medics, who plucked me from the aircraft, onto a trolley and straight into the reception area.

'They discovered to their disappointment that I was not a battle casualty. Being Sunday, they left me there on the trolley while they went back to whatever they were doing – playing poker I think. Eventually they took an X-ray and decided that I had not broken anything. They put this enormous plaster cast on my leg. Now I can't walk. That bottle of vodka has a lot to answer for.' Three days later Michael was gone – sent back to duty with a broom handle as a crutch.

On 14 September, nearly a month after Jim Richmond and Barry Meller had spent the night of Long Tan wounded and alone, the American doctors requested I buy Jim beer. It would act as a sedative, increase his appetite, and give him needed calories. The hitch was that normally no alcohol was allowed in an American hospital. I purchased a crate of beer with Red Cross petty cash and told the doctors *they* had to explain to the rest of the Australians patients at the 36th why they weren't allowed any.

Predictably, Jim Richmond's beer started trouble. At Nui Dat, each soldier was allotted two cans of beer a day (with no accumulation) and, of course, zero alcohol was allowed on operations. The Diggers felt they should be given their beer ration while they were in hospital. There was a little dispute with 36th Evac management, but some swift and forceful negotiation by our doctors in favour of Aussie culture won out. From then on our patients had their daily beer ration. Game, set, match, Australia!

I am sure that all Australian soldiers believed, as I did, that if we treated the Vietnamese fairly and helped rid them of the VC's cruel influence, they would feel protected and able to go about their lives without fear. Our help eventually would result, we hoped, in Aussie lives being saved by the Vietnamese having gained respect for Australians and the values for which we stood. With that aim, the army's Win Hearts and Minds (WHAM) unit was devoted to obtaining the friendship and respect of the Vietnamese. All major Task Force units were assigned a special area of responsibility: repairing schools and market places, and building new dispensaries. ALSG's responsibility was Nam Binh, a fishing village west of Vung Tau settled by Roman Catholic refugees from the North. One afternoon a week our dentist, Major Ron Beynon, drilled the stained, decayed teeth of the villagers. I was needed to amuse and occupy the dozens of fascinated children who otherwise crowded around Ron's dental chair and got in his way while he was working. Hilda did a lot of Medcap work but, for me, the needs of the patients came first. How could I tell a soldier who wanted me to write home for him that I had to go play with Vietnamese children?

At first I went on very few Medcaps. Still, Red Cross was eager for me to get involved, so Harry and I began to administer Red Cross programs ourselves to bypass the ever-present black market corruption. We arranged for Red Cross to send, for example, pencils and exercise books from Australian to Vietnamese children who had few such supplies. I was also able to help at the local Vietnamese hospital, Le Loi, where conditions and the medical care offered there seemed appalling. I went to Le Loi with an ALSG sergeant whose unit wanted to give gifts to the hospital patients at Christmas. Hospital staff suggested that basic toilet articles, such as combs, toothbrushes and soap, were suitable. Collecting and packing the items was a project ideal for Junior Red Cross branches in Australia. Then, rather than distribute the gifts willy-nilly, we asked a WHAM officer to guide us to the neediest. We had learned from experience at Nam Binh that it wasn't easy to introduce the children to toothbrushes and paste. With its smell and taste of peppermint, the children thought the toothpaste was to eat. Toothpaste alone, they found, was not so good. Combined with bread or rice it was wonderful!

How effective the Australians were in winning the hearts and minds of the Vietnamese we will never know. When I returned to Ba Ria in 1995 though, the nuns in the Roman Catholic orphanage/school there proudly drew my attention to the playground equipment built by our soldiers almost thirty years earlier – equipment built to withstand the onslaughts of children well into the new millennium.

Our Red Cross team became the focus of international publicity. Armed Forces Radio (later made famous by Robin Williams in the movie *Good Morning, Vietnam*) was the only English-speaking radio station broadcasting from South Vietnam. The station asked some of the patients and me to make a tape for broadcast to the Yanks. Our program made quite a change from the station's usual diet of Country and Western songs – and the Supremes. Next, CBS television shot a film about army hospitals for nationwide distribution in the US. The show aimed to illustrate the international aspects of Red Cross personnel working together, and the 36th Evac was the only military hospital in Vietnam where that happened. Koopsie and Vivienne (from the American Red Cross) and I were filmed working in the team conviviality that for us was the norm. The Australian Broadcasting Commission (ABC) news division did a feature. United Press International filmed Harry for Dutch TV, and I made an appearance with him. NHQ welcomed the positive publicity our work generated. It helped them raise the funds that supported domestic and international efforts and, of course, kept us in pocket money.

Sometimes publicity could hurt though. One Sunday a WHAM unit took a group of Vietnamese children from the not-so-friendly, too-close-to-Nui Dat village of Hoa Long to the Saigon Botanical Garden and Zoo. As it turned out, that

Sunday I had a rare day off. My thirst for seeing new places couldn't be sated, so I was happy to go along to help. After lunch, we shepherded our group of excited young Vietnamese, all scrubbed clean and dressed in their best, into a Caribou at Vung Tau airport. For probably all of the children, it was both their first ride in an aircraft and the first visit to their country's capital. We rode on the back of an army truck from Tan Son Nhut to the gardens and zoo, which were a long cyclo ride from Tu Do and the Roman Catholic cathedral on central JFK Square. Army public relations had a photographer with the WHAM unit that day – not an unusual event. With some of the children following behind and others fighting over who could hold our hands, we explored the bridges, lakes and lawns of the sprawling gardens and zoo. Once lovely when the French were there, the gardens had been neglected. But the day was a delight and the children gleeful. We were well aware though, that these same youngsters might kill one of our soldiers the next day.

As it turned out, the innocent excursion apparently caused anguish to a loving wife waiting thousands of miles away for her husband to return home. Pictures of her husband, the children and me appeared in nearly every major newspaper in Australia. I hope it was only idle gossip, but some weeks later I heard that the soldier's wife had seen the picture of us on the Saigon outing and thought we were dating – or worse. I felt nauseous. I hardly knew her husband, and I certainly never had been alone with him. I wanted to write to tell her so in order to relieve her worries. I knew it would do no good, so I did nothing. It saddens me to think about it.

Many years later Marie London, who was married for more than forty years to her husband Brian (he did two tours of Vietnam and was recognised for bravery there) told me: 'I know from army life that the "I heards" get changed with each person's retelling. I can only speak for myself, but if Brian was ever to meet any American nurses, or one of our Red Cross ladies or, for that matter, a Vietnamese lady, I would be only too happy for him to have some female company with whom to share talk about home and family. There had to be something normal to break the horror and madness over there.'

The madness wasn't only 'over there'. Australian wharfies, to protest the war, despicably and misguidedly refused to load cargo ships with goods for the war effort. Medical supplies in the hospital were critically low, and we had been out of Red Cross supplies for a month. In fact all units, including our front line warriors, urgently needed goods and equipment of all kinds. 'It's coming on the *Jeparit*,' was the answer to any request. The *Jeparit* was a large container ship chartered by the government to take supplies to the troops and to us. If everything that was said to be coming on the *Jeparit* actually was, the ship would have sunk under the load before leaving Sydney Heads.

9

What Was the Crazy Killing All About?

With its tropical climate, Vietnam at any time would slow us down. Occasionally after lunch I came to a full stop and, dog-tired, escaped to the Villa for a quick bit of shut-eye, having told the guard on the door to be sure to wake me in thirty minutes. That's if I ate lunch at all. Frequently, hungry and in need of a midday break, I'd sit down in the mess tent, take one look at the American hotdogs and sugary baked beans – with food shortages, that often was all the hard-pressed chefs could procure – and go back to work, my appetite suddenly gone.

Winter was just as enervating as summer. We'd been living through some gruelling days, and I longed for the relief of the drenching afternoon rain to cool the air for a few brief minutes, though it meant that half an hour later it was steamier and hotter than ever. We blamed a lot on the climate. Never one to be blessed with good skin, my face was getting spottier each day. That's Vietnam, I thought, and ignored it. One day at lunch, though, one of the doctors took me aside and suggested I stop by his office to get something to heal my complexion. I was astonished and flattered that the doctors would have time for anything so minor. For once, I was grateful to be noticed.

More worrisome than my spotty skin was the itchy problem of my sharing a room with Hilda. It wasn't working out. Hilda had written to Red Cross NHQ four days after my arrival: 'May I congratulate you on your choice of Miss Debelle. She is a charming, delightful person, who, I am sure, will do well in her new posting.' From then on, though, it was all downhill. I was much younger than Hilda, which may account for the fact that we looked at our work and our play from different perspectives. At the end of the day, after work like ours, we all needed someone to sound off to and Hilda wasn't that person for me.

The American Red Cross gals, with their usual 'can-do' attitude, pushed matters to a head. 'Karen Gramke, from Chicago, is coming to help us out for a few months,' Koopsie said. 'You and Karen should share a room and let Hilda move in with one of the American nurses.' No sooner was it said than done. I am sure Hilda was as relieved at the change as I was. Karen's sense of fun kept me laughing, and stories of her on-again, off-again love life kept me intrigued. She was a wonderful roommate.

By October 1966 the American soldiers were feeling increasingly abandoned because their President had yet to visit them. There was always talk of Lyndon Johnson visiting Vietnam,

but would it ever happen? One day people complained inces-
santly of puzzling events. Aircraft were late, or didn't arrive
at all. Telephone calls wouldn't go through. Something strange
was happening, and it was happening countrywide. Early
afternoon someone speculated: 'I bet the President is in
country!' An hour or so later we heard that President Johnson
had indeed made his first trip to Vietnam – a quick and highly
secret foray to the Cam Ranh Bay airbase. All of the communications for the visit had been done many kilometres to the
south, in Vung Tau! The Americans of the 39th Signals Battalion, whose telecommunications equipment dominated the
town's largest hill, had put the trip together.

So secretive was the President's visit that, as his plane, *Air
Force One*, was landing, airmen were still draping bunting on
the reviewing stand. Rumours flew around the Australian
camp that someone had painted a red kangaroo on *Air Force
One*'s tail, but no one could confirm such a daring breach of
American security. President Johnson reviewed troops, had
lunch at the enlisted men's mess, and then jetted out of the
country. He had been in Vietnam for less than an hour.

The President continued on to Australia, and the welcoming
crowds greeted him with a fervour not seen since the first visit
of Queen Elizabeth II in 1954. There were a few anti-war protesters, mostly students who might be called soon to fight in
Vietnam, but clearly Australia was still 'all the way with LBJ'.
The Prime Minister, Harold Holt, capitalised on the enthusiasm
by calling an election a month later, largely on the issue of
whether Australian troops should remain in Vietnam. All of us
at the front voted absentee, then awaited the election results
with great interest. Maybe we would be home sooner than we
expected. The people of Australia voted overwhelmingly for

Mr Holt, who immediately increased the commitment of troops to 6,300 and later to 8,000. President Johnson made a second visit to Vietnam in December 1967, on his way home from attending Harold Holt's funeral. The Prime Minister had died mysteriously in a swimming accident at Portsea, a beach resort near Melbourne. His body never was found.

With no other female staff at the Australian hospital, there was always much to do that was outside basic Red Cross duties: beds to be straightened, ashtrays to be emptied, magazines to be picked up from the floor and tidied, with old ones thrown out and new ones added. Once there was orange peel to be picked up from the floor. Orange peel? I wondered. Where had the oranges come from? I did whatever needed to be done, and it all took time. Hospital personnel were far too busy with medical matters to stay on top of housekeeping duties.

Those who worked at 2 Field Ambulance agree today that in some ways the hospital was not so different in its appearance and operation from that portrayed in M*A*S*H, the film and television depiction of the Korean War. We had no female nurses, but there was a 'Radar' (Jim Townson), and a 'Klinger' (who shall remain nameless). Our Klinger tried to get a 'homer' by lying under a truck naked and shooting at the Officers' Mess with an Owen gun. As in M*A*S*H, nothing Klinger tried got him sent home.

I had been living at the Villa for about three months when all residents were summoned to a meeting in the ground floor hallway. Colonel Honeycutt, forcefully yet with dignity, told us why some of the toilets were clogged: condoms had stuffed up the works. Unlike in M*A*S*H, in which any mention of

sex was greeted with derisive laughter, we listened quietly
and attentively to Colonel Honeycutt. She was brief but to
the point. New rules were to be enforced. No person of the
opposite sex was allowed in our rooms unless signed in by
the front door sentry, and bedroom doors were to be left
wide open at all times when a visitor was there. As the
meeting broke up, Karen reflected on the colonel's words:
'Honey just told us: in the Villa we can do whatever we want
with the opposite sex so long as the guard knows about it
and the door is open for everyone to watch!'

We laughed, but extremely fit young men facing death each
day did have their longings, many of which were met at the
numerous bars and cathouses that had mushroomed in Vung
Tau. What did love have to do with it? In 99.9 per cent of
cases, absolutely nothing. As a resort town, Vung Tau had
long offered its pleasures to visitors. It was a common sight to
see bar girls draped over soldiers, who sometimes chatted on
to their mates, pretending to be oblivious to the attention.

We got to know the bar girl talk. If his mates called a man
a 'cherry boy' (virgin), he was assured of a lot of attention
from the bar girls. Those men who didn't commit to any
special girl or bar were known as 'beaucoup butterfly flit'.
'Didi mau' meant 'Get lost'. 'Beaucoup' and its opposite 'titi'
were just two of many bastardised words we used from
Vietnam's French heritage.

Most of the Australian soldiers, growing up in the
fifties and sixties, had led sheltered lives and had wanted
for little. But when they saw their mates die, they had a
rude awakening. They began to live for each day. One Digger
said the general attitude toward life was get a f--k
today, for tomorrow you may be dead. There were also

those, he said, who thought it was macho to get a 'dose' of VD, despite the fact that condoms were provided free. He told me of what had begun innocently for him when he was exploring Vung Tau with a few hours to kill. His story may be typical of many.

Waiting for a ride back to Nui Dat, he realised he needed a haircut. He found a barber shop that was very clean inside. 'In I went, noticing that the back of the shop was partitioned off with curtains. Halfway through the haircut a delightful young lady came up to me and enquired whether I would like a massage after the haircut. This I readily agreed to. I was taken behind one of the curtains and the massage began. Then halfway through the massage I was asked by the lady in question if I would like "hanky panky", which again I readily agreed to. This was undertaken in situ. Well and truly looked after, I went to pay at the front counter, where there was an incredible array of flick knives, banned at the time in Australia. I bought the most lethal. When I asked the total cost – namely for haircut, massage, f--k and a flick knife – I was informed $5. I returned to Nui Dat a contented soldier.'

The number of prostitutes in Vung Tau grew spectacularly each month. In October 1966 the Aussies set a record of sorts: the highest incidence of VD for any period of time our troops were in Vietnam. Jim (Radar) Townson, the clerical assistant to the 2 Field Ambulance Commanding Officer (CO), said: 'Of course, all the officers caught it from a toilet seat. We thought that was a funny place to have a root!'

The army did everything it could to contain the disease. There was a story that Lt Col Colin Townsend, CO of the Sixth Battalion, had wanted to establish a battalion-regulated brothel. Shock! Horror! The innovative idea never got off the ground for fear of what the Sydney tabloids would say. And more important, what would the mothers of the National Servicemen say?

Graphic photographs of cancer of the testicles shown to the soldiers were making little impact. Men continued to become infected. In 1967, however, the American doctors began to notice an astonishing trend. The *Stars and Stripes* military newspaper had for a long time featured photographs of bikini-clad Australian women. When Sydney opened up as an R&R resort, Australia became a top destination for the Yanks. Before going there though, a soldier had to test negative for venereal disease twenty-four hours before his departure. The American VD rate, and perhaps the Australian also, dropped dramatically.

In Vung Tau at that time, there were few wholesome places of recreation then available as a break from non-stop demanding work. Movies were screened every night in about four different places. We went occasionally, but we were fortunate to have our own entertainment right next door. Vivienne, who had been stationed on many of the world's army bases, knew how to make herself at home in each posting. In the room she shared with Koopsie, she had a tiny TV set with good reception. Karen and I went next door to watch 'Candid Camera', 'Bonanza' and 'The Ed Sullivan Show' as well as old movies. Vivienne said the shows were transmitted from an aircraft the US Air Force (USAF) sent up every evening to circle over all of South Vietnam, enabling the armed forces – including those at sea as well as the Vietnamese – to pick up current American programs. Whether unwinding or on the job, I always learned much about our work from talking to the experienced American women.

Evenings at home were relaxing, but we did love going somewhere special for dinner on occasion. Cyrnos, a fine French restaurant, was our favourite. Dinner served at a snail's pace in the pleasant surroundings at Cyrnos was a welcome change from the food slopped to us in a chow line at the Pacific. Madame Anna, the chic French woman who had run Cyrnos with a firm hand for years, greeted both French weekend visitors from Saigon and us 'locals' with an equally gracious smile and a *'bonsoir'* as we arrived. Like many restaurateurs, she continued to stay in Vietnam during the war, enjoying the boom in business. Perhaps in her late forties, Madame Anna had fine skin the colour of a sun-touched peach, and she seemed remarkably worldly-wise and knowledgeable for her years, which I attributed to her cosmopolitan background. One day I was out driving with patients when I found, perhaps, the reason for Anna's mature wisdom. I stopped for directions at an elegant villa on the seafront. Down a shaded driveway lined with flowering bougainvillea, I saw a bikini-clad woman sunbaking on a chaise longue in the garden. As I approached to ask for help, I couldn't believe what I was seeing. The woman was Anna of the beautiful face, but the body below was wrinkled and aged. I felt I was in a horror movie. I was looking at a face lifted – more than once. Or, did Anna drink formaldehyde with her morning café au lait?

My boss from Melbourne, Commander John Crabb – as urbane, witty and sophisticated as ever – visited us on the 11th and 12th of October to see for himself the conditions in which we lived and worked. Hilda reported to him that I should be more judicious in my conduct off duty. Clearly, despite working long hours each day and being in my bed sober (relatively) each night by 11 pm – she knew as we had shared a room – I was not shaping up to her expectations. I was flummoxed. Did she, too, believe the rumours about 'Jean Jean the Sex Machine'? I don't believe Commander Crabb did, but if so, I think he would have chuckled. On his return to Australia, Commander Crabb wrote to my brother Bruce who, after Dad's death, was listed as my next of kin: 'How much I enjoyed seeing Jean in Vung Tau. She was in great form and doing a fine job, which she obviously enjoys. She works long hours in a hot and sticky climate, and she must get pretty tired at times. She took me around the wards of her hospital and it was delightful to see the high regard in which the patients held her.'

I confess I *had* warned the patients the day before that my boss was going to be there, and in front of Commander Crabb the darling boys greeted me rapturously. Never one for introspection, and with no time anyway to look back, I forgot about Hilda's criticism. Commander Crabb recommended some welcome changes. Although all patients still would be visited every day, each of us was to have one and a half days off a week, which was the practice with American Red Cross. We were to get five days R&C within Vietnam, and we were to get one R&R outside the country! With our morale lifted considerably Hilda, Harry and I started working for the first time as a team. I celebrated by cruising up the river to Saigon on one of the frequent trips of the cargo-carrying *Clive Steele*, a Landing Ship Medium (LSM) of 32 Small Ships. I had been invited on board by a former patient, Jack Peel, but hardly saw him. While I was being entertained by the officers, he was down in the engine room 'pedalling'. Against a background of mortar fire, bombings and other explosions, we sailed through VC-infested country as I devoured my lunch, whooping with joy to see pumpkin on the plate!

The *Clive Steele*'s previous trip had been a fiasco, and it was no one's fault. Near Cat Lo the crew saw heavy fire coming from the Americans and immediately went to their aid, all men at action stations. It turned out to be a firepower demonstration for the American Ambassador, Henry Cabot Lodge, and the Australians were told in no uncertain terms to 'piss-off', which they promptly did.

At Back Beach we had our own problems. The rainy season closed with a torrent. We had driving rain, we had thunderous rain, we had non-stop rain. Everything flooded. The camp was like a series of wading pools, and it stayed that way through the end of October. Unlike the soldiers who in their sturdy boots and gaiters could slosh along nonchalantly, I'd take off my shoes and paddle through barefoot. One time a Digger offered to piggyback me, but thinking of his hands on my thighs and the chances for gossip if my skirt rode up, I declined his offer.

L/Cpl Peter 'Radish' Radford worked for 17 Construction Squadron as a fitter and turner. He spent nine days at 2 Field Ambulance because of eating a 'noggy' roll. The crusty fresh French bread stuffed with salad from the local market was also known as a 'heppo' roll because the germ-laden lettuce and tomato were guaranteed to cause hepatitis, diarrhoea or worse. 'I had diarrhoea bad, *bad*,' Peter recalls. 'There were no bedpans available, so I sat on the throne in a blinding monsoon rainstorm for hours. No roof – just a pedestal out in the open. I was so crook I didn't care. The shiny toilet paper was wet through. It was no fun.' One day Peter thought he was hallucinating: from his hospital bed, he watched a huge snake slither across the tent floor and disappear into another tent.

There was an urgent need to replace the tented wards at 2 Field with permanent Kingstrand huts, which had concrete floors and aluminium walls with louvred windows to keep out the rain and the snakes. Any 2 Field staff who could be spared, plus ambulatory patients who were well enough, laboured with locally-employed Vietnamese to help the engineers build the huts. By the end of October, three Kingstrands had been bolted together and were ready for patients. We had hoped to start some sporting activities, but the volleyball court was always underwater from the rain, and the table tennis table, which the engineers had promised to build us, was delayed once more and was not to be in my time.

Because of the rain, the sand and the conditions of the roads, our vehicles needed a great deal of maintenance. In fact, all mechanical machinery did. The Volkswagen had a series of mishaps, including flat tyres and a shattered windscreen. The nearest VW agent was in Saigon, and getting needed parts from him seemed to be more difficult than climbing Mount Everest in bare feet. For weeks we drove behind a temporary plastic windscreen until Mary Gaynor, with Red Cross in Singapore, sent us a proper replacement. How elated Hilda, Harry and I were when a four-wheel-drive Land Rover, more suited to the local conditions, arrived on the *Jeparit* for Harry. Until then he had been forced to rely on army transport, always willing but often unavailable.

Also on the *Jeparit* were eight tea chests of much needed supplies from NHQ, and thirteen fruit cakes. To an American a gift of a fruit cake is about as welcome as malaria (some of the commercial versions, chock full of candied fruit and preservatives, have turned a traditional treat into a national joke). But the moist sultana and raisin-laden Aussie fruit cake liberally laced with brandy or rum was a universal favourite. Nine of the cakes had to be thrown away though; they had not been packed in airtight tins and so were crawling with maggots or weevils. In addition, another tea chest had been opened and biscuits stolen. It was so hard to get supplies in Vietnam, and those small setbacks were disheartening.

Harry had the use of the Land Rover for only a short time. Australian Red Cross had been active with Vietnam refugee work since the end of the French war in 1954, when the country was partitioned, and hundreds of thousands of refugees, mainly Catholic, had left their homes in the North to settle in the South. Vietnamese Red Cross, already severely overburdened with a million and a half refugees, was trying to assist an additional 60,000 people left homeless by the floods. As part of NHQ's International Red Cross efforts, Harry was transferred to Saigon to work with the Vietnamese. I was sad to see him go. He had been a thoughtful friend, but his new work alleviating suffering among the refugees was important. Harry was a tireless worker, respected by both officers and men alike. His enthusiasm and willingness to do any job since his arrival caused Colonel Rodgers to praise him openly.

I was cheered to get Harry's Land Rover, for suddenly I was responsible for the Red Cross work at 2 Field Ambulance, where most of the patients now came, and Hilda took over my job at the 36th. I thought I was Superwoman when I shifted the Land Rover into four-wheel drive and felt the wheels powerfully grip the loose sand. Even better, because prices of everyday commodities in Vietnam had almost doubled, Hilda increased my allowance by $11 a month! She'd noticed that among the free-spending Americans, I was engaged in an ongoing struggle to make do on my pay.

I still worked occasional days at the 36th Evac, however. Father Larry 'Doc' Donohue, a Jesuit chaplain there, once told of an evening when a Dust-Off came in with Australian wounded: 'They hit a landmine when they jumped out of the chopper. One young soldier (were there any who weren't young?) was terribly wounded all up and down his back – nothing on the front. Sixty-some wounds they counted. I gave the lad conditional absolution and baptism. I always baptised anything that was not nailed down. I carried a nasal spray bottle filled with Holy Water and could hit a guy at three feet! Of course I told him when I saw him in the recovery next morning. He was awake and in good spirits so I asked why he was wounded only on the back. He replied, "Chaplain, ya know we were blown up by a mine when we got out of the chopper?" Yes, I knew that. "Well, Chaplain, it was me who jumped out first and detonated the f--ker!" I almost had a stroke right there. He couldn't care less who he was talking to and was so sincere.'

Doc Donohue went on: 'Another time a chopper of Aussie wounded came in, and after all the men were carried into triage, the last man walked out straight as a ramrod. He was the officer in charge. He looked after his men, and then it became obvious that he, too, was wounded in the legs. He hadn't said a word until his troops were taken care of. I will never forget that man.'

The American nurses at the 36th continued to give our boys special treatment. Ted Harrison from the Fifth Battalion, his chest peppered with shrapnel, was recovering in the post-op ward. Jackie Kennedy thoughtfully invited him to see some aerial movies filmed from a chopper over Vietnam. Ted says of the American medical staff: 'Instead of becoming garden fertiliser, I owe them my life.' All the Australians could do to return the favour was to give spirited support to help the 36th Evac staff win the Vung Tau baseball championship.

A significant number of African-Americans served among the enlisted men in Uncle Sam's army, yet it was rare to see a black nurse in Vietnam. The wounded black men lucky enough to do so couldn't believe their eyes. 'You're a black angel. I must be in heaven,' they'd say to Gert Baker when they came out of the anaesthetic. Gert, the 36th's head theatre nurse, would reply: 'You're not in heaven, but I'm here to look after you.' They'd smile and then fall asleep comforted.

In the 36th Evac's first tour, there were only two black female nurses. One of them, whom I yearned to know better, had an especially beautiful face. In the predominantly 'white' Australia of that day, I had never had a black friend. Once, at a gathering, I heard someone say: 'She's here to add colour to the party'. Naïve about racial relationships, and believing that what I had read in the papers only applied to bigots in the Deep South, I took the remark as funny. With a warm smile I repeated it to her. From beneath the smooth brow of her beautiful face, she directed a cold, flat look at me for a few seconds, then turned her back. Instantly, I understood what I had said. My cheeks flamed, and I stammered out an apology while my hoped-for friend just looked at me. Later I heard there was a Taylor Caldwell novel she wanted to read, and I hastily got it sent from Australia to give to her. I tried to make up for my gaffe in numerous small ways, but understandably she never became a friend. Why should she? While black nurses had been fully integrated in the US military since 1948, at home on civvy street their brothers and sisters were protesting for equality.

At a reunion of the 36th Evac in San Antonio, Texas, in 2002, I asked Gert Baker how she would have reacted if I'd made that remark to her. 'I would have killed you,' she replied. 'In Vietnam, we were working with freedoms that we didn't have at home. Besides, all black women there felt we were needed at home more than in the hospital wards in Vietnam. Our war was the Civil Rights Movement. We didn't need anyone in Vietnam to give us trouble.' I simply had had no comprehension of the depth of racial feelings in the United States.

Few Westerners socialised with the locals, except to do business in the markets, or to take care of that other kind of business in the bars. The girls employed at the PX cash registers were Vietnamese. I grew fond of one teenager, who called herself Lily, a Western name she thought rang with sophistication. I preferred to call her by her real name, Hue, which means fragrant flower. We often joked as she tallied up my purchases. One day she surprised me. 'Miss Jean, would you come to my birthday party on Saturday?' she asked. 'I'd love to,' I replied enthusiastically. I was thrilled that Hue had invited me and that I would have the chance to visit a Vietnamese home. I was as thirsty to know more about Vietnamese culture as I always was for a Coke.

Hue said it was her birthday, but today I know that may have been an excuse for inviting me to her house. Vietnamese do not celebrate their birthdays as we do in the West. They usually celebrate only two events concerning the birth of a baby: the first takes place a month after the birth, the other when the child is a year old. After that, they must wait until they reach sixty, then seventy and eighty, when they celebrate longevity. Longevity is prized among people accustomed to living a short life because of disease, poor medical facilities and especially the killings associated with unceasing war. Gift-giving celebrations are reserved for Tet, when the old year gives way to the new.

I felt I should take Hue a birthday present. But what? She probably had everything she wanted from the local market. I didn't have a clue what was trendy in the singsongy music that floated from every market store. And choosing a suitable book in Vietnamese was out of the question. The biggest handicap, though, was that I had so little discretionary money myself. I settled for a lipstick, bought at the PX, where Hue worked but was not allowed to shop. I gift-wrapped it as prettily as circumstances allowed.

Saturday afternoon arrived. Following Hue's directions carefully, I soon found myself deep in the Vietnamese coun-tryside, far from the military security of Vung Tau and Back Beach. No other round-eyes were to be seen. It was foolish of me, but I wasn't worried. Unless one actually had been shot at, it was hard to comprehend the danger. Besides, Hue spoke French and Vietnamese, as well as English. If I should happen to get into trouble, I knew she could say in three languages: 'The VC have captured my friend. Please rescue her.' God protects fools, and I was blessed with the casual ignorance of youth.

Hue was a clever girl who came from a clever family. Her parents had a simple, one-storey stone house with a small, well-kept vegetable garden behind. There we sat and dined outside, *en plein air* as Papa-san said in French, giving me a courtly smile. The house was by no means a villa, but it was clean and pleasant. It had only one room, which was partitioned with furniture and curtains to provide a little privacy for sleeping. Whole families commonly slept together on a large square bed or in hammocks or on a straw mat covering the tiled floor. Grandmothers, parents and many brothers and sisters slept with arms and legs entangled together, as I had observed when I walked along the streets of Vung Tau on sultry afternoons. The outdoor kitchen and laundry were recognisable by the large tin bowls used for preparing food and by the plastic buckets used for toting water and food scraps. I knew not to use the toilet, as it was generally a hole in the ground with indentations for feet on either side. It was never easy to squat in place, holding my skirt high and at the same time trying not to breathe, look down or fall in.

Hue's family had left the North as refugees but had lived in Vung Tau for some time. With pride they showed me photographs of their son who, they said, was studying in the United States. It was not unusual for Vietnamese families to have no young men around. We always assumed they must be away fighting for either the ARVN or the Viet Cong. I struggled through a limited conversation with Papa-san – apparently not fit enough or too old to be in the military – and hoped that the future of Vietnam would be assured by people like his son. I never discovered what Papa-san did besides tend his garden.

It was a problem knowing when to hand over my gift. After everyone was seated, I pulled it from my purse. From Hue's obvious joy it seemed nothing could have pleased her more than an American-brand lipstick. I had scored a bullseye!

During that lazy afternoon in the family's garden, watching

dogs scratch at food scraps and fleas while children joyfully played the same games that children everywhere play, I was introduced to a banquet of Vietnamese foods. There was red sticky rice, pork roll, pickled pig's ear, jellied fish salad and fish cakes. Everything had to be dipped into the ever-present *nuoc cham*, the pungent dipping sauce made from *nuoc mam* fish sauce, vinegar, garlic, chilli and sugar. I tasted a food that was to become a lifelong passion – *cha gio*, the crispy spring rolls of pork and shrimp wrapped in a light crunchy skin of rice paper. Relaxed and content, I sat drinking Coke and slowly munching those cylinders of delight, savouring the taste and allowing time for Hue's mother and grandmother to fry more. Hue told me that *cha gio*, known in Hanoi as *nem nuong*, were first introduced to the South by those fleeing the Communists in the North.

I ate cautiously. Although my Western digestive system had been seasoned by months in country, I was conscious that the local banquet still might not agree with me. I stuck with the fried foods that had so thoughtfully been provided. Occasionally I'd stop eating long enough to consider whether I was safe there, all alone in a Vietnamese village. As soon as I have another *cha gio*, I thought, I'd better leave. Sunset would be soon, and it could be deadly not to be back in Vung Tau before dark – well before dark.

After I ceremoniously shook hands with everyone, Papa-san held open the door of the Red Cross Volkswagen as formally as though he were the doorman at the Ritz. I drove off, the whole family waving goodbye. As I navigated the car along the pot-holed streets, past the little houses and rice fields, my thoughts were conflicted. What an honour to have been invited to Hue's home. And what was the crazy killing all about?

10

To Nui Dat and a Mine Field

WHEN I FIRST ARRIVED IN SAIGON, I had looked scornfully at the unkempt appearance of the American nurses. Just because they were so few among so many men was no reason not to look tidy. How could they let themselves go? I had not yet learned of the rains that came flooding down every afternoon, ruining any hope of glamour one might have. Or of the lack of a good beauty shop to take care of a woman's necessaries. Or of the sweat that rolled down my cheeks, leaving rivulets across a made-up face. I soon gave up any expectation of being well groomed. I tried to look as good as I could in the morning, but that was it for the rest of the day.

One hot, sticky afternoon I struggled up the steep hill to the ALSG Officers' Mess on an errand, my feet sinking into the deep, soft sand with every step. I suddenly came face to face with two vacationing Australian women who had flown into the base camp for only a few hours. I thought I was dreaming, but they were real enough – so real that today I can remember their fashionable bouffant hairstyles and the ruffled, sleeveless dress one of them wore. They sat in a circle of men who hung on their every word and gesture. To my envious gaze, those blonde women were so elegant they made supermodel Jean Shrimpton look like a reference librarian.

The officers, virile young men that they were, seemed mesmerised. I was so upset that the women looked glamorous, I could hardly speak. It wasn't that I was jealous of their being there or of their depriving me of the men's attention that unconsciously I had accepted as my due. It was simply that they looked so beautiful! It just wasn't fair. They had flown in from an airconditioned hotel, not a hair out of place, well-manicured hands that hadn't cranked open the lid of a tea chest of supplies that morning. They wore stylish clothes that didn't smell of being laundered in an oil drum in a hut built from flattened beer cans. And later they would fly back to their comfortable, well-fed existence. As we were introduced, I was swamped by my insecurities and imagined their eyes sweeping my sweaty body with contempt. They had to be thinking, how could she let herself go?

I have no idea who the women were, but they were enterprising to have visited ALSG in wartime. Most likely they were friends or relatives of a high-ranking officer. I didn't stop to find out. I turned and ploughed down the hill through the sand that stuck like glue to my legs, back to the patients in the tented ward below, stopping only to buy myself a Coke to keep the heat at bay. The Coke jingle went through my brain: 'Things go better with Coca-Cola. Things go better with Coke.' By the time I arrived at the wards, I was swaying, my step in time to the jingle. There were more important things to think about than being envious of visiting glamour girls. Some months later at ALSG I saw another female tourist, a civilian from Melbourne – anyone could come into Vietnam at any time throughout the war if they had a visa. To my astonishment, I had seen travel posters in Saigon encouraging tourists to explore Vietnam's charms!

November arrived, and I had been in country nearly five months. On the first of the month Vietnamese National Day was celebrated in Vung Tau with parades, an aerial display and many speeches by local dignitaries. In gratitude for our aid in helping to overcome Communist aggression, town leaders presented each patient in both hospitals with a Vietnamese doll. In the market, those dolls cost the Vietnamese only a few cents each; for us, it was a dollar. The men also received a stem of red gladioli – red being the colour of happiness and good luck, presumably for their future.

Three days later, the Back Beach boys held their own ceremonial parade. The new Commander of ALSG had arrived, together with a gaggle of visiting politicians. The parade welcomed Lt Col L. C. Chambers and bid farewell to Lt Col Rouse. One thousand soldiers from ALSG marched in unit formation along the hard sand of Back Beach at low tide, waves gently lapping alongside and behind them. The medics who made up the Fifth Battalion's band played that wonderful military music that stirs the resolve of soldiers and thrills the hearts of those watching. Back Beach had never seen anything like it. The crisply starched uniforms, boots that gleamed like patent leather in the blazing afternoon sun, chests puffed out in that special military way, and faultless marching were an astonishing achievement under the circumstances. Not only

The riveting photograph of Sapper Barry Harford that was pinned above my bed in Vung Tau for a year. Barry represented every Aussie soldier to me.

I wasn't happy to be confined to barracks when dust at the 93rd Evac Hospital badly scratched my eye.

The first hospital wards at Back Beach. Patients' beds were higher than the sandbags intended to protect them against incoming mortar fire. Towels dried on tent ropes.

Hilda Zinner offers army bandsman/ stretcher-bearer Private Graeme Davis, shot in the arm during the Long Tan battle, some reading matter at the 36th Evacuation Hospital.

A grand staircase led to the 2 Field Ambulance Officers' Mess and living quarters in tents atop a man-made plateau. Elsewhere we had to plod up the sandhills without the benefit of 'stairs', sinking deep into the soft grains with each step.

Here ALSG sandhills have been flattened and a road of hard-standing built, but there were still floods, scorpions and deadly snakes to contend with. The South China Sea is in the background.

Harry Janssen was transferred to work with Win Skelly, also from Melbourne Red Cross headquarters, resettling refugees for the League of Red Cross Societies.

Dedicated American nurses, like Lieutenant 'Polly' Parrott, loved caring for the Aussies, but complained our boys never dated them!

The Sioux helicopter with its distinctive bubble cockpit, known as a 'Flying Sperm', was ideal for visual reconnaissance missions as it skimmed the tree tops, offering breathtaking views. It also made us an easy target for the enemy. Army aviator Lieutenant Blair Weaver prepares to take me home from Nui Dat.

This sign outside the RAAF airmen's villa in Vung Tau ensured the men never forgot to take their malaria pills.

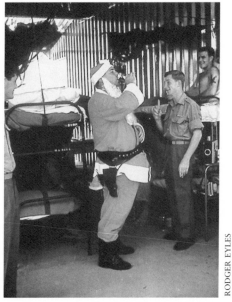

Gutsy and endearing Stumpy, a Viet Cong POW amputee, reminded us that the enemy were people just like us.

Christmas is where you find it. A gun-toting Jewish Santa, Colin 'Doc' Neale, with Peter 'Blue' Hind, quaffs a beer. Beds were double-bunked and jammed into aisles during the Australian hospital's busiest month ever, December 1966.

Barefoot in the sand of Back Beach, Win offers battle casualties a welcome break from hospital life.

Janice, me, Eleanor 'Koopsie' Koops of American Red Cross and Win outside the quonset hut office we shared with American Red Cross at the 36th Evac. The Aussie Red Cross women wore sandals to make walking easier in the soft sand of the Back Beach camp. The shopping trolley acquired from the American PX was used for carrying books to the patients.

Private Russell Copeman, the only SAS soldier to die of wounds sustained in Vietnam, at Nui Dat ready to go out on patrol.

Private John 'Juvy' Matten at right, who carried Russell Copeman to safety, shown some months later with Sergeant Chris Jennison at Nui Dat prior to being lifted by helicopter into the jungle for an SAS patrol.

AUSTRALIAN WAR MEMORIAL
NEGATIVE NUMBER COL 67 0140 VN

An Nhut, 14 February, 1967, after a cleverly concealed mine killed three officers (including the company commander) and three men. Loading one of the wounded onto a RAAF 9 Squadron Iroquois are (L-R, in shirts): Sergeant Ralph 'Rowdy' Hindmarsh, Lieutenant Roger Wainwright and Captain Tony White, the Fifth Battalion doctor. The wounded man arrived in hospital about twenty minutes later.

A Vietnamese boy, accidentally wounded in the fighting, imitates the way I am sitting on the sand, as we watch Maori gunners entertain 2 Field Ambulance patients.

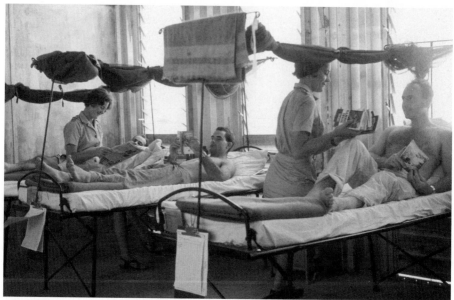

DENIS GIBBONS

With Janice (L) on hospital rounds at 2 Field Ambulance to check on patients' needs.

Watching the ANZAC Day football final at Vung Tau high school with (L-R): Kiwi Gunner Boris August, Private Charlie 'Jock' Creswell and Australian War Memorial war artist, Lieutenant Bruce Fletcher.

With Major Harry Smith MC and Win at 6 RAR Delta Company's party on its last night in Vietnam.

I met my nephew Guy, born while I was away, when the Debelle family greeted me at Adelaide airport on my return from Vietnam. L-R: My brothers Geoff and Rob, Mum, brother Bruce and his wife, Barbara.

On a return visit to Back Beach in 1995, I scrawled 'Remember the Aussies' in the sand.

With my husband Jack, my 'Man from Snowy River', on a winter day at our home in southern Pennsylvania.

DONNA WELLS

were our Diggers great soldiers – they had not forgotten how to drill. Hilda and I beamed with pride as we watched.

The 36th also had a new Commanding Officer, Lt Col James J. DuBois. One of his first orders was that no patient was allowed off the air base. That meant no more Aussie sightseeing and shopping trips, no drives to church or to any entertainment at Back Beach. His decree had to be straightened out pronto or I would have some very unhappy Diggers on my hands. It meant, though, that I could start off on the wrong foot with the new CO, but I never had been one to bother about winning popularity contests.

Colonel DuBois, the man after whom the Villa later was named, was a leader of the highest calibre. When I passionately pleaded with him to allow me to continue the excursions with the Australians, he did an immediate about-face. '*All* patients,' he responded, 'American as well as Australian, will be allowed out on sightseeing and shopping tours. Thanks for setting me straight, Jean.' For the Americans, he instituted daily tours to central Vung Tau, which many of the wounded saw for the first time. A few days later he followed up by inviting me to receive a parcel of books given by an American organisation and to have my photograph taken for American newspapers.

To repay his kindness, the 2 Field Ambulance band played at the 36th. The band, the Fi-Sonics, was known far and wide, having appeared on the top-rated television show *In Melbourne Tonight* before shipping out for Vietnam. The army had not allowed the band to take musical instruments to war, but enterprising Harry immediately obtained instruments for them through his PX connections in Saigon. The Fi-Sonics also performed at the American officers' clubs in Vung Tau, and other gigs included playing for General

Westmoreland and Prime Minister Nguyen Cao Ky at Free World Headquarters in Saigon. When the band let rip at the 36th and the noise drew a larger and larger crowd, once again I felt immensely proud. The Fifth Battalion's band of infantry medics also played for appreciative audiences at the hospital.

That week Brigadier Jackson gave the word that I had been waiting for. Women were at last allowed at Nui Dat on a day visit. Of course no overnights were permitted. Hilda had made her first visit in August just before the Long Tan battle, and then the sharp end was put off limits to us for another two months. Ironically, just as the soldiers couldn't wait to get away from Nui Dat, I couldn't wait to see where the dusty, mud-covered boys I so loved existed.

Lt Col John Warr, unassuming and gentlemanly, was the experienced CO of the Fifth – known as the Tiger Battalion – at Nui Dat. Passionate about the welfare of his troops, he took it as a deeply personal blow when they were wounded or killed. Not uncommonly he would be there waiting, with that great wide smile of his, to meet a filthy and exhausted platoon coming back through the wire after a week on patrol, eager to share a chat and a cuppa with them around the Salvation Army vehicle. His obvious concern for his soldiers, both officers and men, was reciprocated in spades – he was a man they would proudly serve.

Colonel Warr understood that seeing where the soldiers subsisted would broaden my knowledge of the war, and so the arrangements were made. It was a marvellous day. The sun was shining after weeks of torrential rain, and the sky was a dazzling blue as I flew from Vung Tau to Nui Dat in a RAAF Huey. While I silently and rapturously enjoyed the scenery flashing by the open doors, the door gunners' eyes continually swept the ground as we skimmed over the jungle at tree-top level. Choppers had no doors, both for easy boarding and disembarkation, and to give maximum freedom for the door gunners to fire. It was hard for me to believe that the beautiful scenery below hid the guns and mortars of the VC.

At Nui Dat I firmly held onto my hat as I jumped from the chopper and ran, half bent, to avoid the down draught of the overhead blades. I was dressed in my American fatigues and the unaccustomed heavy boots. For fear of standing out as a woman lest a VC should take me for an easy target, I had tucked my hair hard up under my bush hat and tried to look tough, like I had a bayonet hidden on my person. The men weren't fooled. Bob 'Dogs' Kearney could hardly believe his eyes: from his Charlie Company perch – hammering a roof on one of the first buildings at Nui Dat – he was seeing a round-eyed woman for the first time in months. I waved to shirtless men going about their tasks of cleaning, building and repairing. I grinned with only slight embarrassment at men wearing naught but a small olive-green towel heading to or from a shower. The word went around: 'Sheila in the camp, watch the language!'

I explored the sandbagged camp, established in orderly lines among the rubber trees. Sandbags surrounded each tent up to a height of about two metres to protect the men from incoming mortar fire. In the event of attack, each tent was like a little fort. Furniture inside the tents consisted of sandbags stacked to form chairs and tables. Mirrors were nailed to rubber trees; below them, at a suitable height, planks of wood nailed to the tree trunks held washbowls and shaving utensils. In the Messes, I saw relics of battles each unit had fought: VC guns, red NVA flags with the big central

five-pointed gold star, and carvings from Buddhist temples the
VC had commandeered to use as strongholds. To avoid sacri-
lege when the necessities of war demanded the soldiers
destroy a Buddhist temple, they first removed as many of the
religious items as they could. It was sad that temples were
demolished, but there was no good alternative.

Guarding the entrance to one Mess stood a rocket, painted
black, its message jokingly laconic: 'In times of panic, push
button marked P'. Then I came face to face with home. In the
middle of the camp in the rubber trees, a large and familiar
yellow realty sign – undoubtedly an original somehow spirited
to Vietnam – ironically proclaimed: For Sale, L. J. Hooker.

Coincidentally (or was it Colonel Warr's clever planning?),
it was the day of the Melbourne Cup – Australia's premier
horse race, the 'race that stops the nation' – and it did not
pass unnoticed. All over the camp, even at battalion HQ,
soldiers crowded around radios to urge their horses on.
Certain priorities must be maintained, even at the battlefront!

I saw some familiar faces. Captain Bob O'Neill, intelligence
officer and assiduous scholar, was sitting outside his tent
reading. Dressed only in a pair of shorts, bare legs up on a
table, he looked as casual as if he was sunbathing at home.
Bob is one of life's true gentlemen, with a probing intellect and
generous smile. Just the man to quiz: 'Why did the army build
a strategic base in the middle of a rubber plantation?' He
explained: 'We acquired use of the area from the South Vietnamese government, partly for its position in the centre of the
province, partly for its excellent communications potential,
partly because it was well away from many people in villages,
and finally because it offered a good site for an airstrip.'

Dr Tony White, the Fifth Battalion's compassionate doctor,

whose vigorous mind could not conceal his devotion to the 800 infantry men for whom he held medical responsibility, was about to move his Regimental Aid Post or RAP (where minor ailments were treated) from a tent into a concrete-floored permanent hut. With pride he showed me around. Afterwards, leaning on a Land Rover with a red cross painted on the side, I shared a Coke with Tony's driver, Brian 'Dada' Aitken, who had helped me shift boxes on one of his and Tony's frequent visits to the 36th Evac. His slow bushman's way of talking endeared Brian to me – he is a wonderful bloke. The Roman Catholic priest, John Williams – with cauliflower ears and a broken nose from old boxing bouts – was the ideal battalion padre: he drank, smoked and swore like one of the boys. John Bentley, the Salvation Army man whose Red Shield van welcomed exhausted and dirty soldiers back from operations with hot tea and biscuits, was standing outside his tent next to a sign proclaiming 'You're Welcome'.

Before lunch in the Fifth Battalion Officers' Mess, I used the visitors' toilet, more out of curiosity than necessity. Roughly constructed, but in keeping with its importance, it sported a plastic lid embellished with a snarling tiger. As though anyone needed reminding that this was the Tiger Battalion!

That afternoon Colonel Warr and Bob O'Neill were going to call on the commander of the local Vietnamese Regional Force company at Binh Ba – an area that was to become known for much enemy activity and more Australian casualties. For his headquarters, the commander at Binh Ba had acquired a large colonial house originally built for the French manager of one of the many rubber plantations that no longer were in production because of the war. How it happened that I went with them, I can't remember. Maybe Colonel Warr, sensing my interest and believing that seeing a little of the operational area would give me a valuable perspective on my work, invited me. Maybe I did the asking. Although not an unusual occurrence, in retrospect perhaps it was slightly irregular, as I was not a member of the army – only attached to it – but in wartime where does one draw that nebulous line?

With the familiar lurch back, then surge forward that I loved, the RAAF Huey lifted from the chopper pad. Our pilot was Flight Lieutenant Frank Riley, a legend in military lore long before he and Bob Grandin, along with Cliff Dohle, Bruce Lane and their chopper crews, heroically dropped the ammo into the darkness of the Long Tan battle. I knew Frank well, as he took Koopsie and Viv out to dinner frequently. 'Our friends from the "RARF",' Koopsie would drawl. Flt Lt Kevin Sharpley was on Frank's right, and two younger crewmen manned each open door with machine guns, ever alert for the enemy. They explained that it was safer to fly low and fast, as that made it more difficult for the VC to get a target in their sights. Colonel Warr sat next to the door. I sat on the bench next to him, then Bob O'Neill, and on Bob's right, Sgt Bic, the South Vietnamese interpreter. As a woman with no weapon, I always was placed between two men for my protection.

We flew into an area of lovely villas, cream coloured with wooden shutters and red tile roofs, surrounded by well-kept lawns. French people still lived there. The scene was one of utmost tranquillity – like stepping back into the Vietnam of thirty years earlier. Frank Riley prepared to land the Huey in the usual place, but when the chopper was about a metre from the ground, there was an enormous explosion, then another and another. We're surrounded! I remember thinking. Terrified, I shoved myself behind the broad back of Bob

O'Neill as Colonel Warr yelled to Frank: 'Get up! Get up! It's a mine field.' Frank already had lifted the chopper away from danger and was looking urgently for a safe landing place close by. He needed to see if the Huey, or any of us, was damaged. We had, indeed, almost put down in a mine field, the down draught of the helicopter blades having set off the mines. The Vietnamese company commander had ordered the laying of mines around the villa, including the area where the Aussies usually landed choppers. He had neglected to report that little detail to Colonel Warr and other Task Force officers.

Safely on the ground, the pilots made a full inspection of the passengers and chopper. The wounded included Colonel Warr, who was hit in the neck by a fragment, causing minor bleeding – and his only combat wound in Vietnam. A door gunner also was hit. Bob O'Neill, troubled for years by a pesky knee, discovered only recently when the knee was X-rayed that a shell fragment had pierced it from the rear. Despite being in the midst of flying shrapnel on many occasions, he attributes the knee injury to that day in Binh Ba.

There were eighteen holes in the chopper. No vital damage had been done, although the underside of the chopper was pitted with mine fragments, one of which had missed the fuel line by less than ten centimetres. But the chopper was flyable, we were all okay, and no report was required. Just as well. Had it been necessary for Colonel Warr to file a formal report, my presence would have been revealed, and there could have been all hell to pay. And if I'd been injured, there could have been more complications for Colonel Warr. Bob O'Neill remembers the colonel saying to him, 'I can see the headlines in the Sydney papers: Red Cross Nurse and Colonel in Helicopter Incident'. The story never came to light.

Methodically, Colonel Warr and Bob O'Neill set about their information-gathering visit with the Vietnamese commander as I waited with the helicopter crew, marvelling at everyone's calm. Then shame overtook me. In my dreams of heroic fantasy, I'd been fearless in the face of danger, gallantly rescuing others from countless disasters. Yet at the first explosion I had shoved myself behind Bob's protective frame, nearly knocking him off his seat, certainly pushing him off balance. I was embarrassed at my cowardice.

At 2 Field Ambulance, we were relieved when the three-table operating theatre was moved from a tent to a Kingstrand hut, for the patient load was growing daily. By year-end all of the medical departments had been housed in permanent buildings, but only the operating theatre and post-op ward were airconditioned. We had been neglecting the forward area RAPs (we thought our time was better spent with more seriously wounded patients), but once the aid posts were installed in concrete-floored Kingstrands, we stocked them with games and books.

I was beginning to make frequent trips to the sharp end, sometimes flying in the right-hand seat beside the pilot of the two-man Perspex bubble Sioux helicopter, known to the Diggers as 'flying sperm'. The upshot of being a woman was that I often was invited to ride in a Sioux, a privilege I longed for. I'd be belted in, then tapped on the leg and wordlessly handed headphones so that I could hear radio talk; more important, the headphones served as a shield from the roar of the engines. Those choppers, with the bubble extending underneath our feet, offered breathtaking panoramic views of the jungle rushing beneath us. And made us an easier VC target!

Other times I drove the 35 kilometres to Nui Dat with soldiers in a Land Rover. One day I decided to do away with the bother of waiting for a helicopter or other transport and drive myself. Medic Rodger Eyles needed transport to the Dat, so he rode with me in the Red Cross Land Rover as the usual 'shotgun' escort. It may have been wrong for a Red Cross vehicle – not a designated military target, although we carried Australian Military Forces number plates – to be seen with an armed escort, because it contravened the Geneva Conventions of War. But the Vietnamese were not signatories to the Conventions. They had shown their disdain for them by bombarding the 36th Evac hospital. And in those crazy days, to be accompanied by a man with a weapon was as common as being accompanied by a man with a Zippo lighter and a cigarette.

We drove through the 'pearly gates', the tall stone columns that were all that remained of what had probably been a colonial outpost in the village on the edge of Vung Tau, and headed towards Ba Ria. Along the road, fish were strung up to dry like washing on a backyard line, and rice paper lay drying beside the road. We passed paddy fields where Vietnamese women and children worked the fields barefoot, their conical hats shading them from the sun and their loose black trousers rolled up, sometimes to their knees. I drove slowly, leaving ample time to dodge potholes, pigs, chickens, children, cyclists, and rambling pedestrians along the road. Through the sleepy town of Ba Ria we went, and soon we were hurrying through the shabby ribbon village of Hoa Long, known to be sympathetic to Victor Charlie. Shortly afterward we were inside the Task Force base perimeter. The trip had been uneventful.

Rodger and I turned for home again immediately after lunch, aimlessly chatting about the duties that awaited us at 2 Field Ambulance. Near Ba Ria, the road was straight, narrow, rutted, and lined with deep ditches on either side. Paddy fields were on the left and scrub, about 25 metres back from the road, on the right. Suddenly, about 40 metres ahead, two smoke grenades exploded on the side of the road and a hundred or so Vietnamese came out of the scrub, firing in our direction. I hit the brakes.

We were surrounded. This is it! I thought. This can't be happening! Then, adrenaline pumping, heart pounding, I realised just as quickly that it *was* happening. 'What do we do?' I asked Rodger. I could see my terror reflected in his eyes. There was no time to turn around on the narrow road, even if we had been able to do so. Rodger made a quick decision. 'Go like buggery,' he said tersely. Then, 'Get down low.' He had already released the safety catch of the F1 sub-machine gun that was our only protection. Although a good marksman, he knew he had only one 30-round magazine – not enough to shoot a hundred Vietnamese. I put the Land Rover in gear and drove like a woman possessed, wheels slamming through the potholes and ruts in the road. There was no way I could get down low or think of anything except driving. The combination of adrenaline and fear made me sweat so that my hands slipped on the steering wheel. We sped blindly through the acrid smoke and fire, noises of battle drowning out other sounds, and then, amazingly, the road in front of us was clear.

I kept the accelerator flat to the floor and continued to

barrel down the road towards Vung Tau, sending stray hens and dogs flying into the deep ditches. 'Shits were trumps then, girl,' was all Rodger said. He was quiet for the rest of the trip. I, my knees quaking, kept my eyes on the road. Once safely inside Vung Tau I pulled over and stopped. My heart was beating so hard I was gasping for air. I needed time to get myself together. Then I set off again, driving far too quickly through the town. As I screeched to a stop at ALSG, our wheels skidded on the newly laid hardstanding metal plates that kept vehicles from sinking into the sand. Rodger walked off, leaving me wondering just how stupid I had been to have driven to the sharp end. Clearly, people like me, who did not know what it was like to be shot at, had little or no under-standing that the enemy was everywhere.

What we had stumbled into, though, was a South Viet-namese army training exercise, and they were shooting blanks. Several hours later Rodger approached me soberly. 'If that patrol had been Viet Cong, Jean, we would not have survived.' I started to say something, but he had already walked off. Inevitably, the incident made its way up the chain of command. It caused some agitation, and I was forbidden to drive myself to Nui Dat again.

11

A Gun-Toting Jewish Santa

OUR FILM NIGHTS WERE GETTING BETTER. *They're a Weird Mob*, a movie taken from the Australian best-selling John O'Grady novel about an Italian immigrant bricklayer trying to become a dinkum Aussie, was to be screened at ALSG. Everyone was excited to see it, and so was I. But it was hair wash night. Sometimes it took hours to wash and curl my short hair without a modern hair dryer because the electricity went off and on without warning. It all depended on how much dope Papa-san, the Vietnamese employed to keep the Villa generator working, had been smoking.

Wet hair in large rollers, I settled in at home; I was too vain to be seen that way. But my mind kept returning to the movie. What if I just crept in the back where no one would see me? I took off to the camp like a rocket, hair rollers covered inadequately with a scarf. It seemed the whole camp, and more, was there for the film. I hid in the dark behind everyone else. Within seconds, my hair rollers and I were ushered ceremoniously to the VIP seats in the front row, in full view of everyone. Next day, embarrassed, I apologised to one of the officers for appearing in rollers the previous night. 'We *were* all talking about you today, Jean,' he said. 'You made us all homesick. You reminded us of our wives.'

The men weren't the only ones to miss female company. My one longing after nearly six months in Vietnam, was to talk to a woman from home. Yet when nurses from the University of New South Wales Surgical Team arrived – sent to care for Vung Tau civilians – I didn't see much of them. We were all too busy doing our separate work. The surgical team, from the Prince of Wales Hospital in Sydney, initially consisted of three doctors, five nurses, one radiographer and a pathology technician. They worked at Le Loi, the local hospital for the Vietnamese, which was divided in two – one half manned by the Vietnamese and the other by the Australians. As civilians, the surgical team lived at the Grand Hotel close to the beach, but unlike us at the Villa DuBois, they had no military to protect them.

The team was shocked by the lack of cleanliness at Le Loi. 'First,' said Jenny James (now Emeritus Professor at the University of Nursing in Canberra), 'we repaired the water supply and the sewerage, scrubbed and painted the wards, and attempted to get rid of the prolific 60-centimetre-long rats. There were no instruments, mattresses, nothing. We had two patients to a bed and, of course, the ever-present relatives – who cooked for the patients outside the wards – also shared the same bed. We had to be careful,' she laughed, 'to pick the right person when we operated! Also, in the beginning, dogs were tied to the ends of patients' beds, not to protect the patient or the family pet, but to fatten the dogs for eating. By far, the majority of our patients suffered from gross abscesses, tuberculosis (we assumed everybody had TB and treated them as such) and malaria. Our most popular surgical procedure was repair of harelips. And we were never sure whether the patients or the officials we dealt with were VC.'

The worth of that dedicated team was reinforced nearly forty years later. Michael Hall, a 36th Evac medic, fell in love with one of the maids, Minh, who cleaned the 36th Evac men's barracks. In 1967 a fever caused Minh to go into a coma. Michael rushed her to Le Loi, where a middle-aged surgeon – a big man with big hands and sandy hair – saved her life. For three days and nights the doctor never left Minh's bedside, sleeping in a chair by her bed until the fever broke and she regained consciousness. Michael, now Minh's husband and father of their three grown American children, recently implored me to discover the doctor's identity. Jenny James swiftly identified the doctor as Noel (Spike) Lucas, who worked for many years as a general practitioner in Bathurst, New South Wales, where he is now retired. Spike Lucas, touched to hear from Mike and Minh in 2003, wrote back:

Thank you for the exciting news that Minh survived her illness and the war. It is unusual and very rewarding to receive news of the outcome arising from medical and surgical emergencies in which one has been involved in other countries, and you would appreciate that, Mike, from your time as a medic at the 36th Evac. It makes the tough times of medical practice worthwhile.

The surgical team settled in, and when they were not working, I'd see them at parties or dinners. Before long Julie Kearns, the young pathology technician, was frequently seen in the company of Dr Ron Spielman, an American ophthalmic surgeon from the 36th Evac, who often did cataract operations at Le Loi. On one of my trips to Saigon, I joined the other Caribou passengers, including Julie and Ron, in the back of a deuce-and-a-half to ride from Tan Son Nhut into the city. As we crossed the bridge surrounded by shanty homes built on stilts in the swamp outside the airport, I casually asked what their plans were for the day. Julie, slim and olive-skinned in a sleeveless yellow shift, replied calmly: 'We're getting married.' She made it sound as though that was the most commonplace thing in the world. 'Wow,' was all I could manage. I had grown immune to surprises. The truck rumbled into the middle of Saigon, and as they jumped down to set off on their mission, I wished them well. (Julie and Ron lived in the States for many years and raised a family there.)

Soon after that excursion, Hilda and I were invited to lunch on the cargo carrier LSM *Clive Steele*, an outing that had me salivating in anticipation of dining again on Sydney food, served on white linen cloths. In the wardroom, my eyes swept hungrily over the display of fresh fruit and all sorts of produce that I had tasted in Vietnam only as often as the Queen does her own laundry. The 2nd Engineer, Phil Cannane, pulled me aside and told me of his secret cargo on the trip up – a load of medical supplies for the civilian team. 'My wife works at the Prince of Wales Hospital as a dietician cook. She prepares and serves meals to the Matron (head nurse) in her flat. Now Matron Vera Adderley is ex-army, and she's a very take-charge sort of person. When she heard that

I was making trips to Vietnam, she asked my wife if I could deliver some medical supplies to the civilian team. She was facing a long wait to get them on the *Jeparit*, as war supplies had priority. I had to ask my CO, old "Haggis" Jim Wilson, and he said: "Mr Cannane, I don't want to hear about it. You do what you believe is right." So Matron rang all her friends and colleagues in hospitals around Australia and collected a load of medical supplies.

'When we were loading our army supplies in Sydney, this truck appeared. A specific load of cartons was taken on board, and I had them stowed in the forward anchor space and in other machinery spaces that were under my domain. The 2nd Mate, Jim Fletcher, was in cahoots with me. During the trip whenever anyone asked about those cartons the answer was always "See the 2nd Engineer". The men knew better than to ask me, so the supplies arrived here without any hassle. The civilian team was sure glad to see them.' After that, supplies for the team flowed officially through proper channels.

Luscombe Airfield, which was named after Captain Bryan Luscombe, an army aviator who was killed in action in Korea, officially opened at Nui Dat in early December. At last the Caribous of Wallaby Airlines could land there. 'Until Luscombe was built,' Dave Sabben said, 'the PBI (poor bloody infantry) had to go down the main drag to Vungers aboard an Armoured Personnel Carrier or in a supply truck. You VIPs warranted a chopper, but we PBI shared the dust and fleas that are the trademarks of the underprivileged.' Oops. Not everyone was as spoiled as I. Being a woman in

Vietnam gave me a tremendous advantage over the Diggers or GIs and, indeed, at times, over senior officers.

Although the advantages far outweighed the disadvantages, the stage I walked was floodlit. Rumours about my 'sex life' continued to bounce around like tennis balls. I learned from the grapevine that I was being treated for VD and that I was having an affair with Colonel Rodgers, the CO of 2 Field Ambulance! I am not sure if the two pieces of gossip were connected. I *am* sure news of our 'affair' would have astonished Colonel Rodgers. We had never so much as dated.

One morning my mentor, Capt Kevin Hawthorne, approached with a look on his face that I knew meant trouble. 'Little One, you have to be more careful about what you say,' he gently suggested. 'The Post Office guys said you told them "you all want to get me flat on my back, like everyone else around here".' Deeply hurt, my cheeks hot with anger, I took a long, slow breath. I *never* would have said anything remotely like that. Sure, I could be tactless and undiplomatic, but to talk like that? Never. There was a time I would have stormed down to the Post Office and vented my fury, kicking the men all the way to Hanoi. Instead I just groaned and walked off, feeling devastated, to fling myself furiously back into work.

Although wounded by the gossip, I learned to quickly put it behind me. The soldiers' wounds were not so easy to dismiss. The irrepressible Lyall Black, a replacement in the Sixth Battalion's Delta Company, received serious gunshot wounds in his left thigh and buttocks. Doctors put a number of pins through his leg, and Lyall kept us laughing with stories of how he flashed the very visible pins at the Vietnamese cleaning staff, who freaked out and decided to keep far away

from him. He also had a running dialogue with the keeper of
the morgue. 'He's a big black American, Williams I think his
name is. Each day he says to me: "I've got this cold slab
waiting for you, Aussie," and I say, "You're not going to get
me." ' We all laughed. Lyall Black of the indomitable spirit
didn't walk again for fifteen months.

On 2 December, Six Battalion Delta Company's 11 Platoon, hit
harder than any other at Long Tan, was battered once again. I
began to wonder if the platoon was unlucky, and I wasn't the
only one. When a command-detonated landmine killed Cpl
Colin Lithgow and wounded about ten others, even savvy, no-
nonsense soldiers like Platoon Sgt Bob Buick wondered briefly
if indeed 11 Platoon *was* jinxed. Strangely, as Bob observed,
most of those who were injured in the mine blast had been
brought into 11 Platoon to replace those killed or severely
wounded at Long Tan. The casualties all looked like the re-run
of a bad movie – a movie none of us wished to see again.

Pte Peter Ainslie had been in a rifle section at Long Tan,
but when radio operator Vic Grice was killed, he was plucked
out of there to take Vic's place. Only scratched in that battle,
this time he lost his right leg below the knee. When Peter
arrived at the 36th Evac, his leg was hanging by a thread. He
was in post-op for a month, just a couple of beds along from
Lyall Black. Like so many of the Australian wounded, Peter
heaped praise on the caring and skilled medical attention
given to him by the Americans. Today he calls himself an
honorary American: 'There were all these wonderful Yank
enlisted men giving their blood to save the life of a damn
Aussie they didn't know and would probably never see again.'

Peter had joined the Regular Army from the Citizen Military Forces (CMF) for the Big Adventure. He was actually worried that it might all be over before it was his turn to go to Vietnam. He would have been heartbroken if he had been sent to any unit besides the infantry. 'I was pretty young at the time, remember.' He had loved to play Aussie Rules football with one of the Melbourne suburban teams, generally on the wing as he was light and quick. There wasn't much future for a one-legged footballer. He spent the rest of his life in the army, retiring as a Major in Ordnance, and then enjoyed overseas postings with his diplomat wife Meikie Flach.

Warren Pearson lay in a bed near Peter with numerous shrapnel wounds sustained on 8 December from an ARVN booby trap. The extraordinary skill of the American Dust-Off pilot who took him to hospital stayed in the minds of all the Diggers there. Lt Ian Savage wrote in his diary: 'The pilot had to land on a raised and narrow road with low-hanging power lines along one side. To do this he had to tilt the helicopter and slide it beneath the power lines. There was no room for error and the pilot didn't hesitate. Amazing stuff.'

To kick off the Christmas season, the battle casualties were joined by a multitude of sick patients – again mostly from the Sixth Battalion. During Operation Ingham, the men had camped in the Binh Ba area, and a record number of soldiers came down with a form of malaria resistant to the pills they were counting on to protect them. At 2 Field Ambulance, the already hard-pressed medics were double-bunking beds. More beds were placed in the aisles and in the breezeways between the wards. It was the hospital's busiest month yet, and it was for me as well. Harry was no longer around to help, and Hilda was away on R&R. There were so many new patients that I ran out of our Red Cross supplies, and I had to supplement many items from the American PX.

Affable Joe Cauchi-Gera, nicknamed the Maltese Falcon, was a corporal in charge of transport at 2 Field Ambulance and ensured that vehicles were available twenty-four hours a day. He had distinguished himself by exchanging a slouch hat for an American truck, an occurrence that apparently was not unusual. Our Red Cross tent was near the transport tent, and I was forever chasing Joe out for 'borrowing' our newspapers. Joe, in hospital with kidney trouble, was among those returned home before Christmas, which relieved my need to put an armed guard on our dwindling supplies!

Like Joe, all patients in the 36th Evac and 2 Field Ambulance who were not returning to their units were to be sent home for Christmas if possible. That meant I had extra telegrams to send and extra shopping to do. Everyone wanted to take gifts home. The heat and the stress were getting to me, and I began to feel like a mouse running in a wheel. I remember with shame that one afternoon, hot and tired, I grumbled, only half-jokingly, to a ward of patients that all they had to do was lie there on a bed all day while I ran around!

The festive season caused many patients to feel homesick and depressed, and to need as much cheering as I could muster. Before he went to work in Saigon, Harry, a man of endless energy and ideas, had made preliminary arrangements for the ABC's *Hospital Half Hour* to be broadcast from 2 Field Ambulance. A week before the broadcast I asked the patients to list their musical requests to be played and acknowledged on the radio show. Roger Miller's 'Dang Me', with its last line 'woman would you weep for me', was the universal favourite. I sent a priority signal to Northern Command for them to relay the list to the ABC radio station in Brisbane. The rushed timing meant that most patients were still in hospital to hear their requests broadcast. With the poor reception on our ward radios, the show was more crackle than pop, but it was fun to listen. We hoped the patients' loved ones had received their letters telling them to listen also.

The 2 Field staff and I did all we could to make Christmas Day special. For weeks I had tried to enlist the help of the ambulatory patients – most of them suffering the debilitating effects of malaria – to make and hang decorations from crepe paper, cellophane, glitter and cardboard that I had bought in the local market or at the American PX. Day after day I would ask, implore, beg and finally nag the patients to decorate the wards, but each morning the decorations were still in their boxes. The patients' spirits were willing, but their suffering bodies left them too lethargic to help.

Eventually the overworked wardsmen, plus those patients who were able, made two splendid Christmas trees, one from wire and frilly green crepe paper and another from gold paper. They made scrolls to hang from the walls and ceilings. They did a great job, and the wards looked amazingly cheerful. Although I had no time to decorate the wards at the 36th, as always our American Red Cross friends helped me out there, even assisting me at 2 Field while Hilda was away.

Many parcels arrived addressed simply 'To a Digger' – some faceless person doing his darnedest to win peace in Vietnam. The parcels piled up with a very real person – me. Two patients removed the postal wrappings, and we made sure all the parcels looked festive before putting them under our two trees – not to be opened until 25 December. At the

Villa at night, Karen and I taped carols to be played in the wards; in Vietnam we had to work twice as hard as we did at home to make Christmas special. Through it all the Back Beach hospital continued to be overwhelmed with patients. Everyone on staff was worked to the point of exhaustion.

Before I could do everything I'd planned, I lost my timing. I went down with one of those indeterminate fevers that were so common in Vietnam – and not just with a fever, I suspect, but in urgent need of a rest. Hilda returned from R&R to find me admitted for three days to the 36th Evac, separated from the other patients, all male, by a screen. I had galloped between the two hospitals during the Australian medical team's busiest month ever in Vietnam, and I could gallop no more. Hilda took over my planned visits to the Task Force to distribute stockings at the Regimental Aid Posts.

I was discharged from hospital with renewed pep on Christmas Eve in time to don my most glamorous cocktail dress and help American Red Cross serve coffee and biscuits to all patients at the 36th. The Australians there were as amused as I was to see the Americans having trouble with the prospect of a hot Christmas. For those of us born south of the equator, temperatures busting the century and fake holly and Christmas trees were the norm. The Americans, though, yearned for snow, for real prickly-leafed holly and mistletoe, and for the tangy smell of a fir tree in the cold crisp air that meant the season to them. Santa distributed the American Red Cross gifts to both Aussie and American patients and then hosted a party in the wards. Harry had come from Saigon, and after the party we went together to Midnight Mass at ALSG where he played the organ. As we sang 'Silent Night' in the crowded chapel, the words 'all is calm' and 'sleep in heavenly peace', held special meaning. How we prayed that those words could be true for everyone in Vietnam.

On Christmas Day I leapt from my bed to visit all Australians at the 36th again before spending the rest of the day at 2 Field Ambulance. On that day, of all days, when the soldiers needed to be reminded that there was another world – a world where women wore pretty dresses and people walked the streets fearlessly – I wore a white linen dress with a coloured sash. The surgical team, with the women also dressed in their prettiest outfits, was at 2 Field as well. In the monotony of an almost totally male environment, it was a true present for the patients to see other women besides 'Everyday Jean'.

Corporal Colin Neale, never known by anything else but 'Doc', was a wonderful medic with a rotund frame and a comedian's personality. Never once allowing that he was unbearably hot, he dressed in the Santa suit Koopsie lent to us and joked his way around the wards, distributing the stockings sent by Red Cross as well as any presents that were under the tree. Pushing a shopping trolley borrowed from the American PX for the day, I followed in his wake with my 'sleigh' of gifts. Ironically Doc was Jewish. 'You don't see too many gun-toting Jewish Santas', was his shtick, and the patients loved him. No one could have done the job better.

I was proud of the beautifully wrapped gifts from Red Cross, as well as the consignment of toys they had sent to Nam Binh, the fishing village ALSG supported. We understood what the soldiers needed far better now than we had when we first arrived. The books selected were well suited to the men, but it was the giant packs of razor blades that had them all whooping with glee! Razor blades had been unobtainable for weeks in Vung Tau. *Everything* was useful.

Of course the four Kiwis – those highly-skilled New Zealand soldiers – plus the VC patients, were given exactly the same as the Aussies but, for the Vietnamese, I substituted books bought in the local market for the paperbacks Red Cross had sent. The Vietnamese did not give presents at Christmas, but how could we leave them out? As for the Kiwis, there was a slight over-sight. While beer of all brands from every Australian state was available for the patients' daily beer allowance, there was no New Zealand beer – something we hadn't considered. And the Kiwis preferred their own tobacco and cigarette papers, which they claimed were superior to the Australian.

'Is there anyone here from Tassie?' I queried, as I handed out a parcel from a Tasmanian women's group. Brian 'Dada' Aitken, the good-humoured medic/driver for Fifth Battalion's Dr Tony White, was the only voice to respond. 'Make sure you write and thank them,' I suggested, and dutifully he did. Suffering from a perforated ear drum and a wound from a piece of metal, Brian was transferred to the 36th Evac the next day to have his ear checked by the specialist there. He was lying on his bed when a medic told him he had to fill sandbags. 'So here I am in my blue hospital pyjamas shovel-ling sand! When the doctor comes tomorrow, I'm going to tell him if I am well enough to sandbag, then can I go back to my unit,' he resolved. Brian must have got his wish. I didn't see him in hospital again.

There were also letters to distribute. A teacher at a Vung Tau high school had asked her students to send notes, all neatly handwritten on fancy stationery, with the envelopes addressed 'Dear Allied Soldier'. In bold script, a girl named Thinh wrote:

On occasion of the Xmas festival, I wish you a MERRY CHRISTMAS.

Please receive my warmest thanks and deepest gratitude for your sacrifice and service to my country. Affectionately, Thinh.

People all over Australia had sent fruit cakes. An unofficial estimate suggested that every ANZAC soldier had at least three cakes, and some boys had as many as twenty. We gave hundreds to the Vietnamese, wondering as we did what they thought of a food so alien to their diet. As before, many cakes had to be thrown away because they were not cooked with spirits and had gone mouldy. Australia, take note! Remember your fighting men *all* year, not just at Christmas. And put plenty of alcohol in the cake! I suggested to NHQ that instead of sending fruit cakes the following year, Red Cross branches could supply a tree for every ward, as large as they could afford, coloured lights and a Santa costume.

Christmas dinner, traditionally served by the officers to the Other Ranks, was roast turkey with all the trimmings, followed by plum pudding with brandy sauce. Hilda, Harry and I stood in line with the officers, dishing out large servings to one and all, and then we sat with the ORs to feast. After dinner most people adjourned to the ORs' bar for the rest of the day, with the Diggers reading outrageous charges against every officer – each of whom, in turn, was playfully court martialled. It was all in good spirit. Next morning the Diggers slipped seamlessly back into addressing the officers as 'Sir' with no repercussions for the previous day's lawlessness.

Despite everyone being away from loved ones and missing them more than they would say, Christmas Day was fun.

Those men who had been feeling homesick and depressed tossed themselves into the celebrations by pretending to race Stumpy, as short and slight as a teenage girl, up and down the ward on crutches.

Entertainer Lucky Starr, who'd 'been everywhere, man', spent his second consecutive Christmas with the troops in Vietnam, and he and his group made a surprise visit to both 2 Field and the 36th Evac. Later that afternoon I drove Harry to the airbase in time for him to catch the last Caribou to Saigon. I rounded off the day with the men of 145 Signal Squadron (who sent the patients' messages home for us), then a barbecue at ALSG Officers' Mess. Christmas had been lovely.

During the last week of 1966, work started on building a permanent Red Cross office at the end of one of the Kingstrand wards. There was much joy when the soldiers dismantled our tent and we moved into our new workplace. Although plenty big enough to hold our stores, the area was still too small to set up a longed-for recreation area with a table tennis table. We were excited, though, when American Special Services gave us twelve boxes of books; from then on there was a constant stream of soldiers in to look for something to read – and often to liberate our supplies! A short sand wedge shot from our new quarters stood a piss-a-phone, but I never saw anyone using it. One day it was gone – a testament to our new-found respectability.

Just before the new year Koopsie had a birthday. We celebrated with French food at the Bel Air Hotel, followed by a visit to a Vietnamese nightclub that had a terrific local band. A tiny mini-skirted girl barely out of her teens sang current

American pop songs in Vietnamese, and an even smaller girl of five did an eye-popping twist, shake and watusi. Both were a big surprise. Vietnamese nightclub acts were usually as flat as sheet music. It was also time to invite people to farewell Karen Gramke, my American roommate who was being transferred to Long Binh. Always fun-loving, Karen had left her packing until after the goodbye party – not the wisest move. She managed to throw everything together in time for me to tidy up for my long-awaited helper and new roommate, Winsome Ayliffe (now Win Palmer of Busselton, Western Australia).

At the time Win offered to serve in Vietnam, she was employed at the Combined Services Recruiting Office in Perth, where her job was to give aptitude tests to army and navy applicants, both junior recruits and officers. She was a corporal in the CMF and a volunteer for Red Cross transport, driving aged people and disabled children to hospital for treatment. She gave blood regularly (despite fainting every time) and, when Red Cross called for volunteers for its Vietnam Field Force, she was the first to step forward. She was decent, honest, courageous, tenacious and mature beyond her twenty-three years. Without consciously being aware of it, everything she did in life was to make the world a better place. In no time flat, I adored her.

Win had not had an easy life. She was seventeen when her father died, and her mother was legally blind. Her only 'sibling' was a boy her parents had fostered during World War II, Don Mitchell, who still regards Win as his little sister. Despite being considered too young for Vietnam responsibilities, Western Australia Red Cross recommended Win highly. Then when Commander Crabb visited Perth and requested that she drive him around, Win's quick wit and unerring eye for life's absurdities easily matched his zany humour. He was won over. Also in Win's favour, Commander Crabb was 'sick of those girls going over there not knowing the military ranks!'

Hilda flew to Saigon to meet Win. Koopsie, Vivienne and I – waiting eagerly at the Vung Tau airbase for her arrival – wanted to greet Win warmly. Short to medium in height, with brown curly hair that fell in a fringe across her forehead, blue-green eyes and an easy smile, she was bubbling with excitement. Her Caribou had been shot at as it came in to land at Nui Dat on the way from Saigon. 'We all got out on landing, looked at the bullet holes underneath and thanked the Lord this time the VC were lousy shots.' Win hadn't been in the country twelve hours and already she had a war story!

After dinner at ALSG we settled in at the Villa DuBois. We chatted non-stop, knowing we would be sharing everything for the next six months. Eventually we switched off the light, and I fell asleep. Win, however, like everyone on the first night in country, was feeling wary and apprehensive. She was exhausted but her mind was racing. Suddenly, she felt something touch her face. She lay frozen with fear, thinking she must be imagining it. Then she put her hand to her face and screamed.

I jerked bolt upright like a jack-in-the-box. In the dim light coming from outside, I saw the intruder. A gigantic spider covered Win's face. She flicked it off, but the size of the creature, plus Win's scream, was too much for both of us. Trembling as one, we elected to get the front-door sentry to show bravery beyond the call of duty and kill the spider for us. I quickly fell asleep again, leaving Win to toss restlessly all night, wondering what other joys lay in her future. The next morning the Americans at the 36th Evac had eighty-three new patients and more were expected. Koopsie and Viv were very glad to have Win's help, and she had no more time to worry.

The year ended with a New Year's Eve party given by the colonel in charge of the Vung Tau area. John Steinbeck, the 1962 Nobel Laureate for Literature, and his third wife, Elaine, a tall blonde Texan who at one time had been married to the debonair forties screen scoundrel Zachary Scott, were among the guests. Confident, casually dressed in a sport shirt and slacks and smoking a cigarette, John Steinbeck held us spellbound as he talked.

The standard question 'How did you two meet?' received a star-studded response. He had been asked to drive Ava Gardner to a dinner, and when Ava was unable to go at the last moment, the hostess requested that he pick up Ann Southern and her friend. 'The friend was Elaine,' said John, raising his glass in a toast: 'Thanks Ava!' Such sophistication in Vung Tau! From our library next morning I stole Steinbeck's book *Travels with Charley*, a non-fiction account of travelling with his pet poodle, and John willingly autographed it for me, adding 'Vietnam 1967' after his name. Such was his charm that the famous writer made me feel he was hanging on my every word.

John Steinbeck had been a war correspondent during World War II. He was in Vietnam to visit his son Thomas, an infantry soldier who later returned to Vietnam for a second tour as a photojournalist. Soon after I met him, John Steinbeck hurt his back in Japan and then suffered through many months of pain and illness. Less than two years later I saw in a newspaper that he had died.

With many parties and much drinking, 1966 ended for us. I gave no thought to any year-end summary of events, nor did I make any mundane New Year's resolutions. However, my goodnight prayers in the first hours of 1967 for my Every Digger, Barry Harford, were more fervent than ever that the ongoing tragedy we were all involved in would end soon.

12

Overnight at the Sharp End

THERE IS NO PARTY THAT CAN'T BE improved by a sausage sizzle. The shade of feathery casuarinas that moved gently in the breeze along the shore of the South China Sea was the perfect setting for beach barbecues. Sometimes there were as many as five unit 'barbies' each Sunday, particularly if steak was available. The barbecues were made from cut-down 44-gallon drums with legs welded on, and a steel plate for a cooking base. Of greatest importance, they could be transported anywhere by Land Rover.

The 2 Field band with its guitarist/singer, Gerry Stevenson, could really rock and was the bonus attraction at 2 Field's barbecues. Wriggling our bare feet in and out of the deep sand, we'd twist and shout, and shake, rattle and roll our trim swim-suited bodies. We favoured The Mamas and The Papas, The Beatles, The Doors and their anthem 'Light my Fire', as well as Aussie artists like Billy Thorpe, Max Merritt and the

Meteors and, of course, Johnny O'Keefe. 'We Got to Get Outta This Place' with its heavy booming beat was a standard favourite. Sometimes, when darkness fell, we danced under the stars, assuaging our thirst with cans of Australian beer.

The RAAF boys, with their usual enterprise, occasionally had Sydney meat pies to complement the steaks and sausages, or a roasted lamb on a spit. When 9 Squadron or 35 Squadron had a barbecue, a RAAF Huey sometimes flew over and dropped flour bombs, but the practice came to a sudden halt the day the CO of Base Support Flight took a direct hit. Many activities were permitted in wartime that might not otherwise be allowed, but bombing the Commanding Officer was not one of them.

Back Beach, where the Allies swam, was divided into sections – the Australian beach, the Korean beach, the American beach, and furthest away of all, the Vietnamese beach. The American area had all sorts of luxuries: deck chairs, changing facilities, volleyball nets and a real car park, as well as a place to check valuables. In time-honoured fashion, all those from Down Under hid their valuables in their towels on the sand, confident that no one ever would suspect.

On the beach, Vietnamese teenagers sold fresh pineapples for a dollar each. With practised machete strokes they removed the tough skin, core and spiky pips, making a spiral on the pineapple. Macho soldiers walked along the water's edge with pineapple juice dripping down their chins. GIs relaxed with their Vietnamese girlfriends – always a source of fascination to the Western women. We heard those girls could be bought for about $10 a day. With all the troops around, the girls probably earned far more in a week than I did.

Win and I loved the break from our relentless routine that a swim and a beach barbecue afforded, but like everything in Vietnam, nothing was ever perfect. Sometimes there were howling sandstorms. There were bluebottles with long stinging tentacles that wrapped around a swimmer's legs, sea snakes (not poisonous, but a bite often meant a hospital stay) and other sea creatures of every imaginable motivation. Helicopters flew the length of the beaches on shark patrol. A dangerous current had claimed ten GIs in the previous few months, so the Americans had put lifesavers on duty full-time to look after us. And the sun was so fierce that even after seven months I still got sunburned.

After just one week in Vietnam, Win had fallen completely and everlastingly in love with the patients at both 2 Field Ambulance and the 36th Evac – and with the 2 Field medics. She fit in as though she had been there for months. But that didn't stop her from groaning each dawn, when the alarm woke us at six. From her side of the room I'd hear a sleepy: 'It can't be time to get up ye-e-e-t.' Her easy manner and dry humour endeared her to all. At first I had watched like a nervous mother as patients asked her to buy them sex magazines at the PX. After one man had put in his order, Win turned towards the patient in the next bed: 'Do you want what he's getting?' 'What's the point,' the soldier responded. 'You can't do anything about it in here.' With a chuckle, Win moved on. She was aware, though, that soldiers were watching her at the PX as she carefully selected the requested magazines. She did say, 'Some brown paper wrapping would have been nice.'

Before Win arrived, I was well on my way to going crazy with the workload. But with her help, instead of continually operating from behind, I could get things accomplished – such as the mundane writing of my monthly report to NHQ about the busy December that had been anything but mundane. I hunkered down at my desk all day and did paperwork. I didn't escape a sarcastic reprimand from Commander Crabb, though, for the lateness of the report.

Our housemaid Baby-san welcomed Win by inviting us both to visit her family. As we sat on wooden stools in her family's tiny home, she told us her husband was away in the ARVN. Or so we hoped. He might have been a VC. It was a sad fact of the war that we could trust no Vietnamese – not Baby-san, not my hairdresser, not Hue the PX cashier, nor the cheeky street boys.

That night there was a stripper at the Pacific, a rare event. I was interested to view her body of work – I'd never seen a stripper – and besides, it was going to be fun to watch the guys watching her strip. Instead, exhaustion sent me to bed early. R&R was more than a month away, but already I was counting the days.

Wealthy Saigoners still made the road trip along Route 15 to spend the weekend at Vung Tau, paying heavy tolls to the Viet Cong to make the trip. However, that route decidedly was not for us! For anyone of the Allied forces to go anywhere in Vietnam, we had only to head to the nearest airbase and find out what transport – free of course – was going where. And there were always the regularly scheduled Caribous, which were usually on time. Invariably there was a spare seat for any woman who wanted a ride.

After six months in Vietnam I solved the leg wax problem

that had so concerned me on my arrival in Vung Tau. The Embassy women knew of a Vietnamese beautician who had run the Saigon Elizabeth Arden Red Door salon in former days. Her salon had closed because of the war, but she took clients in her home. No appointment necessary. As I was heading to Saigon for a clean up, I heard the pilots joking about dodging the sniper who always took shots at them from one corner of the Tan Son Nhut runway. 'Why doesn't someone get him?' I asked in amazement. The answer was simple: 'He hasn't shot straight enough to hit anyone yet. If we take him out, the VC might put someone there who can shoot straight!' Again, I didn't know if the joke was on me.

Saigon was a city that was indisputably Asian, but evidence of its French heritage was everywhere. Like Paris with its arrondissements, Saigon was divided into districts. Just as the colonising British had left a legacy of railways and cricket grounds throughout Asia, the French – who occupied Saigon from 1859 to 1954 – had built opera houses and restaurants. The National Assembly of South Vietnam had been built as Saigon's opera house. The twin-spired Notre Dame Cathedral in the middle of JFK Square and Saigon's ochre-coloured buildings and broad boulevards were other reminders of the French colonial presence. Occasionally I heard French spoken among those Vietnamese who were better educated and more cosmopolitan.

One time I tried to get a reservation for a future visit at Saigon's modern Hotel Caravelle, but the haughty French reservations clerk gave a Gallic shrug and said: '*C'est impossible, mademoiselle.*' Unless one had a large bankroll, reservations were never available, as foreign correspondents monopolised the rooms there, often filming the war from its rooftop. They also shot footage from the roof of the American Bachelor Officers' Quarters Rex Hotel, where visiting military person- nel could rent rooms and share a drink with the press corps or with the American civilian contractors working for the military. It was in the Rex's conference room that the world's journalists received the daily American briefings, known uni- versally as the Five O'clock Follies, on how the war was going.

I had learned to plan my occasional day in Saigon to accommodate the reality of siesta – shutters drawn, iron gates pulled down over shop fronts, the town sealed tight as a drum. At first I'd mistakenly thought the shops were perma- nently shuttered because of the war! The Hotel Continental, the grand dame of Saigon hotels and definitely a place for those on an expense account, had an inviting courtyard and lovely open verandas. After eating a frighteningly expensive sandwich there, I was delighted to discover a large bookstore on Tu Do in the heart of the city. The shop sold books written in English, and it was open during siesta! I loaded up on books about Vietnam (all I needed was time to read them), then climbed into an ancient taxi driven by an even more ancient driver and went sightseeing.

With its fashion houses of French clothes, bars, and a pro- fusion of stores selling jewellery, silks, lacquer ware, and porcelain elephants known as BUFEs (bloody useless f--king elephants), Tu Do was a good place to start. Known as Rue Catinat under the French, Tu Do was renamed yet again after the fall of Saigon in 1975, when it became Dong Khoi, which means General Uprising. Weaving through the military traffic, rhythmically giving quick toots on the horn, my taxi rattled past the gem of a colonial post office on the right, circled Notre Dame Cathedral and turned towards the white

Presidential Palace built in 1962 to boost President Ngo Dinh Diem's image with his people. Then we headed into Cholon, home to the thousands of Chinese who lived in Saigon, with its swarms of stalls and shops jammed so tightly together one melded into the next.

Ben Thanh, a covered market, was bustling – siesta over – when we pulled to a stop at three in the afternoon; I was happy to abandon the bone-shaking ride. The hodgepodge of stalls and throngs of shoppers reminded me of Adelaide's Central Market, but the aisles were only a metre wide. They were jammed full of every kind of product, from fresh vegetables and fly-covered fish to wonderful old china and porcelain; from furniture and silks to incense and other exotic treasures. There was little that couldn't be bought at Ben Thanh, including beautiful antiques that I had heard about from friends who lived in Saigon before the war escalated. I wanted desperately to explore its aisles, especially to buy some Asian soap of rose or sandalwood. I hovered close to the entrance but didn't dare step inside; I was too nervous in the teeming crowd of Vietnamese.

Reluctantly I turned back to the street, where motorcycles and scooters raced at me in sputtering waves. It never occurred to me to visit the history and art museums of Saigon, housed in grand colonial buildings that no doubt contained wonderful examples of the early Khmer and Cham civilisations. Nor did I ever visit a Buddhist pagoda or the racetrack. The military had been warned to stay away from crowded places. We were not in Vietnam as tourists.

Returning to Tan Son Nhut for the trip home, the taxi bumped across the useless railway tracks – destroyed by the Viet Cong – where children played in the rubbish and weeds.

At the airport, I had to turn my head away from the regular Monday sight of coffins being loaded into American planes for the GIs' final trip home.

As I waited for the Caribou flight back to Vungers, I was singled out to fly instead on one of the very few Chinooks in Vietnam, again, simply because I was a woman. I took my seat inside the large twin-propeller helicopter that was capable of lifting a tank. All of the passengers riding with me were American, and one of them was playing music on a transistor radio. When the flight levelled out, a GI approached me and courteously held out his hand. 'Wanna dance, ma'am?' Grinning from ear to ear, I unbuckled my seat belt and stood up on the lurching floor. Other GIs started to clap to the beat, and my gallant soldier and I dipped in a crazy foxtrot of sorts as we flew above the paddy fields and jungle.

While I was having fun in Saigon, Win had been busy. There were seventy patients to shop for, and they all needed a chat. After a quick lunch, she took off on her shopping trip with two of the patients, Barry Hawthorne (the look-alike brother of our ALSG friend Kevin Hawthorne) and a Kiwi. She was carrying $400 cash (roughly equivalent to $2,500 today) and wanted bodyguards.

Engineer Capt Barry Hawthorne had been in hospital repeatedly in December and early January. While tunnel searching and blowing up a large booby trap, he had become immersed in VC excreta and had taken a good swim in it before he could escape. Parasites had entered every orifice and pore of Barry's body and wouldn't be shaken. Like his brother, Kevin, he was protective of Win and me and couldn't do enough for our well-being.

Barry provided us with an opportunity that was pure magic.

The morning he was to return to his front-line tent on the perimeter at Nui Dat, he told us he had permission from his Officer Commanding, Major Brian Florence, for us to stay the night at the sharp end. We could fly up in a Cessna with Barry that afternoon after he left hospital. So far women had been forbidden to stay overnight at the Dat. Too dangerous. We sped through our work, dashed home at lunch to pack an overnight bag and changed into jungle greens. By 3 pm we were in the Cessna. It had no doors of course, scaring Win stiff, but I was an old hand. As we skimmed over the treetops, I enjoyed the views that today's tourist pays a pretty penny for.

The Task Force engineers treated us royally. When it was dark and we had no way of getting home (no non-essential aircraft were permitted to fly until morning), they told us that women still were not allowed in the camp after dark. The Brigadier did not know of our visit! The whole area had been sworn to secrecy. We never knew if that was true (I believe it was), but the uncertainty added to the thrill of it all.

The Mess was furnished as well as could be expected under the primitive conditions. Other unit officers, including Major John Murphy of 3 SAS – none of whose cunning soldiers had suffered a casualty – came over to say hello. After dinner Barry walked us down to the perimeter, warning us not to linger at a certain spot where we clearly would be visible to any snipers. We scurried along. At the edge of the camp, soldiers in strategic sandbagged sentry posts used starlight scopes (devices that illuminated the field of vision) to scan the darkness for infiltrating VC, who often tried to stir up the perimeter at night. The Diggers offered us a look, and suddenly the darkness turned into an eerie green light that revealed anything untoward. 'See that tree about 100 metres out there?' Barry said ruefully. 'My soldiers have killed it on numerous occasions!'

The Diggers had named that sentry post 'Kamikaze', Barry told us, because it was unlikely that those manning it would survive a VC attack. We took only a brief look. Win and I were scared and anxious to get back to the Mess in case we were distracting the gun pickets from their vital role in the camp's security. Back up the track to the camp, we fairly bolted past the spot visible to snipers. According to the officers, the engineers' area was pretty wild that night. Apparently the ORs reasoned that if the officers had sheilas in the camp, then they could go a bit crazy themselves. Win and I slept beautifully in our tent for two (not, in this case, a two-man tent).

The morning's shower, to our surprise, was hot. The engineers had rigged up hot water for most of the camp during its early weeks, with themselves the last to have that luxury. I put on a dressing gown and hurried down the path to our private, screened area. The simple pulley mobility of Australian showers was the envy of the GIs, and the showers were as prized as slouch hats for barter fodder for whatever a Digger wanted.

I had only to pull on a rope to lift a canvas bucket over my head, turn the rose valve underneath and water would flow. Looking anxiously skyward for passing aircraft, I stripped naked and yanked on the rope. Nothing happened. It was as if the water's weight had cemented the bucket to the floor. I considered settling for a sponge bath, but a decent shower was not a luxury to pass up. On went my clothes, and I went for help, which was waiting at a discreet distance. A muscular soldier hauled the bucket in place with one tug of the rope.

Again I scanned the skies, undressed and reached above my head to turn the valve full on. Before I could even grab the soap, the water rushed out, most of it missing me completely. The bucket was empty. I was still dirty.

I dressed again and headed back to the tent to warn Win. She, with her CMF training, managed her shower beautifully. I made her swear not to tell anyone of my efforts. Back in Vung Tau, I showered at the Villa, where we changed from our jungle greens and army boots into our cooler Red Cross dresses. Thanks to the Task Force starting its day early, we were at work on time. We knew a busy day awaited us. We didn't know it was to be one of the most wrenching.

13

A Quiet Hero

SPECIAL AIR SERVICE MEN WERE TRULY SPECIAL to me. All units were special, but for me, 3 SAS Squadron had an edge on the rest. We had flown to Saigon together. Because of their strategic work, those Phantoms of the Jungle and their singular skills were legendary.

SAS reconnaissance – an effective intelligence gathering source – is one of the most dangerous duties in the military. Usually operating in four- or five-man patrols, the men were trained to carry out surveillance, ambush, combat, and snatch (to capture an enemy for interrogation by the intelligence unit). The professionalism and derring-do of 3 SAS was matched by the whole squadron's good looks and devil-may-care attitude.

On 18 January, the morning Win and I returned from our memorable night at the Task Force base, we heard the sound that signalled bad news: that of a Dust-Off landing at 2 Field

Ambulance. The sole casualty was Pte Russell Copeman, 3 SAS, who had a shattered arm and had suffered serious internal injury from bullet wounds to the abdomen. He was rushed straight into the operating theatre in critical condition. Every Australian soldier in Vietnam was as distressed as I was to hear that 3 SAS had suffered a casualty from enemy action.

Russell James Copeman was born with the army coursing through his veins. He was the grandson of one of the original ANZACs at Gallipoli, Pte Cecil Copeman. Russell's father, Major Jim Copeman, was a highly decorated soldier from the New Guinea campaign in World War II, winning both the Military Medal and later, after receiving a field commission, the Military Cross. Russell was named after one of his father's mates who had been killed in New Guinea; his second name honoured his Dad. It was no surprise to his family and friends when Russell joined the CMF in Wollongong as soon as he was eligible to enlist and trained with them until he was old enough to join the Regular Army. He wanted to serve his country as his father and grandfather had done before him.

Russell's sister, Ann Honess, from her home today on King Island, off the north-west tip of Tasmania, recalls: 'Russ was so proud when he was chosen to join the SAS and took all before him with great enthusiasm. Did you know that he had been asked to go back to Australia in December 1966 to begin an Officer Training Course, but wanted to stay in Vietnam to finish his tour of duty with the SAS? One can only imagine how different life might have been if he had taken up that offer. Russell's decision only shows his dedication to his work and his mates.'

On 16 January, 1967, Patrol 13, I Troop, 3 SAS, was sent out on a four-man reconnaissance. The unit consisted of patrol commander Sgt N. S. 'Norm' Ferguson, forward scout and second-in-command (2 I/C) Pte John 'Bubbles' Gibson, signaller Pte John W. 'Juvy' Matten, and medic Pte R. J. 'Russ' Copeman. When Russ Copeman was hit by VC sniper fire, Juvy Matten carried his critically wounded mate through the jungle to safety. Both men were only nineteen. Juvy, the handsome young warrior who had danced with me on the Qantas flight to Saigon, wrote about the rescue when belatedly, in 2001, he was honoured for his bravery. A quiet hero, he has dedicated his account to the memory of Russell Copeman:

As I remember, on day one, the patrol started off on the wrong foot. Our infiltration landing zone was not correct and we were, as you say, geographically embarrassed right from the start.

On moving away from the infil LZ [landing zone], it was very evident that there were a lot of signs of enemy activity and noise in the area. My opinion is that we were infilled close to an enemy fortified position. That night the patrol attempted to locate to a defined area by the use of map-to-ground, paces and direction. I don't think anyone slept that night as the patrol area was extremely boisterous.

On day two, we first sighted the enemy as we proceeded along our bearing, our eyes like mad cats'. There was lots of noise heard to our front and to our sides. On visual investigation, buildings and VC were seen by the recce party – cooking facilities, clothes lines, latrines – the whole box and dice that made up a VC camp. It was time to get out of there.

A tactical withdrawal was made. That night whilst in our overnight lying up position, RCLs [recoilless rifles] were heard firing and exploding within approximately 3,000 metres, and a vehicle of some description was heard starting up and driving off. Another sleepless night was had by all.

On day three, after morning skeds, the patrol continued on its mission, moving in a northerly direction. ['Skeds', or schedules, are radio contacts to headquarters at predetermined times. Should a patrol miss a sked, the base would go on alert in case the patrol was in strife, and if two skeds were missed, soldiers would go looking.] The forward scout, Bubbles Gibson, had just come across enemy tracks and was sending the appropriate signal back down the patrol. I was third in line and Russell was tail-end-Charlie, facing to the rear covering his arcs of fire.

Enemy fire opened up from my left, and I immediately carried out an Ambush Left contact drill. The counter ambush drill that we had practised so many times in training was now being tested for real. It was my turn to lay down fire so that Russell could withdraw. It was then I noticed that I could neither see nor hear Russ. I yelled out to the remainder of the patrol that I was moving back to the area of contact to see if I could locate our tail-end-Charlie. I don't know to this day if they heard me, but I moved to the rear anyway. Enemy fire was still apparent, so I continued to return fire with my M16 and throw a grenade. I can still remember vividly screaming 'GRENADE!' as I threw it – stupid, over-trained or what? At this stage I was not aware that Russell had been hit. He was the initial target of the enemy fire; possibly the only patrol member seen by the enemy due to the thick undergrowth.

I found Russell in the same place that I had last seen him. When I got to him I could see that he had been hit, but where I didn't know until later. I had to get rid of his equipment so that I could get him out of there. I started removing his kit when I realised we were still being fired at. I emptied his weapon in the general direction of the incoming fire. At the same time Russ was telling me to leave him and get the f--k out of there. I ignored him and continued removing his kit. I threw a white phosphorus fragment forward to enable me to pick him up and piss off out of there. I heard some screaming immediately after the grenade explosion, but could not confirm any casualties.

When I picked Russ up and threw him over my shoulder, I noticed his first wound. My left hand went right into his arm, and I had pieces of bone over my hands. As soon as I had him over my shoulder I cut for it, running through dense bamboo that was ripping us both to bits. When I felt it was safe, and the other two patrol members were with me giving covering fire when needed, I placed him on the ground to attend to his wounds.

It was then I found his second and most serious injury; an entry/exit wound to the lower abdomen. I had run with him bouncing on my shoulder right on top of the bullet wound, but at the time there was nothing else I could do. I attended to his injuries as best I knew how, gave him a syrette of morphine [a squeezable tube of morphine attached to a needle, commonly used since World War II by troops in the field for emergency pain relief], then I had to get comms [communications] as I was the sig [signaller]. Talk about the training that we do: I had the sense to grab the 64 set [radio] and throw it down my shirt before I picked up Russ.

REMEMBER, always leave your med kit and radio on top of your pack.

The antenna was thrown out across the scrub, and I proceeded to key the code words for friendly casualty. I didn't know it at the time, but I was sending Morse in excess of twenty-two words per minute. Back in the sig shack they had to get Gino Jansen* to take the message due to the high speed. Luck would have it comms were great and help was on the way.

I do not remember packing up, for as I was attending to Russ, enemy movement was heard advancing onto our not-so-safe LUP [lying up position]. Picking up Russ again we proceeded to move to the closest winch point. Again he had to endure a third-class ride on my shoulder.

At last that magical sound of a Huey. Our means of communication in those early days was a Zarbie [SRRB – Search and Rescue Radio Beacon]. Norm Ferguson was having a hard time trying to use it, so I offered to do the comms to the chopper and direct him to our winch point. The chopper noise drowned out all sound of the enemy movement, so we had no idea where or in which direction they were.

The chopper arrived. Crewmen lowered a cable and we belted Russ into a harness. He was hoisted above the trees and into the hovering chopper. I sent Russ up first followed by myself and the other two blokes. Looking out the side door, I saw two enemy running towards the winch point.

*Cpl Michael Redfern 'Gino' Jansen was an outstanding signaller and one of the happiest men of the Detachment 152 Signal Squadron that had been an integral part of SAS since its formation in 1957. The Detachment manned the radios that maintained contact with the patrols in the bush, with Task Force HQ and with SAS HQ in Perth. Gino Jansen completed two tours with the Detachment in Vietnam.

I opened fire from the doorway, scaring the shit out of the helicopter gunner who then in turn opened fire and saw the two VC hit the ground, but could not confirm a killing. Sgt Ferguson was also firing from the winch as he was lifted.

We flew out of there straight to Vung Tau to the Aussie hospital helipad. Major Murphy was there to meet us. As I alighted from the chopper, the emergency medics made a grab for me as I must have looked a sight. Blood from Russell's wounds had run all over me, along with all the bamboo cuts from the run through the jungle. I directed them to Russell, and from there it was all out of my hands. Later we were informed that Russ had survived by only about five minutes or less – any longer and he would have been history. Injuries sustained were gun shot wound to the upper arm and to the abdomen (sixteen perforations of the intestines).

Six days after his wounding, Russell Copeman turned twenty. To celebrate, a huge number of his mates drove down from the rubber to see him, for 3 SAS was a close-knit group. We were all determined that he should have a happy birthday and live for many more, but Russ, although he managed to stay admirably cheerful, was not getting better. In fact, he seemed to be deteriorating and was soon back in the operating theatre again.

On 27 January, I wrote to his mother, Mrs Pearl Copeman:

Dear Mrs Copeman,
Russell asked me to write and let you know he is improv-ing steadily. He is thinking of you all, and has appreciated all the letters and telegrams he has received from you and Major Copeman, the Pycrofts, and other friends.

He is a wonderful patient, is in good spirits, and has had more people visiting him than any other patient I can remember. The SAS boys collected and gave him a stereo record player for his birthday, and we had a cake iced with the SAS crest on it, plus candles. He has been moved out into the sun once or twice and enjoys these breaks. You would be really proud of him if you could see the way he has accepted his injury, and he cracks jokes about being in hospital. As soon as Russ was injured, Major Murphy came to the hospital to see him.

Russell sends his love to Sue and the Pycrofts [Sue Pycroft, a Wollongong hospital nurse, was his girlfriend]. He was thrilled when he got your signal and is looking forward so much to seeing you all as soon as he is well enough to return home on medevac.

I hope my letter will help you to feel happier about your son. He is a favourite of all of us here, and we are all urging him along the road to recovery.

With best wishes,

Jean Debelle

Australian Red Cross Vietnam

It was hard writing that letter, knowing that Russell's life was hanging by a slender thread. I had, of course, written as Russell had wished it. When we heard back from Mrs Copeman, it was clear she thought Russell was improving. He wasn't. He had been chirpy when I wrote, but the following day his wounds, which had ulcerated, started to bleed. The doctors had him in surgery for ten hours, but they didn't expect him to last the night.

When Russell was wounded, his father, mother, sister Ann

and brother Darrell were in Israel. Major Copeman was a Military Observer with the United Nations Truce Supervision Organisation at Tiberias. Mrs Copeman and the children were packing to return to Australia for the start of school after the long Christmas break. Via the British Consul in Jerusalem, Major Copeman was handed an army signal with the news that Russell had been critically wounded and was hospitalised at Vung Tau. He asked the UN for immediate transport back to Australia for his wife and children. That same day he drove them to Jerusalem for a commercial flight back to their home in Towradgi, New South Wales.

There was news waiting for Mrs Copeman. Eastern Command in Sydney told her that she was eligible to visit her son under the AUSDIL (Australians Dangerously Ill) guidelines established by the Department of Defence. The army would make the arrangements. Simply put, AUSDIL covered *all* members of the serving forces and allowed the next of kin of a patient who was 'very seriously ill' (defined as illness or injury of such severity that life is imminently endangered) to be flown to visit that person. By necessity it was expected that the patient was conscious and would survive for the next seventy-two hours, and that the visit would benefit the patient. If it seemed likely the patient would be medevaced to Australia shortly, no visit was allowed. Russell was still classed as very seriously ill, and recovery was not certain. We had been told the army was bringing Mrs Copeman from Australia, although Russell didn't know it yet. I prayed that he would last until she arrived.

Numb with worry, Pearl Copeman got on a plane again – Qantas direct to Singapore. She was to be met at the airport by a Red Cross Field Force worker who would escort her to the Hotel Cathay to sleep that night, but due to a communication mix up, Red Cross wasn't there to meet her. Alone, Mrs Copeman took a bus to the Hotel Cathay and walked along a deserted lane to the rear entrance. Recalling her memory of that night in Singapore, she said she never had felt so lonely in her life.

Accommodation was scarce in Vung Tau, and we originally thought Mrs Copeman would have to sleep on either my bed or Win's, with one of us on the floor on a camp stretcher. Mercifully for all of us, a room was made available at the Australian Rest and Convalescence Centre on the beach front. I made the room at the R&C villa as welcoming as possible with fresh flowers picked from the garden plus a few extras, such as nice soap and Kleenex, that the army did not provide.

Two Field Ambulance was blessed to have an amazing surgeon, Major Ron Gregg, who had left his practice at Cunnamulla, Queensland, to work in Vietnam. He met Mrs Copeman at the helipad. Before taking her to see her son, he explained in his gentle way that Russell had suffered extensive wounds internally and that many days of nursing would be necessary before his recovery could be assured. A sedated Russell was waiting for his mother. 'Hello, Mum,' he said. 'What are you doing here? You shouldn't have come.' Then he smiled, closed his eyes and went to sleep.

Russell was existing only on fluids from a drip inserted in his arm. He'd wake from time to time, say a few words, then fall asleep again. Drugs gave him some relief from the pain, but because the wounds had destroyed his digestive system, he was unable to eat solid food and could only drink from a straw. It was clear he was making little or no progress, and no move was made to evacuate him to Australia. In his condition he might not survive even a short plane trip to the RAAF hospital in Butterworth, Malaysia.

His worried mother sent an army signal to her husband in Tiberias and suggested he come to see Russell for himself. Major Copeman flew to Vietnam at his own expense and moved into his wife's room at the R&C villa. An excited Russell had to be sedated again before his father's arrival. Pitifully thin, Russ greeted his Dad with spirit: 'Hello, Dad. I wasn't on the track!' Possibly as a result of his own experience in New Guinea, Major Copeman had warned Russ repeatedly he should keep clear of any open spaces – especially tracks and roads – when out on patrol, so as to be less of a target for the enemy.

Russell's condition remained critical, and he was due to have another major operation – his third. Just how often could a body stand such invasion? It would be an ordeal for him. I prayed each day, and I knew Win did too, that he would make it back to Australia in good shape.

14

The End of Joy is Grief

Even in laughter the heart is sad, and the end of joy is grief.

Proverbs 14:13

HILDA ZINNER'S REPLACEMENT, Janice Webb (now Hilton) arrived in the third week of January, just a few days after Russ Copeman was brought in to 2 Field Ambulance. In her mid-thirties, Jan was soft-spoken, tall and fair. She had been a Field Force officer in Terendak, Malaysia, and clearly was at ease with army protocol. Her quick humour was readily apparent: she grinned wickedly when Hilda introduced her to Baby-san as 'the new Madam!' When we went to the 2 Field Officers' Mess for our first dinner together, it was a winner. The men were delighted to have a new female in the Mess, and as an added bonus, there were two civilian nurses visiting from Long Xuyen. We got back to the Villa to find our American neighbours highly agitated. Koopsie, badly in need of a break, was about to be transferred to Tokyo. Her replacement, in country one week, had declared she hated Vietnam and handed in her resignation on the spot. We were stunned. How could anyone not love the work? We were glad that Koopsie would be with us longer, and Vivienne was able to take her long-awaited holiday in Australia.

The next evening Win and I, exhausted and still in our dirty uniforms, grabbed an early dinner at the Pacific. We returned home for some letter writing and catch up, but there came a knock on the door. It was Jan, and she hadn't eaten. We cooked tinned curry for her on our tiny hotplate on the floor – supplemented with coffee, cheese and dry biscuits, which the Mess had given us – and talked into the night with our sociable new boss. We said goodbye to Hilda a couple of days later after a farewell lunch at Cyrnos, and the new team set about establishing its routines.

We continually walked a weird line between the barbarism of war and civilised living. Both Win and I had scored a guernsey to the Embassy's Australia Day cocktail party, a somewhat surreal event in a country at war. We flew to Saigon after work and, as we often did, stayed at a villa owned by an Australian civilian engineer (working on construction projects for the forces) who offered free rooms to any Australian visiting Saigon. Some years the cocktail party was a really big affair and was held at the Caravelle Hotel, where both the Australian and the New Zealand embassies were located. The New Zealand Embassy was easy to spot when stepping off the lift because of a huge picture of the indigenous, flightless kiwi – the bird whose name has become the nickname for all New Zealanders – on the wall.

In January 1967 the Australia Day party was at the home of the Ambassador, Mr Lew Border, on Rue Pasteur. The large lawn in front of the Ambassador's colonial villa was a sea of army uniforms, elegantly dressed diplomats and civilian men and women. A well-groomed servant offered beer or sangria from a silver tray. Heavily armed guards watched from behind trees and potted plants with weapons drawn. The evening was made for me by one of the Americans. He demanded of a New Zealand diplomat: 'Say man, what's that painting of a fat-arsed pigeon doing on the wall at your embassy?' We spluttered into our drinks while the New Zealander, his diplomatic skills firmly in hand, educated the Yank about the 'pigeon'.

Considerably juiced, about twenty of us then headed into town for a Chinese dinner, with members from Australian surgical teams stationed all over Vietnam providing our transport. The Chinese proprietor was the only person who was happy when we left in a rush at curfew, for we'd been bellowing rousing renditions of 'Waltzing Matilda', 'The Pub with No Beer', 'Advance Australia Fair' and other songs that Aussies love to sing when they are far from home. Next morning I returned to Vung Tau on the first plane for work, but Win, who had barely seen Saigon, stayed on for shopping and sightseeing. As she waited for the last Caribou home that afternoon, an American colonel invited the lucky girl into the busy control tower at Tan Son Nhut.

Although Sunday, 29 January, was a normal working day for me, I wore civvies – tantamount to hiring a skywriter to announce it was my twenty-seventh birthday. Before work, Win and I went to church, followed by a celebratory drink in the tent of the convivial Padre Pres Sullivan. There's nothing like a drop of alcohol to start a birthday! We rushed through our day to finish at about five, for we had Big Plans. Eighteen of us met for pre-dinner drinks at the Pacific, where we could park our vehicles safely on military property. We walked to the nearby Grand Hotel for a Vietnamese banquet in a private room, supervised by Mr Dong, the manager. We had grown very fond of the light and delicately seasoned local cuisine.

At the witching hour of 10 pm, when we all had to be out of non-military establishments, we continued partying at the Pacific. Capt Con Ermert, with 101 Workshop, had his guitar with him, and we sat outside on the large patio under a star-filled sky, singing Aussie songs. The Americans at the Pacific's bar and jukebox soon realised where the real fun was and joined us on the patio. We enjoyed their company and, besides, they were paid more than the Australians and liked to buy. Sometimes, by way of thanking them, we told them terrible whoppers, and to our amusement they'd believe us. We sang the songs they knew, like 'Where have all the Flowers Gone' and 'Cool, Clear Water', as well as Con's favourite about poor old Charlie who was doomed to ride the MTA forever 'neath the streets of Boston for want of one more nickel.

With curfew approaching, Harry – who had come from Saigon – offered to drive some of the men back to their tents in the sandhills. Jan, Win and I squashed in too. Harry took the mountain road along the coast and, indifferent to any lurking enemy, stopped so we could look at the sleeping sea streaked with a wide ribbon of moonlight. Then he drove along the Back Beach sand, and we squealed like children as the Land Rover's headlights shone upon sand crabs scurrying to and fro. It was a lovely evening. For a few hours in Vietnam we had forgotten there was a war.

Win returned to Saigon with Harry to spend her day off there. Touring Saigon at night, the two of them driving around in Harry's Vietnamese Red Cross ambulance, something wacky happened, as it did so often in that country at war. They saw three Vietnamese teenagers (Thanh, Khanh and a girl nicknamed Be) who, for a lark, wanted to drive with them. 'We told them to hop in,' Win said. 'They were all university students, with one of the boys studying engineering and one law. They spoke pretty good English and excellent French, so Harry had a long talk with them as we drove around, with rockets – I don't know whose – lighting up the night sky. Crazy, huh!'

'Next day,' Win went on excitedly, 'the students came with Harry and me on our visit to the German Red Cross floating hospital ship, the *Helgoland*, which was berthed at the Saigon docks to treat Vietnamese civilians. Then to cap it all, when I went to Tan Son Nhut for the flight home, hundreds of Buddhists monks were massed around the terminal. I was terrified it was a demonstration and one of them would turn himself into a human torch. But arriving on Pan Am and first off the aircraft was one of their chiefs, followed down the steps by US General Westmoreland and then our Australian General Vincent.' Win had all the luck – I had been in Vietnam seven months, and I had yet to see General Westmoreland, the commander of all US operations in Vietnam!

As always, there was sadness mixed with any gaiety we were able to grab. The day after my birthday began as a typical busy Monday: we shopped for the patients who were heading home that day. After lunch two men were admitted with hepatitis contracted from eating at the Grand Hotel, the place where we had just celebrated my birthday! By late afternoon there was an influx of badly injured men, one of whom didn't make it.

Less than a week later tragedy struck again. On 6 February the magnificent Kiwi artillery, which, legend had it, could land a round on a postage stamp (and had done so for Bob Buick at Long Tan), accidentally fired on the Sixth Battalion's Delta Company. Four men were killed and thirteen wounded. Jack Kirby, the beloved and seemingly invincible Sergeant Major, who had been awarded the Distinguished Conduct Medal for his reassuring presence at Long Tan as he dashed from person to person handing out ammunition to the encircled men, was among the dead. Three helicopter loads of wounded came in to 2 Field; others went to the 36th Evac. It was a struggle to hold back my own tears as I saw soldiers crying for their dead mates. What made the whole ghastly business worse was that it was friendly fire that had done the damage. Incidents of friendly fire were the hardest for us all to accept. We knew accidents happened in war, no matter how disciplined and well-trained the troops, but it hurt. Badly.

The doctors and medics at 2 Field worked flat out. I phoned to get an update in the late evening and was told they were still operating and would be at it all night. The dedicated medical staff worked nearly a twenty-four-hour stint. Win was to have had dinner that evening with one of the doctors but knew she would hear nothing from him. That night we felt sure God wept with us.

15

Tet and More Bloody Mines

ET, VIETNAM'S LARGEST AND MOST IMPORTANT FESTIVAL, can fall anywhere between mid-January and mid-February, for the timing, like that of Chinese New Year, depends on the lunar calendar. During the February 1967 Tet observations, we were warned to be on high alert. The military was taking no risks and Vung Tau was put off limits in case there was trouble. That was another inconvenience for us, as our work demanded that we be able to drive between the hospitals. Our Villa guards had been doubled; most roads and all bars, shops and businesses were closed; few round-eyes were on the streets. A year later, Tet was to become known for the stunning military offensive in which the North Vietnamese and Viet Cong tried to take over the South, but failed.

We heard explosions all over town throughout the day and most of the night. The Vietnamese had come to Vung Tau from outlying areas to celebrate the lunar new year by setting off fireworks. It was nerve-racking. Each explosion might be a bomb. And for the duration of Tet, Baby-san informed us, 'I no come work' – causing us mild trepidation. We had become spoiled by all of the washing and cleaning she did for us.

Australians and Americans all came to understand that for the Vietnamese Tet is like Christmas, New Year, Fourth of July and birthday celebrations all rolled into one. Tet was the time for gift giving and receiving, all presents wrapped in red, the colour that signifies good luck and happiness. Shops and homes were decorated with red scrolls, inscribed in calligraphy, with assorted good wishes that everyone could relate to: Good Luck, Prosperity, Longevity and Good Health. I saw none that said Peace – too controversial. Small red envelopes of money were given to children with the wish 'May you eat a lot and grow a lot'. An unmarried adult was wished 'May you find a compatible person'. Too late we realised we should have given Baby-san a gift, but we consoled ourselves that we had remembered her at Christmas.

In the middle of Tet, the new Officers' R&C centre opened with a party. As we Red Cross girls walked in, the electricity failed. With so many trigger-happy Vietnamese around, the darkness was scary. We sat in the gloom of the rooftop garden overlooking Vung Tau, sipping our drinks and watching fireworks – accompanied by tracer bullets shot randomly into the air – lighting up the dark sky. Both fireworks and gunshots went on all night. The explosions kept Win and me awake. We worried whether the Copemans were able to sleep.

After a week, Vung Tau opened again for business, and Baby-san returned. To give Pearl and Jim Copeman a break from their vigil, Win offered to take them and three patients for a drive around Vung Tau and along the scenic coast road. They had a lovely afternoon sightseeing for, to their surprise, the streets of Vung Tau were empty of the normal traffic chaos. They were blissfully unaware that minutes after they set off, there had been more trouble in Vung Tau, and again the town was off limits. Win was aghast that she could have endangered her unarmed passengers, including the highly decorated Major Copeman.

Russell Copeman's right arm and shoulder were mending well, but the internal wounds had not healed sufficiently to permit him to have food by mouth. It was a joyful milestone the day he was able to suck on an ice-cream, his first snack since he had been admitted a month before. We all hoped it was a sign that he was going to make it. Major Copeman's ten-day leave gone, he returned to Tiberias to complete his tour with the UN, but not before having a drink with the 2 Field Ambulance Other Ranks, who had cared for his son. It was a gesture they appreciated. An anxious and sad Pearl Copeman was alone again.

With the curfew lifted, the convent/orphanage at Nam Binh invited some officers and our Red Cross team to a Tet dinner to thank the Australians for what we had done for them. The Aussies had made significant contributions by building a sewing room (complete with six new sewing machines), a medical/dental room, and a kindergarten room, and by repairing other structures. They had done similar work at the Ba Ria convent/orphanage, and somehow we came through it all well liked. We, in turn, loved the sweet-faced nuns of indeterminate age who, like most nuns of that day, wore black habits and a mantle of simple dignity. The children, too, were adorable. Dinner, on the other hand, was always risky business, as we never knew whether the food was cooked hygienically.

News came in February of the Tasmanian bushfires. No one was too concerned at first as summer fires were hardly unusual in our sunburnt country. But when we heard of the fires' enormity, we were stunned. Sixty-two people had been killed, and the capital city of Hobart was threatened. One of the boys from Hobart was worried; I could hear the alarm in his voice. 'On Radio Australia,' he said, 'they reported that much of Coningham, the little beach town where we stay every year was destroyed. To hear Coningham mentioned by name on world radio, then I knew the fires must have been bad.' At that time the Tasmanian fires had caused the largest loss of life and property on any single day in the history of our continent. We all worried for the Tasmanians; our hearts went out to our countrymen facing such devastation.

St Valentine's Day, 14 February, was marked by casualties from yet another mine explosion. It was also Major Don Bourne's thirty-fifth birthday, which his wife and children at home in Australia were preparing to celebrate. But someone stepped on an artfully concealed mine at An Nhut, and Major Bourne, the Fifth Battalion commander of C Company, became the first major to be killed in South Vietnam. Also killed were his 2 I/C Capt Bob Milligan, who was about to go home to be married, and Capt Peter Williams, the forward observation officer attached from the NZ artillery, who was to return home following the operation. Command of Charlie Company briefly passed to the senior platoon commander, Lt Roger Wainwright, to whom I had carried the cake from Australia.

In addition to the three officers killed, four other men were wounded at An Nhut that day. Lt John Deane-Butcher, the son of a country doctor, was one of them. Although given a postponement to continue his studies when he was called up for National Service, John had volunteered, knowing he would be sent to Vietnam. Now a chartered accountant in Bathurst, New South Wales, he clearly recalls the operation:

'The village of An Nhut, which was to be searched for VC troops and supplies, had been cordoned off in absolute secrecy so that no VC could escape or fire on us. The walk into An Nhut was an unusual one. A moonless night was deliberately chosen. We tied ourselves together in small groups with toggle ropes, as it was too dark to see the person in front. One of our sections decided to play a joke on their machine gun carrier, Bob Antonio, as they crossed a deep narrow stream. As Bob jumped the stream, they didn't let the toggle rope go. Bob got very wet. With the tension of the night, everyone got the giggles. With the added stress of having to keep silent, we giggled more, like school kids. A few hours later the mine exploded and we had a rude awakening.'

At home that evening Win tallied up: 'That's four dead last week and three this week – so far.' I ached as I realised Win had become as morbidly sardonic as I. That same day Military Assistance Command, the Allied headquarters in Saigon, was almost hit by mortar fire. Casualties kept arriving daily, and more dead. Win and I went to church, but it didn't seem to cheer the soul.

Tired and downcast we may have been, but we were never bored – there was always something new. It was common to see air strikes as we flew around the country, but as I took a chopper – for us, no more unusual than taking a bus at home

– from Vung Tau to the Dat one afternoon, the pilot drew my attention to a distant aircraft. Great gushes of spray were streaming behind it, blanketing the land below. I assumed they were spraying against malaria. Today I wonder if it was Agent Orange or napalm I saw.

At Nui Dat I was invited to take a look at a field operation. APCs had moved in to cordon off Hoa Long, a village near the Task Force area that had been a frequent target of searches by our troops, as it was known to house Viet Cong. There were no Vietnamese men of military age to be seen in the village of 3,000 people – only curious children who, ignoring the tough weapon-bearing soldiers, again pulled at the hairs of my arms and giggled. Straw-hatted women tried to sell baskets of vegetables, the produce beginning to shrivel in the harsh afternoon sun. An ABC radio reporter was there and interviewed me. We squatted beside the dirt road, sharing his microphone, as the Diggers around us continued their work of search and, maybe, destroy. The surreal had become the norm.

Less than two months after arriving in Vietnam, Win had started to party as much as I had at first. While at the Pacific to watch the film *The Agony and the Ecstasy*, she met one of the Aussie doctors and stayed to dance to the terrific band. 'The only problem is that everyone gets kicked out about 11.50 pm as we all have to be in our own barracks by midnight,' she complained. 'Just as well, my gal,' I retorted with a blip of a grin. 'You'll wear yourself out here just like I did.'

Win's mother had written that it appeared Win did nothing but socialise, but the reality was we all needed to relax when we could. The doctors especially had been under considerable

stress in the previous few weeks. When Dr Roger Mitchell had
a birthday, Win, Sixth Battalion's Dr Roger Bampton and I
joined him to celebrate with beaucoup champagne. Keeping
busy was good as it left no time to think about what we were
seeing. That was the absurdity of our lives: one moment we
were partying, the next we were faced with almost unbearable
sorrow that at times could overwhelm us. Rather than tears, we
used alcohol and sleep to get us through. Red Cross had it easy,
though, compared to the medical staff. By the time we got to
see the patients, they were cleaned up. It was the young medics,
mostly National Servicemen, who had to scrub the blood of
wounded men off hospital walls and floors, or dispose of the
amputated limbs so casually handed to them by a surgeon.

Unlike the soldiers and the medics, we women always had
some diversion to lift our spirits. Jan, Win and I were invited
to dine on the *Vernon Sturdee*, a cargo ship docked in Vung
Tau. We sat with the officers and two of the American nurses
at white linen tablecloths and feasted on delicious food
accompanied by Sydney water. It was the first untreated water
I had drunk since arriving in Vietnam, and it beat a gin and
tonic hands down. I was amused that our dinner was noted
officially in the ship's log, 16 February, 1967.

Occasionally the hectic social life caught up with us. We
would decline all invitations, stay home and cook dinner in
our room – combat rations that the Fifth Battalion
bandsmen/medics had given us. We heated tinned chicken on
our hotplate, made coffee and had tinned peaches for dessert,
all washed down by a nice bottle of red from the Mess. All
in all, a pretty good meal. Despite our partying, we wouldn't
quit work until we felt we had done all we could. And
working with Win was a constant joy. We felt as one about

how to do our jobs. Every Australian patient in both hospitals should be visited first thing each morning, as they always needed toilet items or assistance in some way. Patients in the 36th Evac should have an Aussie to talk to as they lay surrounded by Americans. Newly arrived wounded required comforting words, or maybe just someone to listen. There was always a patient who wanted us to write a letter for him.

One evening there was to be an Officers' Mess dining-in to welcome General D. Vincent, the new commander of the Australian force, Vietnam. Although Red Cross wasn't invited to the dinner, I thought flowers on the table were essential for elegant dining, so I scrounged blooms from wherever I could. I picked flowers growing wild along the roadside and considered any flower straggling over a villa wall as fair game. I was proud of my contribution.

Each day we'd spend time going through mail we regularly received addressed 'To a Soldier in Vietnam'. Most of the letters were from fourteen- or fifteen-year-old schoolgirls. We weren't trying to protect our soldiers from predatory teenagers but to ensure that there were no anti-war sentiments in the letters. Most were supportive of the work the Diggers were doing, though one from a twenty-six-year-old woman complained there were no men in Sydney since the soldiers left. If she had a fellow to write to in Vietnam, it would make her come alive, and she would have someone to wait for. And that was just the mildest part of the letter. 'Hmmm. Sounds like she might be a good sort,' Win grunted. 'I'll find someone to accommodate her!' I can't remember who the lucky recipient of the letter was, but the lonely woman would have plenty to make her come alive when Sydney opened up for R&R.

Nancy Sinatra was to appear in a show in one of the hangars at the Vung Tau airbase. The USO concerts didn't happen often, but that one promised to be good, for Nancy was the daughter of Frank Sinatra, the Chairman of the Board. Her single 'These Boots are Made for Walkin' had been one of the top hits of 1966. Thousands packed into the hangar, including us with thirty patients. If the VC had thought to fire their mortars at the hangar that night, they'd have scored their biggest victory yet. Nancy, her long blonde hair reaching well past her shoulders, wore the shortest mini any of us had seen – at least eight inches above the knee. Some of the patients were horrified. To our amusement, one turned to us and har-rumphed: 'I hope they're not wearing those things back home!'

Nancy had bought the mini on Carnaby Street, in swinging London, and because she didn't like her legs, she bought a pair of caramel-beige boots to go with it. She looked great as she strode across the stage in those legendary boots, singing her hit song. Sadly, the rest of the show fell far below our expectations. We were grateful for *any* entertainment, but Nancy displayed no personality and, we thought, was making a living on her daddy's name.

The following day Jan, Win and I were invited to lunch on the *Jeparit*, which had just ferried both Red Cross and army supplies up from Sydney. I had planned to go to church, but in the struggle of God versus gourmet dining, I confess good food won the day. Without shame, again I piled my plate high. We were back at work by two, and Jan set off with Major Donohue, the WHAM team and a load of children on an outing.

That night, like almost every night since New Year, we listened to the bombing and artillery fire as we sat on the floor of our room, dining on tinned ham and a freshly baked French roll purchased in the market. The American bombing was miles away, but the whole Villa shook to its foundation. Maybe it wasn't bombing. Had the VC hit the American ammo dump again?

The bombing procedure was weirdly fascinating. Apparently while bombers were in flight to Vietnam from bases in Thailand or the Philippines, a computer programmed precisely and automatically when the bombs were to be released. All a pilot had to do was to fly the plane four kilometres high above the target area. Bombing by computer is commonplace today, but in the mid-sixties we felt we were living out cartoon character Buck Rogers' fantasies of the 21st century.

To take my mind off the noise, I told Jan and Win about all the things I was going to buy in Hong Kong when I went on R&R the next day. Heading the long list was clothes. We'd all had clothes stolen, and there was nothing we could do but shrug. Win's mother had sent her a blouse for Christmas that had 'walked' by the new year. I had hoped to buy underwear in Saigon but nearly fainted at the prices the shopkeepers asked. If the Vietnamese had wanted our uniforms, we would have been going to work naked!

Eight months in country had been debilitating, and I was physically and emotionally bushed. The feeling of exhilaration as I faced each day had long since passed, and I needed the R&R break desperately. Morning could not come soon enough. As always, Win had the right words: 'You won't need me to drive you to the airbase tomorrow. You'll float to Hong Kong on happiness alone.'

16

To Be Alone Was Perfect

NEXT TO GOING HOME, R&R WAS THE one thing every-one most looked forward to. We were given free transportation to an exotic city for five days of recreation and relaxation. The choices offered were super: Bangkok, Honolulu, Tokyo, Manila, Taiwan, Singapore or my destination, Hong Kong. When Sydney joined the list, it quickly became a popular choice for the Americans, as evidenced by bars named Arizona and San Francisco that sprouted like weeds in Kings Cross. Honolulu, too, was popular, and not just for the taste of home that it offered the Americans. Many went there to marry the girls or men they had left behind – or perhaps had met in Vietnam – only to return again to the war.

In Saigon, the practised efficiency of the American R&R system took me into its care. As I changed my military funny money for American greenbacks, it felt strange to have real currency in my hands again. From then on everything got better and better. The food on the big Pan Am plane we boarded was only the start. As the plane lumbered into Hong Kong's Kai Tak airport just after dark, the lights of that beautiful city were reflected in the water, and we had that theatre-set view of the Chinese in their apartments eating their evening meals. Before we could go to our hotels, we were briefed about the joys and perils facing us in the British Crown Colony. I didn't hear a word. I was taken to the President Hotel, and then, almost giddy with excitement, I was on the town, joyously walking the crowded streets alone. For the first time in eight months, I was not afraid of anything.

I was enchanted by the beautiful harbour, the majestic Peak soaring into the clouds, the three banks that were then the only tall buildings along the shorefront of Hong Kong Island, and the restaurants and hotels throbbing with glamour and sophistication. Instinctively I could sense the intrigue that bubbled just beneath the surface of the bustling city. From the top of The Peak I gazed down on stately colonial buildings, the private mansions and the Happy Valley race track – then retreated to my hotel. I sank into the huge bathtub to wash off the grime of Vietnam and plan my week, for I had added an extra two days to the usual R&R. For starters, I was going to make believe there was no war. The bed was large and luxurious, and instantly I fell into a dreamless sleep.

It was so hard to feel feminine in Vietnam. In Vung Tau I had told anyone who cared to listen that I intended to spend the whole week in Hong Kong in a beauty parlour. My first priority, though, was to meet Vivienne's friend, Julie Wong, who guided me to her tailor. He promised to have a Thai silk cocktail dress finished for me before I left. The style I chose was that of the grey and white frill-necked dress worn by one of the girls whose elegance I had so envied when she visited ALSG some months back. I ordered shoes custom designed to my feet – to me the ultimate in luxury. That done, I hit Hong Kong's best beauty salon for the 'works': haircut, facial, leg wax, body massage and manicure.

When I asked the tiny Chinese beautician to tidy my eyebrows, she bent over my face with a taut triangle of string, one end held between her teeth and the rest anchored in each hand. 'What are you doing?' I exclaimed with horror. 'Don' worry, don' worry,' she said mercilessly, while I lay there, fearful of being left with no brows at all. Her hairless Chinese arms and tiny hands swished over my face in a crisscross scissor motion as she yanked at the unkempt brows with the string. 'Now you look,' she said triumphantly, and handed me a mirror. The Chinese string torture (they call it threading) had resulted in my best brow trimming ever.

After spending all day getting in shape, I felt as glamorous as I ever would be. I thought I scrubbed up pretty well and was ready to hit the town. I dined alone on English roast beef and Yorkshire pudding with loads of vegetables, revelling in the refined atmosphere of a cosmopolitan restaurant. Just as I was tucking into the meal, a businessman made a beeline for my table. 'I can see you're lonely, pretty lady. Okay if I join you?' he asked as he sat down. My brain (had I gone troppo by now?) had no snappy answer. He started to chat me up. It quickly became evident that he didn't interest me at all. Then came the kicker: 'Some men are turned off by tough-looking army broads. Not me!' said my Romeo. All I could think was: a pick-up line like that, fella, will get you a free ride on the Bondi tram. That Sydney tram, of course, hadn't run for years.

I suddenly developed an urgent need to be by myself. Feigning tiredness, I took off for The Peak once more, looking over my shoulder all the way in case he was following. Transfixed again by that magical view, I shook off all thoughts of Romeo.

Back at my hotel, as I rode up in the lift looking forward to the softness of my bed, I became uncomfortably aware that the only other passenger, a European man, was eyeing me. When I got off at my floor, so did he. As I put my key in the door, he walked past me down the corridor. I was about to sink into bed when the phone rang. Would I like to have a nightcap in his room? His room wasn't even on my floor! I checked again that the door was double locked and quickly turned off the light. The beauty parlour must have done its job, but the companionship of strange men was not what I wanted. To be alone was perfect.

Next day was for shopping and sightseeing. At Lane Crawford, I chose a string of Mikimoto pearls for Mum and one for myself. At the Daimaru department store, I splurged on lacy French underwear (never had so much been paid for so little). I also bought a wig (destined never to be worn – it was too hot), as Win's SAS friend 'Ned' Kelly teased me relentlessly about the state of my hair.

I saw the legendary Suzy Wong/Wan Chai nightclub area, then headed to the China Fleet, the famous store run by the British navy. I hired a rickshaw, the local version of a cyclo, to take me from the Star Ferry to the China Fleet, but I felt so guilty watching the sweating runner hauling me uphill instead of pedalling effortlessly behind me, that I got out and paid him off before we had gone any distance. To say the China Fleet was like the American PX in Vung Tau is to compare David Jones with a Mum and Dad corner shop. One whole floor

was devoted to reputable Chinese firms for displaying their
wares. Items cost slightly more than elsewhere, but shoppers
were guaranteed a good brand and a well-made product. Like
a kid in a lolly shop, I selected gifts for everyone. And
I bought the Shirley Bassey LP that 2 Field Ambulance elec-
trician Bill Gleeson had asked me to get for him, as well as a
handbag, luxurious bath soaps, cosmetics and other female
goodies for myself.

I had finished shopping for the moment, when a handsome
GI asked me to lunch. Always happy to dine in the company
of an army man, I readily agreed. That evening I had dinner
at the Hilton Grill with a USAF Major, who then took me
to see British comedian Tony Hancock at the Mandarin
Hotel. I felt much more at home with the gentlemanly
military than with businessmen looking for a good time.

Before dinner, I telephoned my family – my first phone call
home in eight months. 'Your friend Vivienne rang me from
Melbourne,' Mum said, in a tone that indicated she had heard
all my news already. In her old-fashioned fear of the cost of
long distance calls (or maybe she was too emotional), she
hurried off the line. I had to depend on my brothers to fill me
in on what was happening at home. They eagerly told me that
Star Trek had just arrived on television to transport us 'where
no man has gone before'. More amazing, however, was the
news that Aborigines had been on strike for months at Wave
Hill cattle station in central Australia for higher wages and
for conditions similar to those of white workers – unheard of
in those less-enlightened days. The Aborigines were learning
from the American Civil Rights Movement.

The entire week I indulged in an eating frenzy, one great
meal after another. There was a sumptuous breakfast at the

hotel, followed by lunch at Jimmie's Kitchen. For afternoon tea I sat beside the towering marble pillars of the colonial Peninsular Hotel among well-tailored and bejewelled expatriates and Chinese. I selected my own fish for dinner at the Aberdeen floating city of boats at sunset.

Hong Kong was a visual feast as well. I rode the Star Ferry across the harbour to Kowloon and back again on the cheapest fare, just as the Chinese did. I stared in awe at the superbly tailored suits, dresses and shirts they wore as they travelled to their jobs. But unlike them, for whom the ride was business as usual, I looked with shining eyes at the red-sailed junks, the grey Royal Navy ships at anchor and the water taxis whizzing their rich passengers across the glittering harbour. I saw the homes of Hong Kong's poor – shanty shacks clinging to the mountainside – that often were washed away in the mudslides that followed the typhoons. I gave the somewhat garish Tiger Balm Gardens a miss – I wanted a 'Sound of Music', 'everything's coming up roses' week.

Within three days my new dress was ready, and I wore it blissfully when Major USAF (he had become a regular dinner companion, with both of us whizzing around solo during the day) and a friend of his asked me to celebrate their last night of R&R with dinner atop the President Hotel. Despite talk to the contrary, it was evident that there were many men who did not spend their R&R ensconced in a hotel room with a woman. I was not surprised. Months earlier in Vietnam I had figured out that the men who talked the most about the girls they had enjoyed on R&R were usually the shyest and had probably spent their time alone with the TV instead. It was those who said nothing who stirred my curiosity.

With my champagne tastes, I'd intended to spend my last two days at the swanky Mandarin Hotel, but the orgy of spending had left me close to penniless. Barbara Beck (now Platt), a friend from Hobart, worked for the Department of Foreign Affairs as part of Australia's Trade Commission in Hong Kong. I spent the weekend at her small but decorative flat overlooking Repulse Bay in the upscale residential part of the island. She drove me beyond Kowloon into the New Territories, where we saw ancient walled villages, a small monastery, and straw-hatted farmers tending neat rows of vegetables on farmlands extending to what was then the Chinese border. Today the area is all high-rise buildings. We toured Sha Tin and the market at Tai Po where, for about five cents, I bought a bamboo basket that still hangs on my kitchen wall today. From Lok Ma Chau (known to tourists as Look, Ma, there's China) we stood overlooking the sluggish brown river, which at that time bordered the British-controlled New Territories, and peered curiously at the forbidden land of Red China.

During dinner at a Chinese restaurant in the New Territories, Barb taught me a lesson in international economics. She peered at the menu with a furrowed brow and then summoned the proprietor. 'This isn't right. I think you've given us the tourist menu.' Faced with a challenge, he scurried away and came back with a different menu. One glance and Barb said firmly: 'This still isn't right. Please bring me the menu for the Chinese, not the expats.' A third menu arrived, with prices astonishingly cheaper. We settled down to a meal more suited to government and Red Cross budgets.

I had been too busy shopping to explore Hong Kong Island itself. On my last day of R&R, Barb took me to the new

Stanley Market (huge today, but then small and very good), Deepwater Bay, West Town and Cat Street, ending with a Malay meal and a screening of *To Kill a Mockingbird* at City Hall.

Each day had been more wonderful than the one before, but the following morning the bubble burst. Before seven Barb drove me to the President Hotel to catch the R&R bus that took me and my sizable load of luggage to the airport – and back to the war. I joined eighty-three very subdued, very poor soldiers on a plane that, to my surprise, was going to Cam Ranh Bay rather than to Saigon. I didn't care. Cam Ranh Bay, with two airstrips and a deep-water port, was said to be the biggest base in South-East Asia. When it turned out to be huge and unattractive, I realised how lucky I was to be located at our seaside resort.

I stood sweltering in the middle of the vast Cam Ranh Bay airstrip, waiting for a plane to Tan Son Nhut. I had bought butter and a wheel of Dutch cheese as a gift for the Officers' Mess, and I didn't dare think what was happening to it as we sweated on the hot tarmac. Someone tall with a ramrod-straight back purposefully strode towards me and my melting packages. It was General William Westmoreland, commander of all US forces in Vietnam. He nodded in my direction, and I gasped 'Hello, General'. With a strong face and determined jutting jaw, he looked to me as a general should.

I met General Westmoreland again in the early eighties, in a restaurant in Manhattan. He was celebrating his birthday with a party of friends, including Jean MacArthur (General Douglas MacArthur's widow) and others whose faces I knew from the media. I chatted to one of the women in the ladies' room. When she told Westmoreland I had seen him once in Vietnam, the General abandoned his guests and came to talk at length with my husband Jack and me. Words gushed from his mouth in an unstoppable torrent. All I remember is that he praised Australian soldiers to the skies. When we left the restaurant to take a cab home, he again came over and walked with us to the sidewalk, speaking still more of Vietnam. When at last, embarrassed by his attention, I was able to collapse into the backseat of a taxi, I turned to my husband and asked, 'Why did Westmoreland spend so much time talking to nobodies like us?' Jack replied, 'Because he was starved for recognition. He's the only general in recent American history that I know of not to return home a hero.'

At Cam Ranh Bay I caught a plane in time to connect with the afternoon Wallaby from Saigon to Vung Tau. Win had a birthday while I was gone, and our room was adorned with cards and gifts. 'I'm glad to see you,' she said casually. 'It's been a bit hectic, and I want to take a day off.' She *did* look tired, but we were tired so often that in my excitement I made no comment. Dr Paul Lennon had planned a dinner for Mrs Copeman, Jan, Win and me to celebrate Russ Copeman's good progress and my homecoming. Russell had insisted that one of his SAS mates go with us; he didn't want his mother to go anywhere in Vietnam without a bodyguard. At dinner they filled me in on news of friends and asked about Hong Kong.

The next morning I wore the wicked and wildly expensive new French lingerie under my uniform, and as I swished around getting my breakfast at the Pacific, I felt as glamorous as a Hollywood star. The prospect of seeing my cherished patients again made me the happiest person on earth.

But on the drive to 2 Field Ambulance, Win told me what no one yet had mentioned. The past week in Phuoc Tuy province had been no less than horrendous.

17

If You Could Swing with the Vines Like Tarzan

Should you put your foot to that flat rock or the clump of weeds to its rear? Paddy dike or water? You wish you were Tarzan, able to swing with the vines. You try to trace the footprints of the man to your front. You give it up when he curses you for following too closely; better one man dead than two. The moment-to-moment, step-by-step decision-making preys on your mind. The effect sometimes is paralysis. You are slow to rise from rest breaks. You walk like a wooden man . . . with your eyes pinned to the dirt, spine arched, and you are shivering, shoulders hunched.

Tim O'Brien, *If I Die in a Combat Zone*

ON 21 FEBRUARY, 1967, AS I WAS happily on my way to Hong Kong, the Fifth Battalion Bravo Company 4 Platoon was devastated by mines in the Long Hai hills, north-east of Vung Tau. It was the biggest landmine disaster involving Australian troops in Vietnam.

Travelling through the jungle in a convoy, the lead APC – manned by 4 Platoon – ran over what probably was a powerful command-detonated landmine. The massive explosion blew the 12-tonne APC into the air and tossed it three metres away, leaving a deep crater in the ground. The APC came to rest on its side in a heavily-seeded minefield. Some of the men were torn apart by the blast, others crushed to death by the APC.

The most urgent need was to find a safe path through the mine field to reach the wounded. The rescue effort turned into a catastrophe when someone stepped on a jumping jack mine that sprayed hundreds of deadly shards of shrapnel into a group of medics and signalmen, killing or injuring most of them. The company commander, Major Bruce McQualter, 4 Platoon commander, Lt Jack Carruthers, and five other men were killed that day or died later. The Diggers didn't even have the satisfaction of striking back. The enemy was nowhere to be seen.

L/Cpl John Nyhuis, who had been in hospital for surgery the previous October, was riding inside the APC when it ran over the mine. He was lucky. He escaped with shrapnel wounds in his right shoulder from a piece of flying debris. 'When the fireball went through, it took off all my body hair,' he told me one morning, as I listened, horrified. 'All I remember is I was trying to get up from the ground when the second mine went off, but I felt numb from the waist down. I have no idea how any of us got out of that APC. My next memory is of being on the Dust-Off with Lt Carruthers and seeing what a mess his head was.' John Nyhuis was back on operation about two weeks later.

Years later John recalled: 'Only one other guy and I, of the thirteen or fourteen who were actually in, or on, the APC that was hit, went back. A few weeks later the other guy, Pte Richard Edward Lloyd, was killed by a mine. The rest of my time in Vietnam, two months, is just a blank. After getting home, it was almost twenty years before I saw any of those guys again. Of the original thirty-two that went away, there were only about fifteen of us left.' John went home and got on with his life, but today he still has nightmares about the APC tragedy and other bad times he had on operations. When Private Lloyd, a National Serviceman, was killed, he had less than three weeks to go before he would have been cruising home on HMAS *Sydney*.

Like John, each surviving man vividly remembers every detail of the tragedy. By chance, the Battalion doctor Tony White was only a two-minute skim by helicopter from the scene and was able to tend the many casualties before Dust-Offs arrived. On the thirtieth anniversary of the disaster, Tony wrote an article for *The Canberra Times* in which he described himself as 'moving about among the wounded with one hand protectively over my balls, even though I knew that these mines could ablate not only the genitals but the legs and more'. Ignoring their own safety, Tony and the medics moved selflessly through scenes of indescribable horror. Some men, in a state of shock, were mute; others, with dangling limbs and gaping wounds, cried out for relief. So dangerous was their work in the mine field that every one of the medics was injured.

The wounded flooded in to both the Australian and the American hospitals. And I wasn't there to help. Five soldiers were flown straight to 3 Field in Saigon, a hospital better equipped to cope with critical brain and spinal cord injuries.

Win always kept a large Esky-type box in our office, as it was perfect for cooling drinks. One of the medics asked if he could use it. 'I gave it to him, thinking I would get it back,' Win told me a week later, her eyes brimming with tears. 'John, another medic, said "You won't see that box again." They wanted it for one of the dead soldiers – there wasn't much left of him.'

'The hospital was packed,' Win went on. 'They even had to borrow an airconditioned trailer from the Americans to put two of our seriously injured boys in. The medical staff worked straight through until 4 am, then had a couple of hours sleep and went back on duty for another full day.'

For Win, the anguish didn't stop. While Jan took Red Cross paper mugs to the civilian nurses at Le Loi – they had no cups for their patients and were making do with converted beer cans – Win did the rounds at the 36th. There she ran into one of her favourite ex-patients who was visiting his mates. The soldier told Win that while he was away from Nui Dat on R&C, two of his friends were killed in the fray. One of them had taken his place in the platoon when he went to Vung Tau, and the soldier blamed himself for the loss: 'It should be me that's dead. It's my fault he's dead.' Warm and giving, Win wanted to do something to wipe away the torment the young man was suffering and talked to him for more than an hour. 'Pray for your mate, and lead a good full life,' she said. 'Fate has saved you from death.' She drove him back into Vung Tau, where she knew his intention was to get drunk.

Win shed some of her grief at the week's events by writing her mother long letters about the patients. At the 36th there was an Aussie who had lost his leg. His brother, also in Vietnam, sat at his bedside to give him moral support. 'Both boys were very brave and hopeful,' she wrote. 'I guess one can always get an artificial leg, but brains and spines for the patients at 3 Field Hospital in Saigon are hard to come by. I am thinking so much of the loved ones at home worrying.' The next day Win turned twenty-four.

Win's birthday started early. She had to pick up Mrs Copeman at 6.30 am, then drop Jan – on her way to Saigon to visit the seriously wounded Australians – at the airbase by seven. With me on R&R, Win had to look after the patients in both hospitals that day. Before stopping for breakfast, she took Mrs Copeman to see how Russell had fared during the night. She collected another donation of books from the Americans, visited the large number of patients at the 36th Evac, and by the time she arrived to start work at her heaviest job at 2 Field Ambulance, the patients were looking at their watches in mock annoyance at her late arrival.

'I gave them all black looks for their trouble,' Win said. 'To cap off the day, someone backed into our little VW, and 101 Workshop told me what with war needs coming before ours, it would be four days before they could beat out the dent. I picked up Jan at the airbase and was so exhausted I had to cancel my birthday dinner. Jan cooked me C-rations on our hotplate instead.'

My week away from Win had made me aware she was becoming increasingly despondent. She loved the patients as though they were her own flesh and blood. 'Jack Carruthers, one of the boys flown to hospital in Saigon, died this morning from the head injuries he suffered at Long Hai,' she said softly. 'I feel it's a blessing, as he would have had to spend the rest of his life in an iron lung, and he was married with a family. This way he knows no more pain.' Then stabbing the air with her finger as if I'd caused it, she intoned: 'I *hate* this bloody war.'

It had been a bad week for everyone. Beds were in desperately short supply, and 2 Field's staff was pushed to the limits. It was decided to medevac as many of the borderline patients as possible the following Monday, and the fitter ones were sent to the R&C centre to recuperate before going back to their units. On the day I returned from Hong Kong, fifty-one men went home – the largest number yet to be medevaced on a RAAF Hercules C130. Win and Jan had shopped and sent telegrams for them all. The medevac was so large that television channels Seven and the ABC were there to film the departure. Denis Gibbons, a freelance magazine journalist who at that time was working on a story about Jan, Win and me for *Woman's Day*, also covered the event. 'I am thrilled for the boys when they go home,' Win told me with a wan smile, 'but I feel upset to lose them. I get so used to having the cheeky devils around.'

That bleak month more than 360 wounded Americans were sent to the 36th Evac, by no means one of the busiest hospitals in Vietnam. One of the GIs had just had his left arm and left leg amputated when Koopsie received a message from his mother, who was dying of cancer. The mother, not knowing her son had been wounded, asked for him to come home. She no longer could look after the soldier's twelve-year-old brother alone. The GI died a day later – another of the thousands of daily tragedies. And to add to our misery, we knew that in 3 Field Hospital in Saigon there were dozens of patients who never would be mentally responsible again, having to live out their lives wholly dependent on others. My R&R euphoria had vaporised, to be replaced by a massive guilt that I hadn't been at work to help.

* * *

We became adept at switching seamlessly from the tragic to the hilarious or to the mundane. We were ready for a dose of the mundane, and we got it. Red Cross NHQ had been begging us to make a film of our work in Vietnam to be used for fund-raising publicity. We nominated Win and her movie camera for the job. While Jan and I worked with the patients, Win kept the camera running. Early next day, to take advantage of the morning light, we left for Nui Dat to do more filming. Three SAS boys who'd been visiting Russell Copeman drove us, making a stop in Ba Ria to pick up their laundry. Even tough fighting warriors have to take care of their smalls!

That afternoon Major Donohue ran another of his WHAM programs, so Win, camera in hand, and I joined him as he drove into the villages and handed out sweets to the children. They all knew the major and came running from everywhere when they saw him. One of the mothers, her face beaming with goodwill, asked us all in for tea. Saigon tea? The legendary amber soft drink of the bar girls that could cost a hopeful soldier a fortune? It would be rude not to go, and we couldn't decline a gracious gesture when we were trying to win hearts and minds. But we didn't want to get sick. Maybe she'd boil the water well. We accepted, leaving John Donohue outside to guard the Land Rover and watch for the enemy. To our relief, we were offered not tea but watermelon and bananas, which we ate, although even the fruit potentially could give us hepatitis. We sat in silence in the simple, dirt-floored house, smiling at our hostess all the while to show our appreciation. The woman and others of the village filled sandbags for the Aussies for less than a cent a bag. They earned about a dollar a day – less than the bar price of a

Saigon tea – for the backbreaking chore. With the men usually away, it was the women and children who did all the work.

Late afternoon, after a drink at the Dat with SAS to toast Russell's much hoped for recovery, we waited in our green fatigues with a group of smoking, joking soldiers for the chopper to take us on the ten-minute flight to Vung Tau. With a laugh we realised that all of us were squatting over wide-spread, bent knees, our backsides nearly hitting the ground. Unconsciously, we had all adopted the surprisingly comfortable, but for women most unladylike, waiting position of the Vietnamese, which we at first had savagely disparaged as the 'noggy squat'.

As for Russell Copeman, it seemed as though everyone's prayers had been answered. He was going home on the next medevac. Pearl Copeman watched ecstatically as Russ was loaded onto the Hercules with other battle casualties for return to Australia. Dr Gregg advised Mrs Copeman that if Russell survived the exhausting trip home, particularly the first few hours to Butterworth, there was some chance he might make a good recovery. From Butterworth there was the much longer haul to Darwin, Richmond, and then by ambulance to 2 Military Hospital at nearby Ingleburn. Two days later Win escorted Mrs Copeman to Saigon and put her on the first available commercial flight out of Vietnam.

As Dr Gregg predicted, the long trip and ambulance ride worsened Russell's condition. By the time Mrs Copeman arrived at Ingleburn, her son's health was such that she phoned her husband in Tiberias to tell him she thought Russell's time was short. She needed her husband's support during the last days of their first-born's short life. Major Copeman signalled both Australian army HQ and the UN for release from his posting and within twenty-four hours was granted approval. Russell courageously fought on for a few more weeks, then died peacefully at 2.30 am on 10 April, 1967, three months after he had been shot.

When word reached 2 Field Ambulance, we were all devastated. Russell had put up such a brave fight. A great love grows between medical personnel and those entrusted to their care when, for so long, the staff wills them – prays for them – to keep living. Jim Townson summed up the sense of defeat and loss: 'Everyone had fought long and hard to save Russ. Once we got him sitting up and well enough to go home at last, we all thought he would live. And the Copemans were such terrific people.'

Russell Copeman was the only SAS man to die as a result of enemy action during the years the unit was in Vietnam (1966–1971), although one other man, Pte D. J. E. Fisher, was declared missing in action in 1969. Three others died from illness.

Russell was given a military funeral at Wollongong. It was attended by hundreds of people including Juvy Matten, the man who had carried Russ out of the bush. On ANZAC Day, 2001, the SAS Association presented John W. 'Juvy' Matten with a citation for bravery from his 'brothers in arms' in recognition of selfless deeds on that far-off day. Russell's father, Jim, and his sister, Ann, now the mother of four, flew to Perth to witness the presentation. Pearl Copeman, in her eighties, could not accompany them, but is still living on King Island.

As for Juvy Matten's heroic rescue, Ann said: 'We are all forever grateful to Juvy, this *brave* man, for giving us a few more months with Russell. I still cannot understand why he was not officially decorated for his courage that day. Juvy must have had nerves of steel to be able to do what he did, and he was only nineteen. It must have been traumatic for him.'

Juvy says only: 'You can't leave your mate behind.'

18

Bubonic Plague

ONE SUNDAY IN MARCH, JAN, WIN AND I attended Mass in the small white-washed Vietnamese church close by the Villa. Catholics had come to Vietnam as missionaries two or three centuries earlier, and in recent years many Catholics had fled to the South from North Vietnam. With ornate carvings of the crucifix and the Virgin Mary, a side altar and a full congregation, the inside of the church looked like any Roman Catholic church I had been to at home. The Mass was in Vietnamese but we could follow it. There all similarity ended. Men sat on the right side of the centre aisle and women on the left, as they still do today in Vietnamese churches. Alternately, each side responded to the priest's songs and chants; the women in their high sweet voices were answered by the deeper tenor and bass offerings of the men. The Vietnamese language is tonal, and similar words can have different meanings depending on which tone is used, resulting in the lilting singsong of Vietnamese. When raised in joyful sound, their voices are spellbinding, and their chorus swept over us in uplifting waves.

Despite their suffering, these people, who never had known peace, were maintaining the normalities of life and traditions in the face of hardship and danger. They went to church to renew their faith in God and the hope He offered. The Vietnamese were more than survivors. Stoically, resourcefully, they accepted what life tossed at them and kept going.

Each of us left the Mass feeling enriched and otherworldly, but we were jolted back to reality outside the church doors. A raucous jumble of people hawked tawdry religious artefacts in an effort to feed hungry children. Win and I fled that circus to go to work. Fortunately, no one needed much attention that day, and we were able to take time out to attend three goodbye parties. The feeling was widespread that as people came to the end of their year of hardships and were about to return home, they should be given a suitable send-off. We then dashed home after the parties to shower and change, because that night we were taking patients to what was to be the best show we saw in Vietnam.

Beloved Australian trouper Lorrae Desmond was performing with Jim Gussey and the ABC Dance Band at all the Australian camps. We attended the show at the RAAF Airmen's Mess, known as the Ettamogah Pub. Most female entertainers at that time, Aussie and American alike, wore American fatigues for their shows. But Lorrae gave the boys what they wanted to see. She must have been poured into her long tight gown, cut dangerously low to reveal a delicious amount of her breasts. She sparkled with sex appeal at each shift of her voluptuous body. Dinah Lee and other female vocalists wore brief minis or thigh-revealing skirts. The atmosphere from the stage was electric. Jim Gussey and his band were bouncy and joyful, but it was Lorrae the men cheered with whistles and catcalls. Lorrae clearly was aware of what her womanly presence meant to the soldiers, and they went wild. If they hadn't, as Bob Hope put it, we might have needed a new military!

As the only women in the audience, Jan, Win and I were ushered, as always, into the best seats in the front row – the perfect position for the show's comedian to make witty play on our female presence. To cap off the day, the RAAF flew in delicacies from all over South-East Asia and turned on a feast of crabs, oysters, lobsters, asparagus and other exotic foods we hadn't seen in months.

Next evening, the boys from Down Under triumphed again. At a bingo fund-raiser, the 36th Evac staff raised $645, just what they needed to buy some medical equipment. Joe McAllister, one of the Fifth Battalion wounded in the February 21 mine disaster, won the only prize, $100. It was quite a feat, as there were only four Aussies present, including Win and me. Our boys again had upheld their reputation for beating the GIs at whatever they took on.

The original medical team from the 36th went home, and their replacements arrived in about the second week of March, just in time for the first official dance of ALSG's Officers' Mess. The Cabaret on Saturday, 11 March, was a rare occasion to give the officers the old razzle-dazzle. The excitement built all week, and Koopsie decided to glamorise Win for the festivity. She set up a beauty parlour in our room, where she delighted Win with a makeover – pulling her hair off her face and applying eye shadow, mascara, a new lipstick and blush. The results were stunning.

The men arranged amongst themselves who would escort us, and at seven on the dot our partners arrived at Jan's room for a drinks party. We scrounged enough chairs to sit on and there were, of course, the twin beds. We made an elegant group as we sat sipping our drinks before we climbed into our glass carriages – army Land Rovers – for the drive to the Back Beach camp.

The tented Officers' Mess had been transformed. Chairs and tables were scattered cabaret-style outside the tent on a temporary patio of rough-hewn slabs covering the sand. Coloured lights were strung around. Women in pretty dresses moved among the officers. Mess stewards circulated with large platters of canapés. And considering their meagre resources, the cooks outdid themselves with an astonishing variety of food.

Usually we were greeted by a pile of weapons outside the Mess. Although it was mandatory that every man in ALSG have a weapon with him at all times in the camp, a standing rule forbade weapons inside the Mess. That night no weapons were visible. Instead, the tall President of the Mess, Major Ken Petersen, stood at the entrance, greeting each guest as formally as if he were hosting a baronial ball. Ken, who sat with us at breakfast most mornings, failed to recognise the new knock-'em-dead Win and politely introduced himself. 'He shook my hand,' Win gleefully recalls, 'and said he hoped I would enjoy myself as guest of the Australian Mess.' She looked so spectacular that other people asked Jan and me who she was. The non-stop dancing was a true call to arms – and legs. We would have danced happily until dawn broke over the South China Sea but had to head home to beat curfew. Even so, Win and I were the last women to leave. The Cabaret had been a smash.

* * *

Still more of the Long Hai mine explosion victims had become well enough for medevac. One was Mick Dwyer, who had been taken at first to 3 Field Hospital in Saigon for neurosurgery and then transferred to 2 Field. Mick spent most of his day lying on his stomach on a specially constructed stretcher, as he was paralysed from the waist down. Despite his injuries, he charmed us with his engaging personality and radiant smile. He was about twenty-one and had been married just before going to Vietnam. He never once complained.

Win and I decided to celebrate our joy at more boys returning home with a special night out at the Vung Tau cinema. My American PX friend Hue and her friend, Hoa, who also worked the cash registers, had invited us. They knew we had wanted to go to the Vietnamese movies but were scared to mix in a local crowd. Our hostesses met us in the foyer with the tickets, two fans and some sticks of sugar cane. The fans were essential, as the crowded theatre was not airconditioned. So far the evening was going well. As we took our seats though, it was plainly evident that we were the only round-eyes in the theatre. The next couple of hours were anxious ones, for our size and looks made us stand out from the crowd. The show was a double feature. We laughed at Donald O'Connor mouthing French with Vietnamese sub-titles in *Wonders of Aladdin*; the second feature was a Japanese movie with explicit sex scenes that caused our teenage hosts much embarrassment. It seemed forever before the film ended and even longer before we could make our sweaty way through the crowd to the exit.

'Did you like cinema?' Hue asked eagerly. Gamely we nodded our heads. 'Now we go get ice-cream,' she said firmly.

'Where?' I had my usual worries of street vendors' hygiene.

'Cyrnos. It very nice. It okay for you to eat, Miss Jean,' Hue answered. Cyrnos *was* okay for us, and we thought the girls perhaps wanted a peek at its upscale interior. Everything went smoothly until *l'addition* was presented. The ice-creams were nearly $6 each in today's money – a price not suited to our budgets. Whenever Win and I had eaten at Cyrnos, except for Hilda's farewell lunch, we had been treated. Behind the girls' backs Win muttered: 'Remind me never to eat here again when I'm paying.' We seldom had to buy a meal in Vietnam, but money – or rather the lack of it – was always a problem.

An infantry patient, wounded months earlier, had arrived back in hospital – this time at 2 Field Ambulance – as the steamy March air was hampering his breathing. When Dr Paul Lennon was making his ward rounds, he found the patient's chest to be congested by asthma.

'How long have you been like this?' he demanded.

'All my life, Sir,' the Digger answered.

'How do you manage?' the doctor asked.

'When I find breathing difficult, I use my "puffer", Sir.'

'Did you tell the doctor about this when you were called up?' (Asthma sufferers normally were not put into the infantry.)

'Yes, Sir, I did.'

Paul Lennon's brown eyes began to blaze behind his horn-rimmed glasses, and he asked forcefully, 'How would you make out if you ever got into a fire fight?'

'I'd manage, Sir,' the patient quietly replied.

Paul moved on, marvelling about the stupidity of the army for putting him in the infantry, and of the patient for being there. The medic accompanying the doctor on his rounds took him aside: 'I think you should know, Sir, he's the most famous of our National Servicemen, Ron Eglinton. He got the Military Medal for bravery at Long Tan.'

In mid-March, Lt Gen Thomas Daly, Chief of the General Staff and the army's top man, arrived to inspect 2 Field Ambulance. We understood that the General needed to know what was going on. For the working stiffs, however, his visit disrupted the daily battle to complete basic work as everyone flapped around to ensure the hospital was suitably spiffed up. Thinking that all visits from VIPs were a gigantic pain, I muttered to no one in particular: 'Far better to let him see how we normally cope.' We hoped improvements would follow his tour of the hospital.

That evening Win and I attended a special party at Nui Dat to which we had been summoned in rare style: by printed invitation. Not one of those embossed gilt-edged 'invites' that look so grand, but one equally impressive, for the typed white paper had the logo of a fighting infantry company drawn on it.

The Leaders of the Boots and Souls, led by Major Harry Smith, Military Cross, Company Commander of Delta Company, 6 RAR, request the pleasure of your company at the Opening of the new Officers' & Sergeants' Mess from 1930 hours on March 14. Dress optional.

There was a 'Minties Moment' on our late afternoon flight to the party at the sharp end. The smaller Iroquois helicopters generally had seats for four passengers only, plus the door gunner and crewman. After Win and I boarded at 2 Field's

Vampire Dust-Off pad, we stopped at another helipad for more passengers. They turned out to be Colonel Chambers, CO of ALSG, and his VIP guests, two New Zealand colonels and a major. Colonel Chambers' face reflected horror, dismay and 'this can't be happening to me' when he saw that the seats for his VIPs were occupied by two women. Smiling sweetly, we held on to our places and tucked our feet in to give the brass, good sports all, more room to sit on the floor. When the memorable party ended and we were heading home, our pilot took us on a swan around the countryside, showing us bombed villages and ending with a low-altitude view of Vung Tau. But that was about as close as we wanted to get – the town that was our home had been hit by an outbreak of bubonic plague.

Dr Spike Lucas, one of the Australian doctors working with the medical team at the civilian hospital, Le Loi, first diagnosed the disease when he was doing a routine medical examination of a Vietnamese man. Le Loi's resources were meagre, but when the civilian team knew it had a potential epidemic on its hands, all stops were pulled out to prevent the disease from spreading. The staff immediately segregated the infected man from other patients, but after two days of isolation, the family-minded Vietnamese disappeared forever, absent without leave, AWOL. The town – except for our living quarters – was put off-limits to us all.

Bubonic plague, also known as the Black Death, while not common today in the Western world, is the same deadly disease that killed more than a quarter of the population of Europe in the Middle Ages. Fleas that bite infected rats (historically nature's most versatile weapons of mass destruction) carry the plague and infect humans. Huge rats, many of them larger than the average domestic cat, were a common sight around the streets of Vung Tau, and fumigation teams sprayed pesticide in an attempt to eradicate the vermin. Nurse Jenny James recalls: 'Only later did we discover that the worst thing to do was kill the rats. Then the fleas had no host and looked to humans as a source of blood, which caused people to become infected. We were taking all the usual precautions associated with infectious diseases – masks, footwear cover, hand washing – but this was scary stuff. There was no known treatment.'

At the Back Beach camp, Colonel Rodgers was concerned. Many of the locally employed Vietnamese who did the menial work at the camp came from the nearby village where the plague had originated. And rats from the village could come into ALSG. The RAAF officers and men, who, like us, lived near the centre of Vung Tau, were also at risk of contagion. Dirty, rat-infested alleyways backed onto their villas, and the plague-carrying rats might enter their living quarters. Dr Ian Favilla had long complained that those quarters were not of a suitable standard. The RAAF villas were thoroughly dusted with flea powder, as was the Villa DuBois. I wasn't worried. I still felt ten feet tall and invulnerable.

The plague reached epidemic proportions among the Vietnamese. Although both the American and the Australian medical teams inoculated the local population en masse, many people died. Le Loi and a small Korean hospital nearby were pushed beyond their capabilities. We kept our distance from our courageous friends at Le Loi but worried for their health. Vung Tau wasn't declared free of the plague until a month after the initial outbreak, but such were the preventative measures taken that no Australian was infected.

* * *

Western Australian Red Cross senior executive Greg Rowe, who worked in a five-man team with Vietnamese Red Cross at Quang Ngai, helped care for 11,000 refugees left homeless by war and floods. Surrounded by aggressive VC and battles that raged non-stop, the camp had been shelled three times in a month. On a visit to see Win in Vung Tau, Greg told a story that upset us. A couple of weeks earlier our side claimed to have killed a thousand VC and to have captured many more. General Westmoreland and SVN's Prime Minister, Nguyen Cao Ky, congratulated the soldiers at a victory march. The enemy prisoners, their hands tied behind their backs, walked blindfolded through the streets while their fellow countrymen screamed abuse. Then the ARVN took them away to torture them for information and afterwards probably shot them.

Win and I were appalled. How ghastly it was to hear of one Vietnamese torturing another. We hoped our boys, who were so clearly learning to hate, wouldn't carry the hatred home with them. But they *did* hate. It was understandable. One day Win, to my great admiration, severely admonished them. A VC patient, who had ten machine-gun bullets in him, hadn't been expected to make it, but he lived. One of our own soldiers was brought in at that same time. He hadn't seemed so badly wounded, but he died. Some of our patients irrationally blamed the VC for the Aussie's death and taunted him, 'Tomorrow you go Saigon get neck stretched.' Crying, the VC took to his bed and didn't budge for a couple of days. When he felt the danger had passed, he ventured out again, only to face more abuse. Win rebuked the men for their sadistic pleasure. She understood their sentiments, but that was no reason to be cruel. Eventually the VC was sent to

Saigon, and the fate the Diggers had predicted for him doubt-less came to pass.

As for Stumpy, he had arrived at 2 Field Ambulance in September, trembling all over; six months later, on the March day he left us, he was trembling again. The Military Police took him away for transfer to the ARVN as a POW. As we wished him luck and shook his hand, he vibrated like a leaf, but he tried to put on a brave front. I think he had been as fond of us as we had been of him. He was in hospital longer than any other patient. Rumour had it that later Stumpy was tossed out of a helicopter alive.

By the last week of March the days became so hot and steamy that the wet season couldn't be far away. The sea was a deep blue, and the Long Hai hills to the east across the bay looked a magnificent bluish purple – marred only by the smoke from navy shelling and bombing. Long Hai and the Horseshoe further east were the areas from which so many of our casualties now came. Two National Servicemen, Privates Bracewell and Hart, arrived from the fighting in that region by Dust-Off. Dennis Bracewell was paralysed from the chest down; Peter Hart had lost an eye and had critical head injuries.

Suffering a broken spine, Dennis Bracewell also had difficulty breathing and talking. In post-op, not long after regaining consciousness, Dennis whispered: 'You have no idea how good it is to be alive and how dear life is.' Next day, Win was about to write letters home for Dennis, who had been told he was to be on the next medevac flight. 'I'm so excited to be going home to my family and my girl alive,' he joyfully told her. Win had just pulled out her pen and paper when the doctors came in to treat him. She promised to come back after lunch and thought about him non-stop as she went about her duties. She returned at 2 pm to find she still could not see him, because in the bed next to him, his mate Peter Hart had just died from his head injuries.

Win said later: 'I am sure it was for the best, poor thing. Peter never would have been all right again. So with padres and doctors and medics preparing him for his last journey home, I decided it would be wiser to visit Dennis the next day.' Early next morning, before the doctors made their rounds, Win collected her writing materials and went to see Dennis, but a medic met her at the door. Dennis had died half an hour earlier. With tears spilling from her eyes, Win said: 'I guess now he will be going home with Peter Hart. I am going to write that letter to Dennis's family. I'll tell them what a brave and wonderful son they had.'

In light of the death of Dennis Bracewell, who so wanted to live, the story Koopsie and Vivienne told us about a senseless accident at the American soldiers' barracks opposite the 36th Evac was as maddening as it was tragic. One of the GIs had found two halves of a grenade at the beach, put them together, and took the little bomb back to the barracks. The soldiers used it as a ball to toss around. The grenade blew up, killing one of the men outright and wounding three others. It was such a stupid act that we scarcely could believe it.

Easter was approaching, and we'd been flat out preparing. We wanted the Easter Bunny to leave little treats for the patients to break up the monotony of their days. Padre Pres Sullivan already had made Easter cards to go with our gifts. After an almost fruitless search for sweets in all the PXs,

I finally found some chewy caramel Columbines, and for several evenings after work we gift-wrapped them in small festive bundles.

On Good Friday, Win and I took the Anglican and the Protestant patients to the 8 am service in the new ANZAC Chapel at Vung Tau. Jan took the Roman Catholics to Mass at five that afternoon. Pres Sullivan, the Protestant padre and a man of exquisite taste, had made special programs listing the order of service for all churchgoers. It was strange to stand in a war zone singing, as powerfully as we could, the old, familiar hymns: 'There is a Green Hill Far Away', 'Crown Him with Many Crowns', 'When I Survey the Wondrous Cross', and finally, to end the Holy Communion service, 'The King of Love My Shepherd Is'. The collection went toward furnishings for the still sparsely-equipped chapel.

Afterwards we took Hot Cross buns, tea, coffee and hot chocolate around to the patients. The soldiers, who usually had to fend for themselves, loved to be fussed over. In the afternoon we organised bingo, with small prizes for each winner to make it interesting. Everyone knew that small was all the prizes could be, but small was great.

On Easter Day, Win and I went to the Task Force base for Padre Eddie Bennett's service in the newly-built chapel there. Seeming oblivious to the continuous firing of heavy artillery, the clanking of APCs going out to battle, and the endless chop-chop of helicopter gunships overhead, Diggers in their jungle greens reverently rejoiced at the Risen Christ. I didn't have their calm focus. I worried distractedly about where the action was and whether it meant more casualties. The American battery next to Nui Dat had been pounded by mortar rounds a couple of days earlier, with a number of men killed, but the Task Force had not been attacked for some time. Would it be their turn soon?

After church a Digger told of the frustration they all felt fighting an unseen enemy who so skilfully used the areas above and below his native terrain to hide. 'We know positively that we've got the VC completely surrounded. But when we close in, there's no one there. It's like fighting a ghost that evaporates into thin air. Sometimes we bomb the VC and go in next morning for a body count. There's not a body in sight.' He banged his hand on a Land Rover, exasperated. We were back in Vung Tau mid-morning and gave the boys the Easter gifts. Win supplemented each gift with a kiss on the cheek – kisses that some men say they remember fondly today. The Sex Machine abstained.

The Australian War Memorial in Canberra, continuing a tradition extending back beyond World War I, sent an official war artist, Bruce Fletcher, to capture the Diggers in sketches and paintings. Bruce, thirty, was an art teacher from Melbourne who knew his way around the military. He had completed a jungle training course with a promotion to lieutenant before going to Vietnam. Even so, with his sensitive face and gentle manner, he stood out from the battle-scarred Diggers. We liked him enormously, and a good thing too – we saw a lot more of him than we were anticipating.

Bruce had been in country only a short time when he was sitting in a Caribou alongside South Vietnamese troops and a stack of captured VC weapons. One of the RAAF crewmen spotted a weapon he'd never seen and picked it up, knocking a rifle off the stack. The rifle fired, hitting the artist in the ankle. Win, always one to see a glass half full, said: 'I'm going to tell him firmly he can't leave the hospital until we have some drawings to hang on our office wall.'

With a white plaster on his leg, Bruce became a familiar figure around 2 Field Ambulance. He painted many scenes of daily activities and repeatedly asked Win and me to sit for him. Although we knew the paintings would be wonderful publicity for the Red Cross, we had no sense of history or desire for fame, and the constant needs of patients took all our time. I kept saying, 'Next week for sure, I promise.' Bruce gave up waiting for us to sit for him and went ahead anyway. He did an oil painting of me in a ward with patients and one of Win with stretcher patients about to be loaded into a Hercules C130A to return home to Australia. Neither painting was a close-up, but Jan and the medics agreed that we were clearly recognisable.

We never scored anything to hang on our Red Cross hut walls, but both Win and I have our portraits in the Australian War Memorial. Years later I saw the painting of myself hanging there, no doubt with Back Beach sand imbedded in the paint. It was one of the most exciting moments of my life. Impulsively I turned to tourists standing in front of the painting and told them it was me! As some time had gone by since those days in Vietnam, I am not sure they were convinced, although my radiant face surely must have been believable. The next time I went back, the painting had been moved, and Win's was hanging in its place. The large number of Bruce Fletcher's paintings in the War Museum testifies to his prodigious productivity and skill. He was unstoppable. When he was well enough to go out on patrol at the sharp end, he realised the white plaster – still on his leg

– was dangerously visible in the jungle. He camouflaged it with paint.

Cpl Clifford R. Bell from 101 Workshop, an accomplished cartoonist, was our next artist in hospital. Known far and wide as 'The Ghan', for he resembled an Afghan camel driver from Australia's dead centre, he probably was close to forty, considerably older than the other men, and could only be described as a character. The Ghan caused his officers to tear out their hair in frustration, but he kept the rest of us laughing. One officer told me: 'He was mixed up in some shady dealings, but he always had an excuse that just got him off the hook. His flowery eloquence always started with, "My dear chap . . .".'

While in hospital he drew for us a series of cartoons of life in Vietnam. We had planned to get them framed and hung on the walls of the wards – my job. I regret I never got around to it.

19

Beyond Grieving

THE GENEROSITY OF THE AMERICANS WAS UNSTINTING, and we were never shy to take advantage of it. Out sightseeing with a Land Rover full of patients, I spotted some GIs loading mattresses onto a truck. One of the patients, identifiable in his blue hospital pyjamas, displayed a Digger's customary initiative: 'Got a spare, mate? It's rough without a mattress, ya know.' (Corporals and below all slept without a mattress on their army stretchers.)

'You got it, mateys. I love the way you guys talk. There, shove along. Tally-ho,' the Yank said, as he funnelled a mattress into the Land Rover on top of patients already jammed in. Our boys hid their groans at his painful efforts to talk like us. Dumbfounded but grinning, I drove off, with the lucky Digger yelling, 'Thanks, mate,' and gripping his mattress tightly. He would be the only man in his tent to sleep in comfort.

All that excitement made strong men hungry and the patients complained they were starving. I drove to the nearest American Mess and ordered fifty-five hamburgers, most to be eaten on the spot by the ten men, the rest taken to their mates in hospital. The cook said it was his biggest order ever.

In April, we had a tragic reminder of how dangerous life in Vietnam was, even in comparatively safe Vung Tau. One of our signallers was in the centre of town at dusk, photographing the serenity of the glorious sunset, something we all had done. Without warning an ARVN soldier snatched the Aussie's camera. When the signaller tried to stop him, the thief pulled out a knife and stabbed the Aussie in the stomach. Our man was seriously wounded. In no time flat, the MPs were all over the place and closed nearby bars, as they feared the incident would lead to more trouble.

Most soldiers spent a year in country and, except for R&R, saw nothing more than their base. It was a fortunate soldier who got to see Saigon. But we Red Cross women led a luckier life. If we needed a break from the daily reality of trouble and death, we could take it. With only a couple more months in country, Win and I determined to save our days off for some sightseeing. I set off for Long Xuyen, a town on the RAAF's regular milk run of mail and supplies around the Mekong Delta, where I knew I would be welcomed by a civilian nursing team from Prince Henry's Hospital in Melbourne.

The Delta was infested with VC, yet Long Xuyen was free of war. The town flourished under the strong religious influence of the Hoa Hao faith, a Buddhist sect. The Hoa Hao hated the Communists, who had assassinated their leader and thousands of his followers in 1947, and the sect had grown steadily each year since then. No Viet Cong dared set foot in the area.

Richard Papworth, the hospital team's administrator, met me at the airport shed alongside the strip of turf surrounded by rice paddies that served as Long Xuyen's airfield. For most of the eleven kilometres into town, the road followed the course of a river that fluctuated with the tide, even though we were a long way from the coast. Long Xuyen received more rain than Vung Tau. How green everything seemed, and how clean the town. Its people appeared to lead lives hardly affected by the war and the tacky commercialism that accompanied it elsewhere in Vietnam.

The members of the surgical team – fewer than twenty doctors and nurses who were in the midst of a changeover – were accommodated richly in a large, white two-storey French villa surrounded by what once had been a well-maintained garden. Known as the White House, the villa had been home to the French administrator in colonial days, and the Japanese had used it as their headquarters in World War II. With high walls all around and two guards at the gate, it was a reminder of a once gracious lifestyle. Nurse Jennie Antons showed me to my own apartment, consisting of a large bedroom with two beds and an airconditioner, a second room that was used for storage, and my own bathroom. A married Vietnamese couple presided over the dining room, thoroughly spoiling everyone. Even the transport situation was good: the team had three vehicles – a Land Rover painted yellow (the Yellow Peril), an International Scout and a left-hand-drive Holden. They also had a Vietnamese driver. All I had to do was call out 'Pho', and Pho appeared like magic to take me wherever I wanted to go.

With nurses Dinah Gordon and Valerie Reed, I set off for the market. Dinah wanted to have a pair of shoes made – a 'while-you-wait' deal. We found a cobbler with soles on display and watched as Dinah selected the colour and style she wanted for the uppers. While she sat on a stool as the shoes were fitted and made up, Valerie and I chatted outside the store to a toothless woman with a piece of dirty fabric wrapped around her head. She was gnarled and wrinkled, but she was magnificent. Through our interpreter we learned she was seventy-two. We chatted back and forth, none of us understanding a word the other said. The old crone wore only one thong tied with string; the other foot was bare. Valerie bought her a new pair, and the woman wandered off cackling with glee, pointing to her thongs and telling people how she came by them. Had we been taken for suckers? Maybe she hung around that shoe shop every day, wearing only one thong.

Over dinner the team told me about the medical treatment available in that safe and prosperous Vietnamese town. As at Le Loi in Vung Tau, the civilian team had its own section. The Long Xuyen hospital was big for the area, but squeezing two or three patients into one bed was not unusual. When a Vietnamese came in and needed an operation, the team soon learned that the procedure must be done immediately. If the patient was told to report back later, he or she never was seen again. If a patient died, it was up to the family to remove the body as there were no undertakers. The dead were carted away in any vehicle at hand. Recently a body had been removed in the local passenger bus. One little boy who had died days earlier was still lying in the hospital bed, while his mother in the street outside tried desperately to sell his clothes.

There was a small presence of American military advisers at Long Xuyen who had taken the nurses under their generous wing. Next night at dinner, my escort was the actor who, before he was drafted, had played one of the handsome leads in the movie *Peyton Place*. His name meant nothing to me, but Win nearly had a fit of jealousy when she heard.

My two-day jaunt over, I waited at the Long Xuyen airport for the arrival of the 9.30 am Caribou. I saw American aircraft come and go and watched a Vietnamese army parade held nearby. Three hours later I was convinced I'd been forgotten. Then the Caribou arrived for me – its only cargo. I boarded the private aircraft with all the aplomb my importance warranted. Next call on the run was Phu Quoc Island off the coast of Vietnam and not far from the dreaded Cambodian border area that was a hotbed of enemy activity. Phu Quoc was the home of the Vietnamese fish sauce operations, and the smell of *nuoc mam* hovered in the air 15 kilometres out. After Phu Quoc, the pilots demonstrated the skills they had perfected in the dangerous flying conditions of Papua New Guinea. They skimmed so low over the water I swore I could see waves breaking into the open rear of the Caribou. I was terrified we'd go into the drink. 'Pull it up, pull it up,' I yelled towards the cockpit, while the crew, acting as though it was business as usual for them – and it probably was – just grinned back at me. Two more stops, Ca Mau and Can Tho, before Saigon and then Vungers for dinner.

A few days later there was a court martial underway. The accused, one of the most decent men in ALSG, had been charged with manslaughter. I was told that, driving home from town with other officers on a pitch-black night, he had hit a Vietnamese, and the victim had died. The accident was something we feared might happen to any of us. If we drove faster than the speed of a slow bicycle, civilian accidents were a given. The Vietnamese, in their customary black working clothes, and often walking or riding bicycles with no lights along the unlit roads, were impossible to see. Added to that, people cooked, washed and relieved themselves only a few feet from the road, ignoring the military vehicles that continually passed by. It seemed the hearts of everyone at ALSG were with the defendant, an unassuming family man.

Colonel M. J. Ewing, Director of Army Legal Services, arrived from Australia to be Judge Advocate. He stayed at the civilian Grand Hotel in Vung Tau, presumably to maintain impartiality at some distance from the army. I heard our friend was found guilty, given a dishonourable discharge from the army and sentenced to six months in Long Bay Gaol, Sydney. I was so distressed I wrote immediately to his wife. I hoped my letter might help her to appreciate the difficulties of life faced by us all in that unhappy country.

For several weeks around the time of the court martial, the regular Monday medevac flight to Australia did not carry the usual load of jubilant patients, but a cargo of men who had died too young, returning to their final resting place in the sunburnt country they had loved. Lt Kerry Rinkin was among them.

After another of those abominable mine explosions that were happening with increasing regularity, Fifth Battalion Bravo Company officer, Kerry Rinkin, of 4 Platoon, was brought in critically wounded. He died three hours later on the 2 Field Ambulance operating table. Lieutenant Rinkin had been commissioned as a National Service officer. When he discovered army life was exactly what he'd been searching for, he transferred to the Regular Army. He had been in country only a short while and had been a replacement for Lt Jack Carruthers, who died of wounds received in the land mine incident in the Long Hai hills on 21 February. Kerry Rinkin's death rocked everyone. Surely Bravo Company's 4 Platoon had suffered enough.

While Kerry Rinkin was on the operating table, I peered through the glass window into the operating theatre. At that moment, the door opened and surgeon Ron Gregg came out. In a voice angry at his inability to do any more, Ron said: 'Don't bother looking – he's dead.' His tone and expression were those of a man worn down from failure. He had performed many brilliant medical operations, yet it was the failures that he remembered. And they hurt.

I turned away from the window and then stopped abruptly in my tracks. A deep coldness had come over me, and it was not because of the bloody torso of the young soldier I had just seen. I realised with horror that, unlike Dr Gregg, I felt nothing. I was calm and unfazed by the sight. Uncaring would be a more honest word. Dear God! I had grown immune to our daily reality: mutilation and the appalling waste of young men's lives. Had my sensitivities been worn away bit by insidious bit? Did others on the medical staff feel this way? Could they cope with the trauma better than I because they were men? Would I ever care deeply about anything again? I felt revulsion at the emotionless, unfeeling being I had become. Numbed by the tragedies I witnessed every day, I was beyond grieving.

Others on the medical staff did not feel as I did. Even

medic Rodger Eyles, who was caught in the ARVN training exercise with me and was a veteran of many a desperate operation to save a life, could barely speak: 'I'll *never* forget that officer. We put twenty-seven pints of blood into that young man, but when we got him into the theatre proper he was dead. I spent the rest of that day mopping up those twenty-seven pints.'

20

In True ANZAC Day Tradition

NEARLY A THIRD OF 1967 HAD TICKED BY. The heat became unbearable, each day worse than the last. The patients lay listlessly in their beds, bored and sweat-stained from the exertion of doing nothing. On our days off, we had to get out of our rooms at those times of the day when the generator that supplied electricity to the Villa was shut off for maintenance. It was particularly hard on the 36th Evac staff on night shifts. Sleep in the airless rooms was impossible. When the incessant throbbing of the generator in front of the Villa ceased, the sudden silence woke them, and they'd lie in bed and fry without the cooling breeze of a fan.

We began to take an hour or so from work each day to hit the waves to cool off, but the water in the South China Sea was almost hot. The US Army, as always, had a solution. They kept a new fibreglass speed boat at Back Beach, and they always were willing to provide rides or to take us water-skiing.

I thought I was so smart, whizzing over the waves in my two-piece swimsuit against an incongruous background of artillery shelling. Today I cringe at what the modest Vietnamese must have thought of how I looked.

Working seven days a week as we did, with scattered days off, I lost all sense of day and time, and felt eerily detached from reality. The fighting men at the sharp end were exhausted and jittery. Those of us at ALSG were lethargic and apathetic. Our lives settled into a foggy haze. Each day Win and I smiled and chatted with the patients, but we had lost our *joie de vivre*. We were worn out. It had been a rough year for everyone.

One afternoon Win quit work at four to go home to rest and slept for three solid hours. Another morning, I couldn't wake her for work so took off without her. I went home after lunch to check that she was all right, and she awoke for the first time. The following night when I was on a date, she intended to write letters. About six that evening she lay down for a few minutes' rest before dinner; I found her sprawled fully dressed across the bed, surrounded by her unused writing materials when I came in at curfew. I moved them off the bed; she didn't stir and slept until the alarm woke her next morning. She was as physically and emotionally drained as I had been before Christmas. Win had given 200 per cent of her energies to the patients, and her selflessness had caught up with her.

During the first difficult months in Vietnam, in the face of our daily burden of work and worry, I had bonded closely with the soldiers. Year-long tours were ending for most of them and each unit changeover meant there were men to farewell. Win and I had little interest in meeting their replacements and even less in learning new names. For us, staying home to write letters and going to bed by 10 pm had become the perfect evening. From along the hallway, we often heard someone playing a tape of a new Broadway show or some of the music we loved. It would be wonderful to be home again to play our favourite records and tapes.

As a last hurrah before going home, 2 Field Ambulance – in a few weeks those of us staying on would become part of 8 Field Ambulance – paraded formally on Back Beach. With everyone feeling we could melt away, Colonel Rodgers took the salute as the doctors, medics and support staff, spruced up and sharp in jungle greens and slouch hats, paraded on the sand. I felt both proud and sad as I watched. I would miss the men I had come to know so well.

To give them a suitable send-off, Red Cross invited the entire hospital staff to a morning tea. There were no complicated stage directions; just come prepared to eat and have fun. The ALSG Officers' Mess cooks, who had done such a splendid job with food for the Cabaret, agreed to make small pies, pasties and sausage rolls – favourites that none of us had tasted in a year. They decorated a cake as beautifully as any Royal Show prize-winner, with 'Goodbye Good Luck 2 Field Ambulance' on it. All of the 2 Field staff took time away from work to show up, and I was thankful no casualties arrived to tear them away. They were great men – always supportive of us, always looking for fun to relieve the burden of suffering they shouldered each day.

On 25 April, ANZAC Day, we were awakened – as thousands the length and breadth of Australia were, and are today – by the clanging of an alarm about 4.30 am. As I explained to the curious Americans who wondered what it was all about, ANZAC Day is a day of deep and genuine spiritual feeling, and for some Australians, it is even holier than Sunday. Every year, no matter where in the world they may be, Australians commemorate 25 April, 1915, as most believe that date marks the proudest day in their history. On that day in World War I, the Australian and New Zealand Army Corps, all volunteers, landed on a narrow beach at Gallipoli in Turkey. Under orders from their British commanders, they advanced up impossibly steep cliffs while being showered with punishing fire from the Turks (on the side of Germany) entrenched above them. During the nine-month siege, the Australians suffered ghastly casualties, and the men of ANZAC who survived became national heroes. The last of those heroes, Alec Campbell – who raised his age by two years to eighteen in order to enlist – died at age 103 in May 2002, just a few weeks after he had ridden at the head of the ANZAC Day parade. His death, like that of Roy Longmore, who had been the only other living ANZAC, was reported in big headlines in newspapers all around the world.

Celebrating ANZAC Day in Vietnam, where many brave men already had earned nothing more than a grave, would be especially meaningful. As we readied ourselves for the ALSG Dawn Service (others would be held in Nui Dat, Saigon and anywhere Australians were to be found in Vietnam), I was reminded of all of the dawn services for which my father had risen before daybreak. First off, Win and I had to collect those patients from 2 Field Ambulance who were well enough to attend. We drove the Land Rover through the pre-dawn darkness to the camp, conscious as we jolted along the dirt roads that the twin beams of our headlights made us easy targets for any lurking Viet Cong. The rice paddies and road merged in the cloaking darkness – quite frightening. The rustle and chatter of monkeys in the trees near the entrance to the camp were the only sounds we heard.

Jan, who had driven alone in the Volkswagen, took one look at me: 'Jean, where's your hat?' I hadn't worn my Red Cross hat since the day I arrived in Saigon, but ANZAC Day demanded full dress. Leaving Jan and Win to ferry the patients, I took off at full run, threw myself behind the wheel of the Volkswagen and raced alone into the inky darkness. Grabbing my hat at the Villa, I sped back to the camp, no longer worrying about the VC. Instead I was praying out loud: Please, God, don't let me hit a Vietnamese in his black pyjamas pushing his unlit cart to market! I sped safely through the S-curve entrance to the camp, and then swerved abruptly. By only feet, I missed ploughing into troops marching through the dark to the service. Dear God! I had nearly run down thirty Diggers.

In Australia the Dawn Service begins at six. As the Last Post is played, the sun starts to peep over the horizon, and the magpies and currawongs sing to greet the dawn. In Vung Tau, as the Service started, so did the rain. We were used to ignoring dripping faces and plastered down hair, and there were so many men I wanted to pray for, yet all I could think of was what the doctors might say when we handed back their sick, and now soaked, patients. As the service ended, the downpour stopped. ALSG units had attended in unit formation, and they marched back to their areas as crisply as any soldier can when sloshing through pools of water and drenched right through.

At 8 am Jan took patients to the Roman Catholic service, and Win and I followed up with the Protestants half an hour later. Woomera Naval Association had sent money for gifts for the patients, so we parcelled together two beers, two soft drinks, one carton of cigarettes, one packet of sweets, and one ballpoint pen for each man.

That morning the largest body of medics yet from 2 Field Ambulance was going home on a Hercules transport, leaving only a small rear party, and we made sure we were there at ten o'clock to give them a good send-off. During their time at 2 Field, the staff – many were National Servicemen pulled from comfortable safe environments into a vicious war – had built a fully-operational hospital from bare sand. They had coped with supplies that did not arrive, floods, scorpions and worse. The medics had proved to be capable, dedicated, and technically proficient at their jobs. Under the most difficult of circumstances, they ably had cared for and treated 2,747 patients, a number greater than their successors were to treat the following year. The later decrease may have been due to the steadily improving sanitation and health facilities in both the camps.

Two Field Ambulance had consisted of more than the medical staff. There were those unsung heroes who silently supported the medicos – specialist cooks, drivers, clerks, engineers, those who ran the quartermaster's store (the Q), kitchens, orderly room, administration, messes and accommodation areas – all essential to the efficient and sustained running of a hospital. Bob Kearney, an infantry soldier who knew what it was like to put his dead and wounded mates on Dust-Offs, said it best: 'The staff at 2 Field Ambulance gave the infantry hope that if the wounded got to hospital, they had a 99 per cent chance of making it home alive. I call them "Bloody Angels".'

In true ANZAC Day tradition, there was a football game

that afternoon. If I remember correctly, it was rugby union –
played between the muscular 17 Construction Squadron
engineers (Ginger Beers) and the Royal Australian Electrical
and Mechanical Engineers (RAEME), derisively referred to by
the Ginger Beers as Engineers Minus Experience. All men
played in their army boots. Win and I were in a dilemma
about which side to support. We had to choose, as football
without partisan barracking can hardly be called a game. The
engineers had always been especially kind to us. However, the
RAEME mechanics kept our Volkswagen and Land Rover, as
well as our radio and typewriter, working soundly despite the
impossible conditions. The decision was made for us by one
of the RAEME boys: 'Support who you like, but you'll look
pretty silly driving to work in a bulldozer!'

We bought ribbons and balloons in the colours of the two
teams for the patients to barrack in true footy style, but we
hadn't had time to blow up the balloons. Any patient fit
enough to go to the game, held at the local high school on the
other side of Vung Tau, had to pay for his ride with hot air.
We stood along the sidelines at the high school – Win and I in
our grey uniforms amongst a sea of blue pyjamas. There was
a large crowd of Australians yelling for their favourite team,
Americans wanting to share in the fun, and Vietnamese
looking to see what the round-eyes were up to now. Every
time Win and I cheered and waved our balloons when
RAEME got the ball, there was an outbreak of snickering
amongst the patients. 'What's funny?' I demanded. 'Nothing,'
they murmured and pretended to watch the game, grins
dancing across their faces. Something was up, and the joke
seemed to be on us. Ignoring their looks, we focused on the
game, waving our balloons excitedly. Later we heard that

those white balloons our little lambs had given us were inflated condoms!

The day ended with a barbecue, where we heard a funny story making the rounds. Dave Sabben put it in writing years later:

The Six Battalion Delta Company Officers' & Sergeants' Mess had hosted an entertainment troupe. At some stage the lone female, a dancer, needed to powder her nose. The Mess, *much* to her embarrassment, held an auction to determine who would escort her, for no one there matched the essential criteria to accompany the lady to the loo, i.e., another woman. The married men confirmed that women *always* went to the loo in pairs. This provided ribald comment about what the other woman was there for. All this time the dancer was suffering – her ears not wanting to hear and the other end wishing the decision be made.

The outcome was that the youngest married man would go with her – for her protection and his education. I was given the task. The loo was in the open, away from all tents and other facilities. It was two seats in a shed, with a front wall that only came up to the waist so the users could see out over the forward defence line [FDL] wire. We must be alert to VC in *all* circumstances. The FDL sentries also, had they wished, had a view of the top half of any officer or sergeant who sat on the loo.

In the normal course of events, not a scrap of attention would have been paid by the sentries to the loo. This was *not* the normal course of events. Our arrival caused the usual population of the sentry post – two – to swell to ten or so in the blink of an eye. With my back turned, I took up a position many yards to the loo's front, and the lady entered. The task appeared to take an inordinately long time, but I suppose a lady with an audience had an excuse. The Diggers, absolutely without shame, took up their observation positions facing me. When they rose as one and offered a hearty round of applause, I guessed the job had been completed.

The lady met me out the front and, in good sport, offered a curtsy to the audience. She got off comparatively lightly, because it was *me* who was grilled back at the Mess about every detail, culminating in the inevitable questions as to whether the paperwork had been completed.

Listening to Dave's story, we laughed until our stomachs hurt. As Jimmy Buffett sang several years later, without laughter we'd all go insane.

21

One Day at a Time

DALAT IS A RENOWNED MOUNTAIN RESORT IN the Central
Highlands of Vietnam, where non-tropical fruit and
vegetables grow abundantly on the fertile hillsides and
roses bloom in profusion. By the end of April, I badly needed
another break from work and from the tropical heat, and the
cool air of the high ground held great appeal. Dalat was considered relatively safe, and some advisers from the Australian
Army Training Team Vietnam (AATTV) were based there.

Men of the AATTV had been the first Australian soldiers
into Vietnam in 1962 and were the last to leave when Australia pulled out ten years later. For their exploits in Vietnam,
the AATTV soldiers were awarded four Victoria Crosses and
110 other Australian decorations, as well as numerous
American and Vietnamese honours. Members of the Team,
I heard, were usually sent to Dalat for a 'rest' after putting in
the hard yards in hot spots elsewhere.

Wallaby Airlines called at Dalat twice a week, so I packed
a bag and headed for that highland Shangri-La, about 200
kilometres north-east of Saigon. Two men in familiar jungle
greens – hoping for supplies, news and mail from home –
were waiting for the 'Bou as it taxied along Dalat's airstrip.
I walked up to them and introduced myself: 'Can I stay with
you until the Wallaby comes through next?' I'd like to say an
AATTV man is surprised by nothing, but I'd be a liar. Their
mouths gaped as their stunned eyes met mine. Each swal-
lowed nervously and looked anxiously at the other. Regaining
composure, they hesitantly nodded their heads. After ten
months of being almost alone in a wash of men, I was
unmindful of the impact of my request for a bed in a house
where men had not seen a round-eyed female in months.
Team member Jack Peel, whom I had known when he was
with 32 Small Ships, told me later: 'It was not uncommon for
the AATTV to have a visitor. The chaplain would sometimes
drop by with the mail, and the occasional politician might
visit at election time, but having a female visitor to stay? That
was unusual, to say the least!' More important, the advisers
knew Dalat was not as safe as I had thought. They had been
in a recent dust-up with the North Vietnamese Army and
knew that it would be a while before the NVA were convinced
they were not welcome in Dalat.

In blissful ignorance, I climbed into the Land Rover, and
we headed up one of the hills to their villa. My hosts were
Norm Hardy, Taffy Fairfax and Jim Copeman (no relation to
Russell Copeman), who had just replaced Bill Tomlinson. All
were slightly older than the young Diggers I was used to and
were quietly confident in their skills. Located across the road
from a Vietnamese police station, their villa was built on three

levels into the slope of the hill. The advisers occupied the top two levels, which could be entered from the street. Below were the quarters of the Vietnamese who did the housekeeping. Each adviser had his own room, and there was a spare room for me. They told me about some of the sites I should see, including the private golf course of the last emperor, Bao Dai. Then I set off on foot to explore the pretty town, distinguished as much by its lack of barbed wire, sandbags and trash, as by its cool climate and hilly terrain.

Dalat curves around Xuan Huong Lake, named after Vietnam's most famous erotic poetess. There French commanders and the wealthy of Saigon built spacious villas among the pine trees on the hills to recuperate from the oppressive heat of the lowlands. There Emperor Bao Dai maintained a two-storey summer palace, which is open to tourists today. A university town, Dalat also had a steepled Catholic church where the French priest spoke English and was glad to practise it on me, a rare female visitor. The once glorious Palace Hotel, today restored, was built in the French architectural style, with huge public areas, ornate fireplaces and high ceilings. For decades Dalat was the best known resort in Indochina and before the war was famous as the base for tiger hunts.

People dressed in woolly hats, scarves and coats. After Vung Tau's heat and humidity, the climate was refreshing and the hilly terrain no problem to navigate after the steep sand hills of Back Beach. Wanting to be back at the AATTV villa before dark, I hailed an open pony cart with dozens of little bells on the harness, and we clopped up the long hill, the bells jangling merrily.

The advisers cooked a hearty meat-and-potatoes dinner,

and I did my best to clean up afterwards. They told me there were more than a hundred of their team scattered throughout South Vietnam, working with the American Green Beret Special Forces to train Chinese mercenaries, the ARVN and the Montagnards (French for mountain people). Dalat and other central highland areas were home to the Montagnards who, like the Australian Aborigines, are a people of many tribes. The Montagnards' reputation was mighty – they would stand and fight to the last man, while Chinese mercenaries or the ARVN would often drop arms and run. The advisers had Montagnards guarding the house. It was critical for the advisers to have the mountain people as allies, and the AATTV shoulder patch, depicting an Australian boomerang with a Montagnard crossbow, indicates the advisers' close involvement with them.

There was more talk among the men, and I listened with fascination to their tales. Then it was time for bed. With the other two watching, Taffy quietly handed me a rifle. 'You might need this if the VC pay us a visit in the middle of the night.' I'd been ten months in a battle zone and thought I understood war's deadly consequences, yet all I could manage was a gasp. 'What?'

'They could come up that valley there and into the house and be here before we know it,' Taffy said. Jim and Norm nodded their agreement. Now it was my turn to gape. Fear of the VC wasn't my problem – it was the gun that terrified me! I had never been trained in using a weapon. Once I had fired a rifle at a tin can on a fence post, but after one shot, I was done. In the confined area of the Dalat villa, with a weapon in my inexpert hands, I might shoot one of *us*.

'If the VC come, I'll dash to the nearest one of you,'

I protested. The men argued that I should take the weapon. Just as vehemently I refused. How wrong I was! I still didn't have a clue. All men, especially soldiers, believe they must protect women from danger. If the VC *had* attacked the house during the night, my unarmed presence might have caused the advisers to focus on me, rather than on the enemy. My ignorance could have cost them their lives.

The night passed uneventfully. Next day I walked around Dalat again before going to the airport to take the Caribou home. I asked if it was safe to leave my camera on the bed. 'No problem. No one here will steal anything from us,' I was told. In Dalat's modern, architecturally-designed market I jostled with the other shoppers. With a seller who wore a snug-fitting blue woollen beret beneath her conical straw hat, I haggled to buy traditional Montagnard weapons, similar to those used in medieval times – a crossbow, arrows and the slim basket that is slung across a warrior's back to hold the arrows. An intricately woven length of Montagnard cloth in the typical vivid orange, red and black colouring also was a must have. It would look perfect on our bedroom table at the Villa. To round off, I bought some lush strawberries, as many as I could carry, to take back to Vung Tau for friends to feast on.

When I returned from my walk, my camera was gone. 'Why did you tell me it was safe to leave it?' I whined. I was not happy. With no money to buy a new camera, there would be no more photographs for me in Vietnam. When word of the theft reached adviser Bill Tomlinson sometime later, he set me straight. 'I had a similar experience when I first joined my ARVN battalion at Tam Ky. During the first few weeks there, they pinched everything I owned, including my rifle magazines. Once I'd proved myself and been accepted, I think

I could have left a million dollars lying around and no one would have touched it. In fact, they'd have protected it for me. It must be something to do with the Vietnamese psyche. When my replacement arrived, I assured him that his stuff would be safe. They took it all! He wasn't happy with me,' Bill said.

I packed my newly acquired treasures, and the advisers took me – happily, I'm sure – to the airstrip. Wallaby Airlines arrived promptly, and I was home in time for dinner. Win and I sat on the floor of our bedroom with friends and devoured our gourmet meal of strawberries sweetened with a tin of cream bought in the market. A few weeks later, as they had predicted, the Dalat Training Team came under enemy attack from rocket and machine-gun fire in the early hours of the morning. They were able to repel the attack with a heavy volume of return fire from the windows, but Norm Hardy was wounded. When I heard of the assault back in Vung Tau, I went cold. I was still so stupidly naïve.

As April plodded into May, Jan, Win and I officially became part of 8 Field Ambulance (the following April the hospital formally was named 1 Australian Field Hospital). The new CO, Lt Col Ralph Meyer, his officers and men settled easily into the hospital that the men before them had laboured day and night to establish in the sand. Eight Field was all spit and polish. Its ways of treating the patients were different from those of its predecessor, and we began to hear rumbles of discontent from those 2 Field men left in the rear party. One day medic Rodger Eyles got angry with a newly arrived doctor who had reduced a patient's medication. 'Here I am, a private with basic skills, telling a medico his decision was premature! I still think I was right, though,' he said grinning. With many months of extraordinary nursing experience under his belt, he may well have been.

In early May the Australian army nurses arrived – the first women, apart from the Red Cross, to work in our military hospital. Captain Amy Pittendreigh and her Lieutenants, Colleen Mealy (now Thurgar), Margaret Ahern (now Hopcroft) and Terrie Roche, took the patients to their hearts and quickly earned the accolade 'the Fabulous Four'. They were soon joined by Kiwi nurse, Margaret Torrey. Colleen still remembers my words of greeting to her: 'You have no idea what you're in for.'

As usual, the first word of the nurses' expected arrival had come not from the top brass but from the men in the Q store. A large supply of women's sanitary products had arrived some weeks earlier. Not knowing of that special product privilege for army women, we always had purchased our own. Only half jokingly, one of the ALSG officers said: 'I guess your nose will be out of joint, Jean, with competition now.' On the contrary, I couldn't wait to talk to another woman from home. As it turned out, our lives rarely meshed. The nurses threw themselves into transforming the hospital from rough-and-ready to shipshape, as only nurses can do. The medics had done a great job, but the nurses saw things that would give a matron apoplexy.

The staff at 8 Field was kept busy with the continuous arrival of casualties from the newly arrived Seventh Battalion that had replaced the Fifth at Nui Dat. Far too often the injuries were from exploding mines. Our battered spirits plummeted when we heard the news that two ex-patients and another soldier had been killed in a car crash after returning home.

The American nurses at the 36th continued to give our boys devoted care. For their part, the Diggers lived up to their roguish reputation and gave the nurses the laughs they badly needed. Juliet Gordon (now Day) remembers an Aussie patient whose jaw had been broken in a brawl at the Red Horse Saloon. He was incensed to be going home with medical records that stated: 'Wounded in Line of Duty?' 'No.' He believed he had been fighting to defend his unit's honour!

On 9 May Sapper John (Jethro) Thompson, 1 Field Squadron, arrived at the 36th Evac in dire shape. John had been in the Australian army three years when he was sent to Nui Dat in January 1967 to drive the earth moving equipment required for building roads and establishing the camp. When he wasn't doing that, he was one of the Rats of Dat. 'Just me, not my 'dozer,' he'd say. Like Barry Harford, he explored enemy tunnels. While laying mines along the infamous barrier mine field from the Horseshoe north-east of Dat Do to the coast – the area that spawned so many of our casualties – John Thompson put his foot in the wrong place. Many soldiers were wounded by the spray of shrapnel from a jumping jack mine, and two men later died. John's inventory of wounds was shocking: one leg amputated high into the thigh; chunks of flesh missing from the other leg; right arm removed to a few inches below the elbow; left hand retaining only a thumb and forefinger. Fortunately a caring American surgeon thought it important to save the remaining two digits on the one intact arm. John's abdominal area and back are riddled with large scars from much stitching and the surgery clamps. He still carries shrapnel, which frequently gives him trouble.

How does one find words to comfort a soldier who has had limbs torn away? Perhaps there are none. How could I assure John, then only twenty-one, that with his wealth of charm and good looks he was still attractive to women? How could I help him cope with his grief, knowing that if he survived, he faced years of living with never-ending pain? I thought John Thompson might kill himself when he returned to Australia.

Because of the severity of his wounds, John was placed in a bed next to the nurses' station, where his every breath could be monitored. Many times he nearly died. One day a large wooden supply box was wheeled into the ward. Knowing his condition was critical, John was convinced it was for him. To keep a slender grip on reality while he struggled for life, he listened to the nurses chat as they worked. He learned which nurse was married, which one had a new date, which one didn't get on with a colleague.

The nurses used silver nitrate extensively to treat burns, and the acid ate holes in the nurses' clothing. One day Annie Philiben, assistant head nurse in ICU-Recovery exclaimed: 'The way this silver nitrate is eating my uniform, it's going to fall right off me one day.' From the bed closest to her, John moved for the first time. He lifted his head and said: 'I hope I'll be around then!' The nurses were overjoyed at that first indication that he might live. John's engaging personality, witty turn of phrase and iron-willed determination endeared him to the Americans.

Before his vital signs stabilised enough for medevac, John had seven operations. He claimed to hold the 36th Evac record for the longest stay in post-op: forty days – certainly much longer than most American patients. (Australians were not evacuated home as quickly as Americans because the RAAF's C130s were not as well supplied with medical equipment as the Americans' larger aircraft.) John was in RGH Heidelberg, Victoria, for more than two years before he was finally discharged. But his mother had her son home again – that was all that mattered.

Back in Vung Tau, the American medical team, despite a steady flow of new patients, missed John. Nine of the doctors, nurses and medical corpsmen each wrote a page of a letter to John, telling how they loved him and admired his humour, courage and determination. They were not to know that for the next thirty years, whenever John felt overwhelmed by pain, he pulled out that nine-page letter and read it for the cheer it offered him.

Somehow, word falsely reached Vung Tau that John had died. John tells the story today: 'Two of my mates went drinking when they heard and told some Yanks, "Our mate died today." That didn't impress the Yanks. "What's the matter with you? Americans are losing hundreds every day!" That started it. My mates knocked the Yanks senseless, and then they started fighting the White Mice and the MPs before they were locked up. I don't know if they repeated it when they heard I wasn't dead!'

When he left Heidelberg hospital in Melbourne, John met his first wife, Judy Hosking, who had lost her first husband to cancer, leaving her with two young children; she and John had three daughters together. In 1975 Judy died from bowel cancer. Always moving forward, John married Perle Butler, mother of two boys and widow of a Seventh Battalion sergeant who was killed in a motor cycle accident after returning from Vietnam; John and Perle then had seven children to care for.

For years John tried a wooden leg for mobility but gave it away in 1985, as the Queensland humidity made using it difficult. Never one to shirk a challenge, John now travels the world on two crutches with Perle, his dark curly hair today showing only a few flecks of grey. In the nineties, when he visited the United States to get in touch with the doctors and nurses who had saved his life, they all greeted him joyfully.

I didn't see John for almost forty years. I met up with him again in the United States, at a reunion of the 36th Evac medical staff in 2002. Sitting on a chair, his crutches nearby, John's radiant face reflected joy at being alive. He vividly recalls his days at the 36th Evac. 'I remember you, Jean! You were writing a letter to my mother, and you said, "Drat, I've spelled Heidelberg wrong."' When I confessed to John I had feared in Vietnam that he might commit suicide, he replied: 'I don't know the meaning of the word.' Today John has more energy than a playground of rowdy children. He has mowed lawns at army bases when other physically able 'sorry arses' (John's words) wouldn't. To help other veterans obtain benefits due them for war injuries, he has tirelessly fought bureaucracy, and has held official positions in many ex-servicemen's organisations.

John, also a diabetic, is never without pain, but will mention it only if asked. 'I have pain from nerve storms at amputation sites and unexplainable bouts of pain in my stomach. Then there's the pain caused by the futility of war.'

The army gives no medals for John's brand of enduring courage. He has only the medals that I, and everyone who served at least six months in Vietnam, received – plus John has a medal for previous service in Borneo. Unlike GIs, Australian soldiers are not awarded medals for being wounded.

John Thompson's story, both appalling and inspirational, is the story of many wounded who return from war to a lifetime of pain. Their constant lot is to go the extra mile to live a normal life. They battle on, one day at a time.

22

On the Countdown to Home

ALL THROUGH MAY THE HEAT WAS SO intense that I wore a path to the hospital's drinks refrigerator. Then the rainy season arrived. Each day dawned for wetter or for worse. We endured twice-daily downpours, each one seeming heavier and longer-lasting than the one before. The camp flooded again, although nowhere as badly as in October, and soldiers with brooms worked steadily to keep the water out of the Red Cross office. I waded through water for the rest of my time in Vung Tau. But nothing mattered. I was on the countdown to home.

My year, beginning in June 1966, had been tough. I had been in Vietnam for what history has recorded as the worst battle for the Australians, that of 18 August at Long Tan; the busiest hospital month, in December; and the worst landmine disaster, that of 21 February in the Long Hai hills. There had been floods, the black plague and critical supply shortages. Casualties continued to arrive too regularly.

Our work was the only thing that was going smoothly. Jan, Win and I had settled into a well-oiled team, with an established office and a streamlined operation that Harry and I had built from nothing. Because of the improved transport situation, our supplies from Red Cross NHQ in Melbourne arrived without a hitch. NHQ seemed delighted with our work, especially as it was generating publicity for them. Photojournalist Denis Gibbons' article and pictures about us appeared in colour in the 15 May, 1967 issue of *Woman's Day*. 'Our girls in Vietnam: they're mighty game little things' said the front cover line and the heading atop the three pages. And then Win met an ex-patient at the Vung Tau airbase who told her proudly: 'Remember when I was in hospital and had a picture of you and Jean taken with me? I've sent it off to *PIX* magazine, and it's going to be published in the "My Favourite Australian" section.' Win retorted: 'When MGM hears about all this, they'll revoke my contract', but we were tickled at his gesture. It was all good fun. It was the Diggers, though, who deserved the kudos and the bouquets.

When Win finished the movie of our work and life for NHQ, she bought a projector so that we could view it. Because Jack Wilson was a RAEME officer, we felt he had the electrical and mechanical credentials to master a projector and requested that he be in charge. The Aussie and the American Red Cross workers sat together on our twin beds and watched the screen. Win had done a fine job, but the movie needed narration. I got the gig. On Monday we movie stars were back to reality as it was a busy medevac. We were relieved that the patients were going to have a slightly more comfortable ride on the homeward-bound wings of the RAAF's newer, quieter C130E silver birds.

Major Laurie Doyle, of 161 Reconnaissance Flight, in whose Sioux choppers I so loved to ride, had a wonderful Irish sense of humour and a passion for telling witty anecdotes. He was one of our favourites. He invited Jan, Win and me, when we were on a visit to the Task Force, to sit in on an intelligence briefing to be given to all unit officers about matters such as VC positions that had been discovered. Undoubtedly Russell Hill Army Headquarters in Canberra would not have approved of the Red Cross presence at the briefing, but the invitation indicated how trusted and respected we three women had become by all ranks of men.

The rag tag existence we had once known was headed into history. Each day there were more signs that our environment was improving. A recreation area was planned at Back Beach in memory of Major Peter Badcoe, AATTV, whose bravery had earned him a Victoria Cross, an American Silver Star and numerous Vietnamese decorations before he was killed by machine-gun fire in April 1967. Work had begun on a bar gazebo outside the Villa DuBois. And, after a year of the Australian presence, dead Vietnamese bodies – seen by convoy drivers on their first trips to Nui Dat – no longer lay along the road.

When Major Donohue sent a vehicle to take us to the Ba Ria convent/orphanage school break-up concert, the drive along the Nui Dat road was beautiful. We had come to know the nuns and the orphans as friends. The children, all in freshly ironed clothes, danced barefoot. One child forgot her lines, one little boy kicked another when he thought no one was watching, and a church relic was in danger of being toppled any moment by the performers. The simple concert refreshed our jaded souls.

I was robust when I arrived in Vietnam. Photographs show that by the end of my year I was woefully thin. My skin, like that of many others, had a strange yellow tint – who knows from what – but we were accustomed to The Look. We didn't know it, but newcomers could tell from our faces who of us had been there many months.

Less than three weeks remained before Win and I were to go home, and I was getting antsy. Driving home alone one night after dinner at ALSG, as I bumped along the dirt road now so familiar that I knew each rut, tree and house along the way, the sturdy Volkswagen slowed down and stopped for no apparent reason. When I turned the ignition key, there was a sickening click. I tried again. Nothing. It was pitch black, and the VC owned the night. I panicked and my mind raced: I have a Vietnamese friend who lives nearby – I'll use her phone to call for help. Think again. Vietnamese farmers don't have telephones. I let my fears take over, abandoned the VW and started to run. It was the only time in Vietnam I was certain I might die: I was utterly alone, with no soldier close by with a weapon to protect me. Near an intersection of the dirt roads, I heard the noise of an approaching truck. It never occurred to me that it might be the VC. 'Help, help,' I called, almost strangling on my fear. I heard a soldier say: 'I think I hear a lady out there!' The truck slowed, and I saw several GIs. I ran toward them through the darkness, an unexpected and eerie figure. The surprised Americans probably wondered what was in the cigarettes they had been smoking! They walked me back to my car. It started immediately. Nothing wrong. The bumpy road may have knocked the battery loose. Who knows? I drove home with the truck following, feeling like a total jackass.

The Second Battalion arrived on HMAS *Sydney* at the end of May, and a jubilant departing Sixth Battalion took their bunks on the Vung Tau ferry. Soldiers returning from a combat zone need time to unwind and re-adjust from the months of carnage before rejoining their loved ones. The sea voyage on the *Sydney* was a great relaxer. Responding to an invitation we treasured, Win and I had attended Six Battalion Delta Company's farewell the previous afternoon. In both the Diggers' and the Officers' & Sergeants' Messes, every man was deliriously happy to be going home – alive. Delta Company had suffered more casualties than any other in the past year. After our goodbyes, we took the last chopper of the day back to Vung Tau with OC Major Harry Smith MC, who added lustre to his legendary résumé (he had led Delta Company at the Long Tan battle) by farewelling so merrily he barely made it back to the *Sydney* next morning before she sailed. The sun slid toward the horizon as we flew home, its brilliant hues reflected in the water of the paddy fields below. Everything looked serene in that beautiful country where so many men had died.

With only eight days, a wake-up and a greasy egg before I was to leave, I had my first visitor from home. Pte Tom Young, from Adelaide, had arrived with the Second Battalion. When Tom was called up for National Service, he'd been naïvely delighted. Now that he had seen his first casualties, some from booby traps and mines, I noticed how philosophical he'd become. Choosing his words carefully he said: 'Of course you can't fight a war without losses, but it's a terrible tragedy when blokes you know are taken from you. The battalion yesterday was a very quiet one, with church parades both morning and afternoon.' Although Tom was too busy to be bored at Nui Dat, he came up with an ingenious way to escape the routine. He started a camera club, darkroom and studio, the only hitch being that photographers had to provide their own female models! His studio caught the attention of the Battalion's CO, and it was used for battalion intelligence photography.

Our last days in country were marked by a splendid round of farewells from the Officers', Sergeants' and ORs' Messes. Some Messes had gone out of their way to prepare what for us was a banquet – sweet and sour fish, curry, fried rice and chicken salad. The CO of ALSG, Lt Col Laurie Chambers, wrote the following unsolicited testimonial to Red Cross NHQ:

I cannot let this opportunity pass without telling you of the sterling work that your Red Cross team is doing in Vietnam. Each member of the team has fitted into the Army way of life and is a credit to your selection. We will all be sorry to see Jean Debelle and Winsome Ayliffe leave this country. Their friendliness and sincerity have done a great deal for the wounded and sick. Janice Webb, your senior member, is outstanding and has won the affection and respect of all the soldiers.

When the doctors summoned us for the army's regulation exit check-up, Win and I laughed, wondering if they thought we might have VD! We didn't relish the prospect, though, of having a physical examination by men we knew as good friends. The doctors, bless them, asked only a few questions to fulfil the army's requirements for our military records. Our clothes stayed on.

We were to fly home with other troops on a Hercules, so excess luggage was not a concern. Win had worried, though, about how she would pack all the souvenirs she'd collected. She would have taken home a helicopter if she could. What *was* a problem was the gastric upset Win had suffered for two weeks; she had lost about 10 kilograms (more than 20 pounds). Then I caught Win's bug and was unable to pack. Win's replacement, Robyn Harris, from Adelaide, packed for me. Jan wrote her mother a last impression of us that was telling: 'I didn't really know whether to laugh or cry when the girls left. I've grown fond of them both, but they looked so awful and thin and sick and yellow under their suntans. I'm half expecting a letter from NHQ asking what I did to them!'

As Win and I lay in our beds on our last night in country, we listened to the sounds that had become part of our lives. Medical staff played music as they relaxed after a gruelling shift. The guard patrolled outside our window with his slow, steady tread. There was nothing more to be scared of, no more curfews to rush home for, no more tinned or powdered food. Unspoken was what we both knew – the casualties, on both sides, would continue and we both would miss the beloved 'boys' who had made an indelible impression on our lives. Then we'd retreat to the bathroom with another gastric attack. Being sick at the same time bonded us even more – there was mutual support in misery.

On 14 June (I had been in Vietnam one day short of a year), that's how we boarded our freedom bird, as the planes home were known – with both ends going happily. We faced a Hercules flight of many hours. To help us keep our dignity, army doctors gave us some white chalky mixture that tasted vile, but worked. The trip was a blur.

Except for Darwin, that is. There we faced Customs, and Win gave Her Majesty's welcoming committee a giant headache. In Vietnam, she had been given a Browning .22 pistol. Customs officers surrounded Win and fired questions. 'A handgun may not be brought into Australia without a permit from police in your home state. Do you have one? Do you belong to a pistol club? Do you have a gun licence?' The answer to everything was 'no'. It was clear that the Customs officers were sympathetic to a woman returning from caring work in Vietnam, but it was equally clear they had a job to do. After much back and forth, and with Win's promise she'd make everything legal as soon as she arrived in Perth, she got the pistol back. But as she didn't have a legitimate need for a gun, the police in Perth confiscated it. They no doubt feared that she might turn to a life of crime!

At Darwin we changed to a commercial flight to Sydney, staffed by pretty air hostesses instead of an all-male crew. Knowing I was flying over my beloved country, my natural resilience bounded back. I had a zillion questions to ask the hostesses. How short were women wearing their skirts? What colours were fashionable this winter? What was new with hairstyles and makeup? I felt I had been on Mars for a year. But none was interested in talking to Win or me – it was the handsome soldiers travelling with us whom they wanted to greet as heroes, and rightly so. I settled for cribbing my fashion updates from the onboard women's magazines. As we approached Sydney airport, we pulled Red Cross cardigans over our cotton dresses and headed into the toilets to cover our bare legs with nylons in preparation for stepping off the aircraft into the winter chill.

Sydney gleamed in the early morning light like the jewel

it is. Both Sydney and our next stop, Melbourne, were a flurry of media interviews, with pictures of us appearing in major newspapers and on TV. We were too wrung out and exhausted to acquit ourselves well. We visited former patients still recovering in army hospitals in both cities. I didn't know it then, but one of the older Red Cross stalwarts was horrified at my knee-length skirt; the shorter, cooler hemline sent her into orbit, where she stayed for some months!

At Adelaide airport, my family waited. Mum, normally unemotional, burst from behind the security barrier and rushed to hug me, tears wetting her cheeks. No official moved to stop her. She had awakened the house at 4 am to bake scones, as she couldn't sleep. Win headed on to her home in Perth, and I was sorry to part with her. She had been a constant source of good humour, understanding and tolerance and had been the perfect roommate, the ideal friend. She and I were remarkably different, yet we had become as close as sisters. Together we had given every fibre of our being to everything we did in Vietnam.

Adelaide hadn't changed. Men in short shorts still ran around ovals in the Parklands on Saturday afternoons kicking footballs. On television Harry's Menswear still advertised two pairs of trousers for $5. The comfortable sameness was reassuring, but the chill I felt in the air was not only the chill of winter. In the mundane world of everyday life, nobody seemed to care that men were being killed in Vietnam. It was more important to be the first to have the new Holden HR in the driveway – or so it appeared.

Although being home was wonderful (I was welcomed at eighteen dinners and fifteen lunches in a month), I felt confused, out of step with my friends. If anyone grizzled about a bad haircut or of dry cleaning not being ready on time, I'd want to snap 'Grow up!' I had no tolerance for the self-absorbed, for falseness or hypocrisy, for those who couldn't take pleasure in the small joys of life. Like so many of the Diggers, I thought there was something wrong with *me*, and kept my thoughts to myself. Sometimes tears briefly filled my eyes, and I attributed them, unknowingly, to exhaustion. What I did know, though, was that I was angry at the contemptible treatment some people gave soldiers returning from Vietnam, yet I rarely had the guts to say anything. I was on a roller-coaster of emotions; one moment wanting to get on with life, make some money and find a husband, and the next thinking non-stop of my heroes. Not those savvy people making millions then in the stock market mining boom. My heroes were sweaty men in dirty greens in the jungles and paddy fields of a country at war.

I spent a month with my family, then worked for a year at 4 RAAF Hospital in Butterworth, Malaysia, fulfilling my contract with Red Cross. Much as I loved being back in Asia, the slow pace and relaxing lifestyle of Butterworth, which most people welcomed, bored me senseless. I looked forward to the weekly medevac of patients on their way home from Vietnam and was glad I understood something of what they had suffered. For the rest of each week I never truly fit in. Dashing in and out to play tennis, to go to cocktail parties or to play bridge was not the activity I wanted. Just as that Melbourne Red Cross woman had focused on my shorter uniform hemline rather than on the real mission of Red Cross, so, too, the RAAF hospital matron blew a gasket and rebuked me for allowing the wounded I had known in Vietnam to call me by my first name. At the end of my second year with the Red Cross, I returned to civilian life. Neither Win, who before going to Vietnam had volunteered extensively for Red Cross, nor I ever did anything for the organisation again. Unconsciously, perhaps, we wanted to mentally shut out the horror of Vietnam – to remember only a sanitised version of our year there.

I doubt there is any war veteran who can say he or she returned home emotionally unscathed. But my tough, no-nonsense soul had been formed years earlier in a childhood lived close to the soil amongst the wheat and sheep of Silverweir. I emerged from Vietnam less emotionally troubled than Win. More sensitive than I, Win still has gut-wrenching nightmares, such as sorting out who should go into the operating room next when a large group of casualties arrives. In the way of dreams, that was not work she did, but the nightmares are real enough and leave her shaking and drained. I am fortunate to have escaped that torture. I had gone to Vietnam expecting to have a fascinating experience. What I got in return was the discovery, beyond naming and knowing, of the depths and heights in the human soul, the richness of love of my fellow man, and the opportunity to witness countless acts of ultimate human decency that enriched, ennobled and enlivened me.

I was one of the lucky Vietnam returnees. For many men, going home was traumatic. Trained to kill, they were discharged at the end of their tours and sent home, without any counselling, to begin new lives as civilians. Some soldiers couldn't get a date; girls refused to go out with those who had served. Some soldiers woke in the night screaming and sweating, terrifying their families, as they relived in recurrent dreams the horrors they experienced. Other men abused and mistreated their wives. Many soldiers divorced, often more than once.

Three years passed before I finally cried. On the day in 1970 that Prince Norodom Sihanouk of Cambodia was deposed in an American-backed coup that led to the Khmer Rouge genocide, long-held-back emotions about the futility of war finally spilled out. I sobbed like my heart was broken. I cried for all the Australians who were wounded or had died in Vietnam. I cried for the Americans, the Vietnamese and now for the Cambodians, who only wanted to get on with their lives and live in peace.

The war in Vietnam escalated and dragged on – as bloody as ever. Australian, New Zealand, Vietnamese, American and other forces continued to die. Australia, in the face of rising casualty rates, increasing resistance to conscription and negative public opinion, pulled its forces out in 1972. The war went on for another three years, and its repercussions continue to this day.

When I heard about a group of American nurses, Red Cross workers, USO women and others returning to Vietnam for three weeks in 1995, it was an easy decision to go with them. My husband understood. When we arrived in Vietnam, the villages and farms, the smells, the pot-holed roads etched into my memory thirty years earlier were still there, but we found a country at peace. Happy children carried books everywhere they went, for the Vietnamese cherish learning. No one lived in fear of crops being confiscated, or of being forced from their family to fight a war. People whom I had thought might be bitter and unforgiving were gentle and welcoming – and willing to talk about what they called the 'American' war. They stared at us curiously, knowing by the sites we asked to see that we were not the usual tourists.

It was more than strange, indeed frightening at first, to talk to men who had fought against us as our enemy, especially those who had been in Phuoc Tuy province in 1966 and 1967. Thirty years later we found Vietnam to be one of the world's safest countries, where women could walk fearlessly, day and night – except, perhaps, in Saigon (now Ho Chi Minh City). But we also saw a country still pock-marked with bomb craters.

However, without the military vehicles and the gaudy foreign presence of the war, the country seemed more beautiful than ever. In serene, enchanting Hanoi, I attended a classical music concert. I watched men I had considered 'bloody uncivilised VC in pyjamas and thongs who caused us so much grief', dressed in white tie and tails, playing Mozart and Beethoven superbly. It was a shock to see the flag of North Vietnam with its five-pointed gold star – representing farmers, workers, intellectuals, youth and soldiers – flying over buildings that the Americans had built to last well into the new century. Even in Vung Tau, the red and gold flag waved from the roof of the Villa DuBois, now a hotel. At first I thought the hotel rented by the hour, because the entrance hall was lined with photographs of women. The pictures were simply of the staff, who happily opened the door to Room 116. I looked out onto the barbed wire, thirty years rustier, that still lay atop the wall.

Little had changed in Vung Tau's centre, although there were several fancy new hotels to accompany both the now-faded Grand and the Pacific. The market area looked the same, but The Flags sign of the countries supporting the South and the door-to-door bars were long gone. About a kilometre from the market though, Vung Tau was dramatically different – oil had been found off the coast.

The Vung Tau airbase where the 36th Evac had been located was under Russian control – top secret. There were no paddy fields along the road from Vung Tau to Ba Ria. It was all one large town. Phuoc Tuy province had merged with another and was no more. Reassuringly though, laughing kids still teased and begged for whatever we could give them, while toddlers ran around with bare bottoms. And a cyclo ride cost less than it had nearly thirty years earlier with wartime inflation. In 1995, for one US dollar, I hired a cyclo driver for the day.

Following a smoothly paved corniche around the headland to Back Beach, I could find no trace of ALSG, as the sandhills the Australians had laboured to flatten were built over with grand houses. The broad beach that had offered us sublime relief from war had narrowed considerably with time. Barefoot, I knelt in the wet sand and with a stick scratched: Remember the Aussies. As the tide inevitably washed over my words, I thought of the line we had sung so many times in the ALSG chapel our engineers had built in the sand: 'Time, like an ever-rolling stream, bears all its sons away.'

Epilogue

I<small>N</small> F<small>EBRUARY</small> 1973, <small>TWO YEARS BEFORE THE</small> fall of Saigon, Australia established diplomatic relations with North Vietnam and opened an Embassy in Hanoi within months. There is today a sound and lasting marriage between the two countries. Australia continues to provide skills, technologies and ideas to help Vietnam in its economic and social development. The United States only normalised diplomatic relations with Vietnam in 1995.

Pam Spence, now Pam Werner, the first Red Cross woman to work with the soldiers in Saigon, returned to Vietnam in 1970 to work at the Australian military hospital in Vung Tau. She is now a masseuse in Hepburn Springs, Victoria.

Hilda Zinner worked with the Immigration Department in Sydney for the next twenty years, serving as a welfare officer helping newcomers adjust to life in Australia. She died in 2000.

Harry Janssen continued to work for the Red Cross on his return to Australia. He fought for those who served with philanthropic organisations in Vietnam, such as the Red Cross and the Salvation Army, to be eligible for the same repatriation benefits as service personnel. Eventually those benefits were awarded. He now teaches music in Melbourne and, with his wife Ria, takes pride in their three adopted children.

Winsome Ayliffe returned to work at the Perth Combined Services Recruiting Office and remained in the CMF. After marrying Peter Palmer (ex-RAAF), she and her husband ran hotels, food businesses and service stations in the Western Australia towns of Jennacubbine and Goomalling. Today they are manager/caretakers of the Legacy Holiday Camp on the beach in Busselton, Western Australia, where Win, as nurturing as ever, continues to care for the widows of the soldiers of Vietnam and other wars.

Janice Webb returned with the Red Cross to Singapore, where she met a British army officer, Ian Hilton. After marrying in Australia, they lived in Germany, England and Northern Ireland with their three children, before settling in Mount Eliza and then Benalla, Victoria. Jan now works on her golf and tennis games, and still has a splendid sense of humour.

Eleanor Koops died in Mobile, Alabama, in 1995, after working many years with the American Red Cross and US Government disaster relief. Unfortunately I wasn't able to find any information about Vivienne Ollila. Karen Gramke lives in Mobile, Alabama, and spent most of her working life with the Red Cross.

I returned to journalism in Sydney, working for the *Sydney Morning Herald*, *Australian Women's Weekly*, *Woman's World* as editor and *Woman's Day*, as co-editor.

The John Fairfax media group sent me to work in its New York bureau, and in Manhattan I met my husband, Jack Lamensdorf, a stockbroker. I continued to work in international publishing in Manhattan and, at age fifty-five, retired with Jack to rural Pennsylvania. Still as Australian as a meat pie, I teach Australian history at the University of Delaware's Academy of Lifelong Learning program for those over fifty.

Acknowledgements

AS WITH ALL OPERATIONS IN VIETNAM, THIS book was a team effort. I thank Bob Buick MM, who gave me the idea, nagged me to get on with it, and patiently filled in the copious gaps in my military knowledge.

I especially am indebted to Katherine Ward for creative guidance, for countless hours working much-needed editing magic and, good friend that she is, for pushing me the extra mile.

Renate Meundel provided insightful criticism and support; Roger Wainwright checked for military accuracy; and Drs Marshall Barr and Tony White answered my questions about medical matters. Roberta Ivers, my editor, was always there with constructive suggestions.

My Vung Tau roommate Win Palmer shared the letters she wrote daily to her mother from the war zone. Red Cross colleague Harry Janssen dug out my monthly reports from Vietnam to Red Cross NHQ. Former ARVN officer Nguyen Van Ninh and Tran Thi Kim Hien provided insights into the

Vietnamese culture. Australian Red Cross Secretary General Leon Stubbings, to whom I am forever grateful for sending me to Vietnam, died while I was writing this book.

I could not have written this book without the recollections of Vietnam veterans themselves. To the Vietnam veterans who contacted me with the ideas, anecdotes and recollections that have enriched my story, I give my deepest thanks and good wishes. I fear I may omit someone, but among the Australians were: Trevor Anderson, Dot Angell, Len Avery, Dennis Ayoub, Ben Azzopardi, Wayne Brown, Louise Checkley, Bob Coker, Anne Coulter, Jennifer Mary Cox, Nev Cullen, Greg Dwiar, Rodger Eyles, Ray Firth, Denis Gibbons, Ted Harrison, Jan Harvey, Barry Hawthorne, Ann Honess (née Copeman), Tanya Honey, Bob Hutton, Bob Kearney, Barry E. Kelly, David Lewis, John Lindner, Brian London, Sandy MacGregor, Bernie McGurgan, Kate McKillop, Ernie Marshall, Frank and Trevor Maunder, Alec Mead, Bob O'Neill, John Pritchard, Janet Rice, Adrian Roberts, Barry Rust, Rick Ryan, Dave Sabben, Pat Slee, Graham Smith, Charles Stewart, Colin Symonds, Noel Tinning, Bill Unmeopa, Lou Wagner, Arthur Willemsee, Jack Wilson, Terry Woolmer, and Tom Young.

Americans I must thank include Maurice Charette, Antonio Rafael Serrati Gallardo, Geraldine 'Polly' Parrott Bednash, Anne Philiben (who holds the 36th Evac community in her hands), and Donna and Tom Wells, who were always there with help. Sharon and Bob Coffey, and John Correia helped me with photographs.

Lastly, I thank my husband Jack for keeping me laughing – and for a million other reasons.

Bibliography

Fitzgerald, Frances, *Fire in the Lake*, New York: Little, Brown and Company, 1972.

Haran, Peter, and Robert Kearney, *Crossfire*, Sydney: New Holland Publishers, 2001.

Hall, Michael H., *The Medic and the Mama-san*, Cortland, N.Y.: Hawkeye Publishing, 1993

Monohan, Evelyn M., and Rosemary Neidel-Greenlee, *And If I Perish: Frontline U.S. Army Nurses in World War II*, New York: Alfred A. Knopf, 2003.

O'Brien, Tim, *If I Die in a Combat Zone*, New York: Delacorte, 1973. Excerpt reprinted with permission.

O'Keefe, Brendan, and F. B. Smith, *Medicine at War*, Sydney: Allen & Unwin, 1994.

O'Neill, Robert J., *Vietnam Task*, Melbourne: Cassell Australia, 1968. Reprinted 1995.

Pemberton, Gregory, *Vietnam Remembered*, Sydney: Lansdowne, 1990.

Sarnecky, Mary T., *A History of the U.S. Army Nurse Corps*, Philadelphia: University of Pennsylvania Press, 1999.

Glossary of Terms and Abbreviations Used

2 I/C	Second-in-command
64 set	A feather-light radio set, with the ability to send high speed Morse code
AATTV	Australian Army Training Team Vietnam
ABC	Australian Broadcasting Commission
ALSG	Australian Logistic Support Group
ANZAC	Australian and New Zealand Army Corps
APC	Armoured Personnel Carrier
ARC	American Red Cross
ARVN	Army of the Republic of Vietnam (South Vietnam)
AUSDIL	Australians Dangerously Ill plan
BOQ	Bachelor Officers' Quarters
Casevac	Casualty evacuation from battlefield
Chopper	A helicopter
CMF	Citizen Military Forces
CO	Commanding Officer
Comms	Communications
Contact	Firefight, any exchange of weapon fire between opposing forces

Cpl	Corporal
C-rations	Combat rations
Evac	Evacuation hospital
FDL	Forward defence line
Flt Lt	Flight Lieutenant
Gnr	Gunner, a private in the artillery
GSW	Gun shot wound
HMAS	Her Majesty's Australian Ship
Infil	Infiltrate
IV	Intravenous; fluid or medication given into a vein or through an IV line
L/Cpl	Lance Corporal
LSM	Landing Ship Medium
Lt	Lieutenant
Lt Col	Lieutenant Colonel
LUP	Lying up position
LZ	Landing zone
MACV	Military Assistance Command, Vietnam
Matron	Head nurse
MC	Military Cross
Medcap	Medical civil action program
Medevac	Medical evacuation
MID	Mention-in-Despatches
MM	Military Medal
MP	Military Police
MPC	Military Payment Certificates
MTA	Metropolitan Transit Authority
NHQ	Australian Red Cross National Headquarters in Melbourne
NVA	North Vietnamese Army
OC	Officer Commanding

ORs	Other Ranks
PFC	Private First Class
Picket	Camp guard or sentry, also piquet
POW	Prisoner of War
Pte	Private
PX	Post Exchange, a department store on base
Q	Quartermaster
R&C	Rest and Convalescence, taken in Vietnam
R&R	Rest and Recreation, taken outside Vietnam
RAAF	Royal Australian Air Force
RAEME	Royal Australian Electrical and Mechanical Engineers
RAP	Regimental Aid Post
RAR	Royal Australian Regiment
RCL	Recoilless rifle
Recce	Reconnaissance
RGH	Repatriation General Hospital
Sapper	A private in the Royal Australian Engineers
SAS	Special Air Service
Sgt	Sergeant
Uc dai loi	Vietnamese for Australia or Australian
UN	United Nations
USAF	United States Air Force
USO	United Service Organisations
VC	Viet Cong
VD	Venereal disease
Victor Charlie	Viet Cong, in the military phonetic alphabet
WHAM	Win Hearts and Minds

Index